To Hell with Tanks!

To Hell with Tanks!

KEN TOUT

ROBERT HALE · LONDON

ISBN 0 7090 4810 6

Robert Hale Limited
Clerkenwell House
Clerkenwell Green
London EC1R 0HT

Photoset in Palatino by
Derek Doyle & Associates, Mold, Clwyd.
Printed in Great Britain by
St Edmundsbury Press Ltd, Bury St Edmunds, Suffolk.
Bound by WBC Bookbinders Ltd,
Bridgend, Mid-Glamorgan.

Contents

Dedication

In memory of those who, in some of history's darkest years, kept the hope of Liberation alive in occupied countries, and especially those who died, innocent civilians, Resistance fighters, unknown heroes who held that ground until we could arrive to complete the task of Liberation.

Preface

'Stand still there! Silence in the ranks! Squad ... squad, 'SHUN!' How often did we hear those orders as they tried to prepare us makeshift soldiers for the realities of battle? Fortunately since those days there has been no embargo of silence. We have been able to share our memories in dozens of carefree encounters over the years.

It is in no small measure due to the work of the late RSM George Jelley MBE that the Northamptonshire Yeomanry, no longer an extant regiment, should still be represented by an association which numbers more than four hundred, when more famous units have lost touch with wartime veterans. This has meant that the present volume could be drawn from the memories of many who have participated in our return visits to the battlefields described.

My previous books, *Tank!* and *Tanks, Advance!* were simply personal reminiscences. They reflected my own perceptions and attitudes, often erroneous, of that time. This book depends on the assistance of so many friends that to name them all would occupy too many pages in the present binding. Suffice it to say that none of the incidents which are described have been included without eye-witness evidence from surviving veterans.

It is obviously difficult, at this remove of time, for even the heroes of this drama to remember the precise words they said at a particular moment. So they have kindly permitted me to write what I thought to be a reasonably accurate script. Obviously, as a ranker with 1NY, I was nearer to the life of 'other ranks'. I have been fortunate to be able to draw on material from some of our wartime officers as well. Whilst the gulf between officer and trooper was probably as reduced in 1NY as in any armoured unit, there were aspects of officers' lives, attitudes and decisions which were not obvious to the trooper of 1944–5.

7

In this respect I have been able to rely on the advice of the late David 'Hank' Bevan, Tom Boardman (now Lieut-Colonel Lord Boardman, MC), Michael Rathbone and 'Sandy' Saunders in particular. Lord George Scott is still with us as the chairman of the regimental association.

For the interested historian I should refer to some sterling work done by 'other ranks'. Les 'Spud' Taylor was largely responsible for showing that the German tank ace, Wittman, was knocked out by 1NY at Saint-Aignan and not in quite such heroic circumstances as previously retailed. 'Spud' has written his own full account of his extensive memories and has kindly allowed me to use these as basic material. Reg Spittles has tape-recorded episodes of the history of 2NY. Robert Hale has also published Keith Jones's story of 2NY under the title *Sixty-four Days of a Normandy Summer*. As recorded in these pages, 2NY, which had common origins with 1NY, supplied many valuable reinforcements to 1NY when the 'second line' was broken up.

The Northamptonshire Yeomanry Association Magazine (of which I have the honour to be the editor in succession to George Jelley himself) has also carried useful historical material such as the write up by Rex Jackson and Michael Hunt of the crossing of the Rhine.

Most NY veterans will remember with gratitude the collaboration with the infantry of the 51st Highland Division. For a time we worked together as virtually a single battle group. So I thought it fitting that a thread of infantry experience should be woven into the story, taking advantage of the recollections of our good friend, Major Charlie Robertson of the Black Watch. Charlie, like so many, is a reluctant hero, and felt that I should mention how much we, tank crews as well as infantry, owed to his immediate commanders, Major D.L. 'Sam' Small, Lieut-Colonel Charles Cathcart and that outstanding leader of Highlanders, Brigadier James Oliver. The same deference should also be paid to our own brigadier of 33rd Armoured, Wilf Mylan's tank commander, Brigadier Harry B. Scott who stood further out of the top of a tank than even Ossie Porter or me!

The poems owe something to George Jelley and his collection of *Rhymes of the Northamptonshire Yeomanry – World War Two*, wherein Edward Vaughan Green's poem is included, by kind permission of Walter Johnson, esq. I'm sure that Rex and Ralph will take a long time in forgiving me for exposing their very moving verses to public view.

A closing word of gratitude must go to Jai, my wife, for encouraging me in the organization of battlefield tours and other reunions, and also for accepting the disruption of personal arrangements which the writing of the three *Tank!* books has inevitably entailed.

Prologue
To Hell and Back!

'Haven't we, together and upon the immortal sea,
wrung out a meaning from our sinful lives?
Goodbye, brothers! You were a good crowd.'
                    (Joseph Conrad, *The Nigger of the 'Narcissus'*)

Like so many regiments in that war, our orders sent us down
into the very manifestation of hell. Most of us attempted the
journey. Some of us did not come back.

It was ordained for us to drive through seven very special
hells.

The first: the reeking charnel of heat-bloated bodies that
was Caen the night before its liberation.

The second: the black and green flashing horror of the
Night March through the German defences along Bourguebus Ridge.

The third: the bitter, exposed advances across the lethally
elevated dikes of Brabant.

The fourth: the Stygian mists and morasses beyond
Helden, Limburg.

The fifth: the inhuman freezing within steel prisons on the
blizzard-tortured slopes of the Ardennes.

The sixth: the final river, the braving at night in
impromptu boats of the trackless, rushing waters of the
Rhine – Götterdämmerung!

And the seventh: through these, and beyond these all, the
unremitting mental hell of motion within the closed-down
battle tank for 'in a moment our mobile home can be
transformed into

> a self-igniting crematorium ...
> a self-sealing mausoleum ... or
> a self-detonating bomb!'

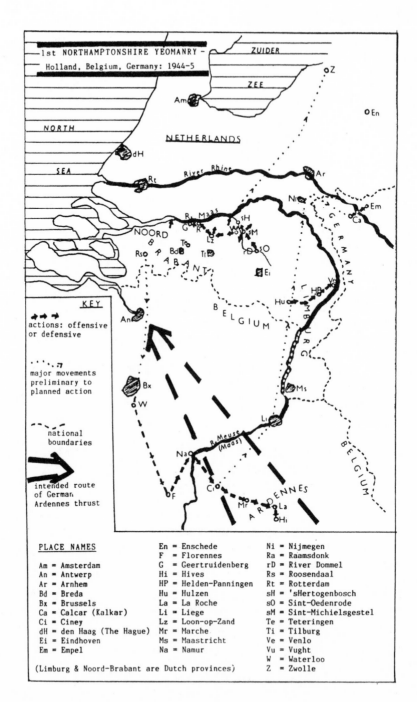

1st NORTHAMPTONSHIRE YEOMANRY –
Holland, Belgium, Germany: 1944-5

INY in Holland, Belgium and Germany, 1944–5

1   Waiting for the Starter Gun

'So this is Holland?' grumbled Trooper Tommy 'Tittlemouse' as we called him. 'I don't see any of them girls from the holiday adver*tise*ments. You know, the ones in clogs and billowing pantaloons and seagull-wing hats.'

'Trust you to be looking for girls in no-man's-land,' chuckled Corporal Hughie McGranahan, oiling his revolver carefully. 'Don't you know there's a war on?'

'Got us here by false pretences,' insisted Tommy. 'No way could I have afforded a holiday in Holland on my screw back home. But here they send us to Holland, and I don't see any sailing barges, or even any windmills, or any Dutch cheeses or, least of all, any beautiful Dutch Madame Oyzels.'

'They don't have mademoiselles in Holland,' corrected Hughie. 'That's French. Here they're *meisjes* or *juffrouws*. It's a different language.'

'Don't tell me I've got to learn another ferkin' language when I've just got my tongue around *parlez-vous* and *avez-vous des oovs?*'

'You surely must, Tommy. Certainly if you want to make progress with any *juffrouws* you eventually find.'

'Not much chance of girls here on this strip of road, with Jerry sitting either side,' said the driver, looking down from the engine covers of the Sherman tank towards the group of tank crews listlessly cleaning equipment for the umpteenth time.

'I don't believe that,' argued another voice. 'It's crazy to say that all the way from here, Saint 'Ole-in-the-road, or whatever it's called ....'

'Saint Oedenrode.'

'Snap! ... to say that all the way from here, up to Nijmegen and Arnhem – what? thirty miles or more? – to say there are Germans dug in each side of the road, breathing down our necks, and waiting to ambush us if we wander off behind a bush to do our daily nature worship?'

'Not exactly breathing down our necks. But near enough,' stated Hughie, who was a tank commander and one step nearer to Montgomery, 'at least that's what we've been told. And orders are to watch out.'

'Well, Jerry won't see much of us in this weather,' said Tommy. 'Rain, mist, fog, drizzle, low cloud; there's more water vapour than oxygen in this air. They certainly don't show that on the holiday adver*tise*ments.'

'Complaining again, Tommy?' barked Sergeant 'Balbo' Warren, who was trudging past in the mud. 'If orders says Jerry is just out there, you better believe it, boy. Or you'll be getting a bullet where your brain should have been. Or a bayonet up your ass, which would be messy for Holland.' Sergeant Warren was a fearsome little man who reminded one of a farmer angrily chasing unruly trespassers off his land. Sergeant Warren *was* a farmer and still looked it, even in best battledress. More so in soaked oily denims. Normally a tank commander, he now commanded a troop of four Shermans because of our heavy losses of officers in Normandy.

'If I was you, Tommy boy, I would be looking out sharpish for the old Hun in them woods there. He might shoot you where it won't amuse them "me-frows" you're planning to catch up with,' and with a sound somewhere between a snort and a guffaw Balbo moved on, placing his farmer's feet carefully between the deeper sumps of mud.

'I don't believe it!' exclaimed Stan Hilton to himself, looking out from the turret of his Sherman tank. 'There can't be any Germans out there in this weather. They're not that daft.'

Stan squinted into the driving rain. His tank was the sole sentinel in this forgotten spot where the First Northamptonshire Yeomanry sheltered under tarpaulins spread out from their tank tracks in the bitter weather. He was 'spelling' the tank commander, taking a spell to watch while the commander rested his eyes. If one watched too long there tended to be a short circuit somewhere between the retina and the brain, so that grim, huge Germans appeared out of the mists where no enemies should be. Many a tank commander had ordered all guns blazing to wipe out such non-existent marauders. But, worse still, the short circuit of the eye might mean *not* seeing an enemy movement when there really *was* one.

Like so many other 'Yeomen' of the regiment Stan was hardly more than a schoolboy and still had a rounded cherubic face. Earlier his commander had smiled at him affectionately.

'You don't seem soldier enough to frighten a Jerry, Stan. With that baby face you look stupid wearing that pudding-basin tin hat on your head and nursing a Sten gun. You'd belong in a tableau, dressed in a long white angel's robe and nursing a golden harp.'

'Please God he doesn't get his golden harp before time,' chirped another voice over the tank intercom, 'and before he's had a chance to do a bit of populating of the earth.'

So Stan, who was already, according to the records, a 'veteran of Normandy', continued to peer out into the misted, twilight emptiness of Holland, muttering, 'I don't believe it! I don't believe it!' to cheer himself up, 'I don't be ....'

Something hard and angry smacked against the turret flap raised up an inch or two above his ear. The buzz seemed to follow the smack. 'A bee? Or wasp? At this time of year? In this weather?' He bent over to pick up the grey crumpled body lying on the turret, a tiny piece of expired anger. It stung. Its sting was white heat. Stan jerked back and, as he did so, another 'bee' smacked into the other turret flap where his head had been.

Realization blazed in his mind. And terror. 'It's a bullet!' he yelped, automatically squeezing the microphone switch. 'Not a bee. A bullet! Two bullets!!'

The anxious face of the commander appeared somewhere around his shin. 'You hurt?'

'No, I'm not hurt. Only brassed off. Somebody shot at me. A rifle bullet. Two bullets. But God knows where from, out there ...?'

The commander squeezed up alongside him in the narrow turret opening. 'Using a rifle with telescopic sights at a thousand yards? From those woods? Easy! Any nearer and they would be calling you "four eyes" by now. Do you want a spell inside?'

'No, I'm OK! But I'm not showing even my eyebrows above board after that. I'll use the periscope. He can try to smash that.'

'Well, lad, it pays to listen to information from on high, even if we don't believe half of what we hear. I'll be up soon.'

And Stan was left alone again on watch, ducked well down and muttering to himself. 'I still don't believe ... oh, well, I'd better believe! Gawd, that flaming bullet's still hot.'

'There's something brewing other than tea. And other than Sherman tanks,' suggested Tommy. 'Big officers' conference going on. Colonel, majors, captains, little lieutenants, all the lot.'

'Time for us to get shooting again, I suppose,' Hughie McGranahan replied. 'They've left us sitting here long enough.'

'I thought we'd done enough in Normandy. Thought they'd bring some reinforcements out and give us some leave. First Eisenhower says we have destroyed the German army in Normandy. Then Monty says it will all be over by Christmas. Now it's mid-October and we're not halfway up Holland yet, never mind into Germany.'

'Sitting here, all together in reserve, we see lads from other squadrons we don't normally see when we're living as single troops,' said Hughie.

'I've seen blokes from A and B Squadrons that I haven't seen since we played them at football in England,' added Alf Rushton, one of the squadron's regular first XI forwards.

'Hey, Lance-Corporal Reboles! What are you doing, trespassing in C Squadron lines?' called Michael Hunt.

'I didn't see any "trespassers will be prosecuted" signs,' grinned Reboles, squatting down at a distance. 'In any case we from a decent squadron need to patrol C Squadron area as well as our own, in case C Squadron are as great duffers at war as they were in the football competition at Bury St Edmunds.'

'Poof off!' growled Alf Rushton, throwing a boot from which he had been vainly trying to prise solid mud. 'We only lost because our dear RSM Jelley had been nobbled, and gave those two penalties against us.'

'Old George Jelley is un-get-at-able, either as an RSM or as a football referee.'

'Yeah, sure. He's the world's best. More like an uncle to us young 'uns. But we should have won. If only young Shellam had ... oh, but he's dead now anyway, isn't he. Caught by that bloody Panther waiting around that corner in the Bocage.'

A group of officers strolled through the afternoon twilight, a dimness due as much to the incessant mists and drizzle as to a westering of the sun. Captains and lieutenants together, walking without urgency but conversing intently.

'Any news, sir?' asking Alf of a short, slim lieutenant with a gaunt but pleasant face, in which an aquiline nose was the prominent feature.

'You'll have to wait until after troop leaders' conferences, won't you, Rushton,' smiled the boyish lieutenant, his accent a thick but well-educated Scots.

'Seems a nice guy,' observed Reboles, still squatting watching. 'What's he like to work with? That's McColl, isn't it?'

'Efficient. Dry. Quite humorous. A good officer, seeing he can't have been out of school more than a year or so,' replied Alf. 'You ought to be an officer, Mike. And you, Hughie. Got the schooling for it, not like poor ignorant Manchester me, all footballing feet and no brains.'

'Strange, friend Reboles being here,' said Michael. 'Remember, you and I were both offered commissions at the same time. But in the infantry.'

'God, yes! And after seeing the way the infantry live out here, I thank a thousand lucky stars that I turned the offer down. But that's the one gripe with this regiment. Not that the colonel can do anything about it. It's the system. Do you know they have made me a commander as a lance-corporal?'

'We've had a lance-corporal, young Ken over there, commanding the squadron captain's tank for long enough, would you believe?' said Mike.

'That's what I mean. If we were crew in the RAF we would all be sergeants. And some of the turret crew might be officers even. But in the tanks we have sergeants commanding troops, and lance-corporals commanding fighting vehicles with massive guns on them. And any number of us have passed our test to go for officer training, but there are no vacancies. And yet you have a lance-corporal having to command a captain's tank. Doesn't make sense!'

'But it's a good regiment anyway, lads.'

'Yes, and look at this lot of officers coming along here.'

'What's that, Corporal?' A captain of somewhat more mature age had approached, accompanied by another lieutenant, also clearly older than McColl. He stopped and looked at the group. Close to the line of battle in moments of relaxation, such formalities as standing to attention and saluting every passing officer were dispensed with by the NY.

'When I left school, sir, I was just looking forward to being able to hobnob with the masters in the local. Then I find myself in the NY and here is the entire school common-room dressed up in officers' uniforms and I have to start calling them "sir" again.'

'That's true!' replied Captain Rathbone, 'I did have the misfortune to have to teach you at school, but at least we don't have to stand you rounds of beer, which we would have had to do if we had still been masters and you had been old boys.'

'*We?*' queried a trooper.

'Yes, that's right. Lieutenant Vaughan Green here was also a master at the same school. And, what's more, our dear adjutant, Captain Llewellyn is another of the same schoolmaster breed. Well, we must move along. More conferences coming up for commanders. Your days of idleness are over. Duty calls.'

When the officers did move along their pace was still unhurried and their conversation apparently lacking in any sign of urgency. Rathbone and Green certainly had imported the schoolmasterly walk, and the donnish bowing of the head, into military activities.

'One disadvantage for Captain Rathbone which he doesn't complain about,' said Hughie. 'His school nickname of "Ratters" has followed him into the army. But he doesn't seem to worry about it.'

'He wouldn't worry about anything, old "Ratters". He's totally unflappable. It would take a thousand pounder bomb to hasten his footsteps half-a-mile an hour. Typical Yeomanry officer!'

Corporal Reg Spittles was still some way down the line of communication, urging his tank on through crowds of happy liberated citizens and masses of supply waggons, looking for the regimental harbour. Trying to take short cuts down side roads from time to time.

As often happens in the confusion of war, Reg had no clear idea as to where he was and, as the border of Belgium and Holland was quite close, was not even sure as to which country he was in. The massed traffic had slowed to a halt for the twentieth time at least, when a man in civilian clothes suddenly leaped on to the tank, climbed to the turret and embraced Reg in a grip so tight that Reg was afraid of being throttled.

'Let me go, man!' he exploded. 'Leave me! Let me breathe! Stand back a bit. That's better ....' and waving his Sten gun, which was lying on the turret top, he demanded, 'Are you Dutch?'

The man stared at him for a moment in something like fear.

'Dutch!' snapped Reg impatiently, tapping the gun on the turret. 'Are you Dutch, *Kamerad*?'

'No! *Nein*! *Nee*! Not *Deutsch*! Not *Deutsch* – me!'

'What are you then? Belgian? – if you're not Dutch?'

The man was nervous, pale-faced, scared, hesitant. 'No! Me – is not Belgian. Not *Deutsch*. Me – is *Hollander*.'

'Oh, Holland. So we *are* in Holland, then, and you're Dutch!'

'No! Nee! Not! Me – *Hollander*. Not *Deutsch*. *Deutsch* is *allemand*, enemy, *Bosche*, from *Duitsland*. Hitler, Himmler. *Duits*! This – Holland! Me – *Hollander*!'

'Oh, I see. So a Duitsman is a German, not a Dutchman. And we *are* at least in Holland. But you had better jump down, friend, because we shall move on again any moment.'

'But, please, I want thank you. I meet you Englishman. I hide from *Duitsers*. In trees. Now I come. Say thank you, Englishman, for my country. Please, this to thank you,' handing to Reg a small coin. And with that, the unnamed man jumped off the tank and hurried down the road, waving to soldiers in other vehicles.

'Well, I'll be ....' spluttered Reg, bending to speak inside the turret. 'Look what this silly Hollander has just given me. For kindly liberating his country. And risking my neck and yours. Look! A Dutch shilling. Or something like that. Well, in Normandy and Belgium I've been offered wine and Calvados and cheese and apples, but never had my price set at a shilling. Perhaps he thinks we still get paid a shilling a day, like the song says. Must have a screw loose. Bomb happy, I expect.'

A scrabbling noise on the outside of the turret jerked Reg into instantaneous defensive reaction, even although there appeared to be no enemy troops within miles of that spot. But the disturbance came from another Hollander wearing the orange armband of the Resistance.

'*Welkom*, my friend,' said the Resistance man, smiling. 'Everything OK? Can we help you?'

'Just two questions: are there any Germans about? And, where are we anyway?'

The Dutchman's smile turned rather sour, and he drew a finger across his throat in the universal sign of assassination. 'Boche *kaput*! All gone. Much way ahead. And we are here near Eindhoven. You have a map, please?'

Reg reached for a map but found the Dutch coin still embedded in the palm of his hand. 'Oh, yes, look at this,' he smiled back. 'One of your mob just gave me this little coin. As a present for liberating his country. Must have a screw loose?'

'Screw loose? Ah, yes, one tile fallen off the roof? Please, I look at money? Wait! This is two and half guilder coin. This very important.'

'Two and a half shillings, not one. But not very valuable?'

'Ah, you do not know. This coin have some, what you call? – silver. Yes, silver. From before the war. Look. Nineteen thirty and eight years date. When the Germans come they take all coins have silver and ... and nickel. Take all those coins and put cheap, poor coins instead. So in the war it is crime, great crime to keep coin with silver or nickel. Germans find this, you *kaput*! The man give you this, he keep it many months, years, a great crime. Danger for his life. To give to you for liberate his country.'

'I didn't realize that,' answered Reg, very much taken aback by the story. 'I thought it was a worthless coin, and that he was a bit imbecilic. And yet really he was ...?'

'A man the Germans must punish, prison in concentration camps, perhaps shoot. So you will always think, friend, that the little coin is the value of a man's life.'

A long way ahead the column started to move again. The Resistance man descended to the ground and began to usher out of the way of the vehicles those excited spectators who had come across the fields from nearby cottages.

Around the main 'laager' of tanks, troopers splashed through the mud in pursuit of a dilapidated football. Enthusiasts like Alf Rushton, young Ripley, Pete Pedder, seeking to reactivate limbs twisted, it felt, like thorn branches from hours of cramped sitting in unnatural positions in tanks, sometimes for as much as thirty-six hours. Jimmy Sables wondered if his legs would ever move freely again, or whether this war would spoil his chances as an apprentice on Newcastle United's books. But another tank man from another regiment, Tom Finney, had played his way into an England team. Perhaps there was still hope for Alf Rushton to impress Manchester City, or winger Yo Preston the Wolves.

Harry Graham, rugger player, shouted insults at the soccer sops, but wondered if there might be an idea for a football skit for the next squadron concert party, an impromptu, trooper-led rollick. After all RSM George Jelley was a football referee of professional standard, and Harry could brilliantly mimic George's parade-ground bellows. There was room for fun, like 'Take that man's name, Corporal, for unfair body charges, goalkeepers for the abuse of,' or 'Take that man's name, Sar'nt-Major, for mud on his boots in the penalty area.' In dire moments of battle despair, tank men survived, relatively sane, by chortling at echoes of the concert party's mockery of their own heroism.

Hank, alias Major David Bevan, commanded C Squadron when he wasn't acting as second-in-command of the regiment in some emergency. Now he stood before his other eighteen commanders (he himself commanded one of the squadron's nineteen tanks in action).

A long rambling living-room in a nearby farmhouse, the only building in sight, had been borrowed for the conference. Out of deference to the Dutch family, which still occupied the farmhouse, all ranks of the 1NY fighting squadrons lived out in the drizzle and mire of the fields along the Arnhem road. But, for a conference, a drier area was convenient and the Dutch family had refused to allow the commanders to meet in the barn.

'Now listen closely,' Hank began. 'I had hoped that this conference would have been ordering you to fan out beyond the Arnhem bridge and begin to exploit country opened up by the parachute attack. But that was not to be.'

'Another bloody miscalculation by the geniuses on high!' growled Bill Fox, Captain, 2 i/c squadron, and Hank's alter ego. In so many ways they seemed opposite. Hank tall, apparently lazy, Eton educated, immaculate, always the City gentleman on the way to his stockbroker's office. Bill,

shorter, tough, bow-legged, wiry, the classic horsey man,
always looking as though he had just returned from a
splashing, stumbling ride over a point-to-point course, or
maybe, more exotically, from rounding up a herd of
longhorns on the Texas plains. Tough old Bill, some years
older than Hank who was not yet thirty. But troopers had
seen tears in Bill's eyes when teenage lads were killed or
terribly wounded in Normandy.

'That's as may be,' intoned Hank, imperturbably. It was
well known that during a practice scheme on Salisbury Plain
Hank had been roundly and nastily 'bollocked' in front of
other ranks by a major-general, red in the face, because he,
Hank, had refused to use textbook tactics. Acting with
improvised armoured movements the squadron had been
umpired as having annihilated an entire regiment of
well-bred cavalry in a way which was considered not quite
'proper'.

'But let's get back to reality. We have another most
interesting job to do instead.'

'Which means more damn casualties' – Bill.

'We had better assume that. You will all remember how
we began to close the Falaise Gap by the Night March and
the battle at St Aignan in August. This is a similar situation.
There is a massive river, the Maas or the Meuse, behind the
Germans who are *behind* us! A small German army which
will have to retreat across the Maas as they had to cross the
Seine in Normandy. If we capture or destroy the bridges up
to a place called – to put it phonetically – "Her-true-den-
burg", they will be cut off, as the Germans at Falaise were cut
off. Right! We are to advance to clear the south bank of the
River Maas. Bill, you have the order of march.'

There was a stirring of excitement among the commanders, ranging in rank from captain to lance-corporal. Also
present were important functionaries like Squadron
Sergeant-Major Farnham, fitter Sergeant Bill Needham, who
looked what he was – a mechanic in uniform, and the
squadron clerk, bank clerk John Pearson. Also the squadron
Quartermaster-Sergeant, the popular, soft-spoken Pete
Mapley, another Northamptonshire farmer-in-uniform,
totally incapable of looking like a Grenadier Guard. Pete was
very tall where that other dishevelled farmer, Balbo Warren,
was short. And, as might be expected, Pete put his orders in
the form of gentle, quiet requests, whereas Balbo stormed

and raged in a mighty voice, almost as loud as the voice of RSM George Jelley, who had been practising parade-ground orders since 1916.

'Yes, well … ' began Bill Fox, 'he only puts me up to speak because neither of us can pronounce these damn stupid Holland names.'

'Not worse than Normandy: Saint-Aignan-de-Cramesnil or Saint-Julien-le-Faucon, sir?' interrupted Stan Upstone, who had joined the regiment at the same time and with the same rank as Bill and other officers, but who had neither the ambition nor the social standing to ascend as rapidly in the promotion pyramid. Stan commanded a single tank, a Firefly, armed with the later 17 pounder gun and with a crew of only four, to allow space for larger ammunition.

'You wait until you hear the names. Have you looked at your maps? Well, hear the first start line! I won't spell it fanatically, David. Letter for letter. Jot it down. Locate it. S-c-h-i-j-n-d-e-l. Now, how the hell do you pronounce that? No prizes will be given. No doubt one of our eggheads can say it for us. Porter, Dwight, McGranahan? Don't worry. We're giving it code name "Charlotte".'

'Even I can pronounce that,' muttered Stan Upstone, as pens squeaked on perspex tracing-sheets covering maps.

'And Sergeant Warren's troop in the lead,' continued Bill.

'With Sergeant Warren as lead tank,' barked little Balbo.

'Now you know the squadron leader, and the colonel, don't like troop leaders taking lead tank role, Sergeant.'

'Your last word changes it all, sir. The squadron leader does not like lieutenants taking lead tank. I, sir, am only a sergeant. And likely to remain one. Sergeants take lead tank role. So I am entitled.'

'Aye, we've had this argument before. Well, you lead, Sergeant Warren. But you will need a Firefly well up the formation. Corporal Dwight!'

'Sir!' Arthur Dwight was a tall, pale, 20 year old, only a few months out from the training regiment and only a day or two old as a full corporal.

'Keep close on the troop leader's tail. There may be 88s about.'

'Yes, this is to be the tactical problem of Holland,' intervened David Bevan. 'We associate the Hun with brilliant blitzkrieg advances. Sedan to Dunkirk in 1940. Von Runstedt in Russia. Rommel in Africa. We forget that the

Germans are also defensive geniuses. Now, we attack as a squadron with nineteen tanks. But in these flooded fields, and between the Dutch canals it is often going to be line ahead, like Nelson at Trafalgar. One tank and one infantryman abreast on a narrow road, with the rest tailing behind. So the German is not going to face us with a squadron of his own. Just one 88 self-propelled gun with modest traversing ability. Or just one lookout man up in the local church tower, and one valiant infantryman at a bend in the road aiming one Panzerfaust – the rocket-firing hand-held bazooka, as we call it. Then we must halt, deploy, wait, inch forward, delay ....'

'So no massed armies as in Normandy. No shedding of gallons of good British blood,' rounded off Bill Fox as the group began to shuffle around on its bottoms impatiently. 'The blood will be spilled in precious pints at lonely corners of the road. But it might be the fatal pints of YOUR blood. And YOURS. And YOURS. So be damned careful. Be godamned careful of the invisible Hun.'

2   Back to Battles

'Ready for off, then?' barked Bill Fox.

'As ready as we can be,' smiled Hank Bevan, as the three Squadron HQ officers watched their crews mounting the three Shermans of C Squadron's HQ(F) Troop – fighting headquarters.

'Not being a professional soldier, I had hoped that we would not have to fight in Holland. War over by Christmas. Montgomery's famous aberration. Germans destroyed in Normandy, and all that,' suggested Captain Todd.

'Holland will be worse. Damn country,' observed Hank. 'Good people. Strong Resistance groups. But damn bad tank country.'

'Worse than the Bocage?' asked Todd. 'Fourteen-foot high Normandy hedges? Not even Shermans could see over the tops. Fields fifty yards square. Panther tanks in every hedge. Thick cornfields. Ripe to harvest. And all that. Infantry bazookas in the corn.'

'Hank's right,' continued Bill Fox. 'Yes, we do have long open spaces for tanks to roll over. If they don't sink in the bloody mud. But look at those distant woods. Shelter for anti-tank poachers. And all those dikes and canal banks, for SPs to lurk behind, and tanks to have to ride across. Lovely skyline targets we'll make. And more flaming, blazing beacons than warned about the Armada.'

Reinforcements from two badly bruised regiments sacrificed in Normandy (2nd Northamptonshire Yeomanry and 148 Royal Armoured Corps) had made 1NY up to strength again after its own Normandy casualties. This had, among other results, caused senior officers to step back a place, Hank from 2 i/c regiment to squadron leader; Bill to squadron 2 i/c; Toddy to 'spare captain'. But there was no animosity between the three.

'At least we have an experienced squadron now. Not the

greenhorns of June. Been through the fires of hell.' Toddy paused, possibly remembering the gusher of fire which drove him from his own tank on the fields of Saint-Aignan.

'Apart from some of the young officers coming up,' growled Bill. 'Not ready to sit a Shetland pony, some of 'em.'

'That's my worry,' concluded Hank. 'So far, some of my NCOs have been better commanders than some of my junior officers. I would prefer to commission my own troop leaders. We have the material for that.'

'Little Napoleon Warren, for instance. He looks least like a soldier, and acts most like a soldier, than any man I ever met.'

'Too right, Bill. I've talked to Colonel Doug. Said we can put fresh-faced lance-corporals into officers' roles without loss of efficiency. He agrees. The brigadier is also sympathetic. But says the system must be justified. And, at this precise moment, that means mounting up.'

Hank drew himself up to his full slim height, prior to mounting the sloping front of his Sherman. Tall, elegant, relaxed, he was in total contrast to his friend Bill, who stood head thrust forward, hands behind back, legs bowed, a shorter man seemingly composed of tight steel springs. Todd added a third dimension, younger, middle height, dark, serious, handsome – possibly a film star or, at least, a film star's brother.

'Let's go find Gertrude, then,' laughed Bill, in that superficial hilarity with which all tank men disguised the inner terrors of sealing themselves into their mobile crematorium.

'Who's Gertrude?' grinned Toddy, already on his way to the third 30 ton tank in the row.

'Ain't it Gertrude's Berg we're headed for? Our eventual target? The last bridge where the Hun can escape from these parts?'

'Don't be such an ignoramus, Bill,' Hank called, giving his metal steed a rap with the riding-crop which so many Yeomanry, and cavalry officers, carried when out of the line. 'It's Geertruidenberg you should be looking for on the signposts.'

'Which signposts ain't there!' This last quip came from the lips of Sergeant Dick Bates, Hank's driver, whose black beret, ruddy cheeks and jovial smile were all that could be seen of him as he peered out of the driver's hatch. Like the commander, the driver could adjust a seat to look out of the tank for normal 'marching'. But unlike most commanders, when the 'fun' started, the driver would sink down, close the heavy hatch over his head and rely on periscope vision. Dick was already revving his engine up into a crescendo of sound as loud as that of a modest aeroplane. Behind him other tanks added their din in a huge wash of reverberations which could blot out the loudest of natural thunder or the greater part of the heaviest artillery barrage booming overhead.

All down the rows of tanks (nineteen of C Squadron, then B Squadron, and A, and three RHQ Shermans, with a couple of lighter Stuart tanks of Recce Troop up front) drivers and co-drivers were already mounted in their front compartments, gunners and operators were climbing up to their turrets or already easing into tight seats, commanders were exchanging last comments – a few pertinent instructions, a fair amount of deliberately perky banter, and, like early morning travellers on a city-bound train, a majority of totally irrelevant and purposely uninstructive verbal quacking and neighing.

Bristling Balbo Warren, bounding towards his tank, paused to stare at Arthur Dwight, a tall, pale-faced youth, who looked as much student-in-uniform as the sergeant was farmer-in-uniform.

'Cheer up, lad. We're winning. Your first day as full corporal. Keep close up, lad. We may need your bloody big gun. Terrifies Jerry, does your 17 pounder.'

'OK,' Sarge, I'll be close at hand.'

'Cheer up, Arthur,' shouted McGranahan against the increasing noise of engines and nearby artillery. 'There's always tomorrow.'

'So you say. But *will* there be a tomorrow? Not for somebody!'

'That's not the way to look at it,' bellowed the sergeant. 'Take life by the throat. Grip her as though you're going to throttle her. Make your own destiny. That's me.'

'Don't we know it!' McGranahan was only a little senior to Dwight, and only a little less student-in-uniform.

'Yes, Corporals both. Berlin or bust! That's me. Give yourself a goal. What's it that Shakespeare bloke says in Macbeth: "When shall we three meet again?" What about in a bar on the Unter den flaming Linden in Berlin. Sink a pint together.'

'Only I don't drink,' murmured Arthur, a strict Methodist, and still finding it hard to be amused at this hour.

'That's me ... Berlin: "old Adolph he will say, Hoch, hoch! Mein Gott! What a bloody fine lot", etceterah! See you there, lads. Now, get out of my way, 'cos I'm heading straight off now to Berlin. No turning right or left. Look out, 'itler. I'm on my way.'

'Just one thing, Sarge. This part of the war we are going the opposite way. We're headed west, not east,' chuckled McGranahan.

'All the same, boy. I never could tell east from west. Just point me at the Hun ....'

'Good luck, Arthur!'

' ... think I may need it, Mac.'

A few tanks beyond, a trooper on his turret bawls to another trooper passing by, the first man's feet high above the second's head, so high in profile is the Sherman. 'Hey, Harry! Hello, Harry! Harry calling Harry. And not Hari Kari, either.'

Operator Harry Brown, at ground level, looked up at gunner Harry Graham on his turret. 'Harry receiving Harry loud, but not very clear.'

'Not in all this lovely hullabaloo. The genuine bloomin' brouhaha. *Le bruyant* warfare,' from Harry upstairs.

'And they said it would all be over for Christmas in Blighty,' from Harry downstairs.

'Been thinking, Harry boy. Must mobilize the squadron concert party for a Christmas show. Start rehearsing. Get some ideas going.'

'With suitably seasonal sacrilegious words, no doubt.'

'Yeah, you're the poet. While you're sitting in your tank today with nothing more to do than thinking about having a nice old Grable with Betty, start on poet-ing some suitable words, like, for e.g. and viz. and i.e., "Sergeant Warren last looked out, on the feast of Stephen"?'

'I'll give it a go. I'm not expecting to win the Victoria Cross today.'

'You'll get that for the Christmas pantomime. Or else discharge from this man's army on the grounds of insanity.'

'Aren't we all!'

Other files of Sherman tanks! Pressed in close by the wayside. Just beyond a village marked on the map as 'Schijndel' but, fortunately for Sergeant Warren and others, marked on the glassy, transparent map-covers in marker pen by the Yeomanry code-name, for this battle, of Charlotte. With Emily, Anne and Bronte further along the road.

Other files of Shermans! Engines shut off. Guns traversed front (or, for the immense 17 pounder, rear: the back, engine end of the Sherman being much longer than the sloping front portion). Crews lolling on turrets and out of drivers' hatches. Grimy with smoke and dust. Dragoon Guards. In theory a more historic, regular and highly polished outfit than the Yeomanry. But here everyone masked by the anonymity of battle grime.

Other files of Shermans! Crews lolling, and looking relieved. They liberated Schijndel at break of dawn. 'Charlotte achieved'. And now the Dragoon Guards rest. And the Yeomanry tanks squeeze past. With the Stuarts and Sergeant Warren in the lead. Again at the tip of the arrow-heads on the war correspondents maps. Or ahead of the assumed arrow-heads as the attack goes well and proves bloodless so far.

'Hello, Able 2. Move on to Emily now,' radios Bill Fox, commanding the first half-squadron of Yeomanry. And growls to himself, 'That's if Emily has no objections.'

'Able 2,' Sergeant Warren commanding 2 Troop, 'am clear of Charlotte and moving towards Emily now, over.'

'Able 2, good man. Off.'

Sergeant Warren stares intently ahead, trying to pierce the mists and discern enemy tanks where they are not. His crew jam their eyes tight against periscopes, trying to enlarge the meagre fields of vision; they grasp their icy controls more tightly; they thrust their buttocks hard into seats, as though for security, but keep their feet a-tiptoe, as though about to sprint from their marks; and they think nothing but ... ACTION!

But, farther back, it is the familiar waiting time, the nothing time, the haunting time, the time to fiddle with some totem or superfluous tiny duty. Arthur Dwight is near enough to the front to keep a casual watch forward, binoculars pressed to his eyes, earphones over his ears, hand holding microphone and finger on switch ready to transmit within the tank or on the wider radio waves of the 'A' set. Farther back, McGranahan pulls out a cigarette and a lighter, studies them for a moment, then pockets them again. He will do that a hundred times this day.

Farther back still, with 3 Troop, young Bobbie McColl finds his mind wandering, now that the troop has entered the vacuum of inaction. Back, thinking back to Scotland, and his father's wish that he should one day take over the successful newsagents' business which was now invading the whole of Scotland. And his own desire to do something other, something more committed to the welfare of mankind, with his life. If he survives. For even in this war young lieutenants have the longest odds against them. Bobby has survived the whole of the Normandy campaign. But still the need continues, to go into battle, head out of the turret, and sometimes body too, in order to get the clearest view of vital events.

Behind 3 Troop, Major Bevan can see the head of young Bobbie protruding from his turret, and remembers the despairing words of an older man, a father, met in England, 'Take care of him, of young Bobby. He's all I've got.' But how can you take care of a lieutenant who is an excellent troop leader and the only surviving pre-D-Day officer in that role in the squadron?

Even way up front, in the trundling, shunting Shermans just behind the lead recce tanks, nothing is happening with such interminable monotony that minds begin to wonder, to function at various levels; hands on control and immediate brain cells concentrating on hands, eyes, viewed landscapes; deeper brain cells switching themselves to memories, fearful forecasts, or frivolous imaginings. Operator Harry muses:

'Sergeant Warren' ... (up there, a pair of boots and trousered legs alone visible to the crew) ... 'last looked out on the feast of ... no, Harry, I can better that ... Sergeant Warren last looked out At Sint-Michielsgestel, Where the ... FOE lay round about, Deep dug in and .... Now, what on earth rhymes with gestel ... wrestle? trestle?'

At the opposite end of the line of fifty Shermans, as rear watch, Lieutenant Vaughan Green has nothing to watch. Like Harry up front, rhymes are pulsing through his mind but unlike Harry, Vaughan is an established serious poet of the kind that Harry hopes to be. And so, whilst military, unwilling military Vaughan Green watches out into the rear nothingness of Dutch drizzle, the poet Vaughan listens to his own magical, automatic pilot of mind, mechanizing words about the memories of past battles:

'Rouen ... flags at windows ... our chariots thunder

through ... Caesar in dusty triumph ... fruits and flowers for the visitors ... smiles ... and tears ... and fuss, we read all about it in History ... and now it has happened to us!'

'Hello, Dog 1. Hello, Dog 1.'

All the way down the column hands tightened, heels dug in, eyes switched to Most Urgent focus, as the leading Stuart tank reported.

'Hello, Dog 1. Road blocked ahead.'

Sergeant Warren was a man who acted more quickly than he thought, usually with positive results. Detaching his headset, he swung his short legs out of the turret and, in the continuing movement, leaped off the tank some nine feet to the ground. Staggered. Registered Black Watch infantry treading carefully up behind his tank. Trotted round the corner to find Recce Corporal Clague. Warren's thoughts caught up with his body. Better a little insignificant man trotting round the corner than a huge, clumsy tank if the Fritzes had an anti-tank gun hidden among whatever obstacle was up front.

'Oh, Sergeant. It's a huge tree felled across the road. Come, look. Right bang on Emily. Code-named Emily, I mean,' said Clague with a sudden vague smile. 'No sign of Jerry.'

'Probably run off with Emily,' grunted Warren with a rare attempt at humour in a moment of crisis. 'Let's go look.'

It was indeed a colossus of a tree, carefully felled so that even a bicycle could not find a path past it; screened with branches and leaves so that a distant view would suggest it might be defended, whilst a closer inspection might still not be able to pronounce it free of booby-traps; and dug in solidly at both ends, so that a quick tug from a tank tow-rope might not be enough to shift it.

Befitting his one nickname of Balbo, after the fiery impetuous little Italian general, rather than his other nickname, the obvious one of Bunny, Warren strode forward down the middle of the road and stood with hands on hips directly in front of the obstacle. Once again his thoughts caught up with his actions. Nobody had fired. Nothing had happened. He wasn't dead. Therefore: the obstacle was not defended.

He waved to the watching Black Watch infantrymen and turned to the recce corporal. 'No way through. No way over the hedge. No local defence. Have to go round. Job for big

Shermans. Not your squitty little Honeys. I'll go round. That's me.'

'With care, Sergeant. Might they perhaps have an anti-tank gun lined up on just where you will have to swing round that tree?'

'Bugger 'em if they do. What you think I got a gun for myself? You keep Emily company, boy. I'm off. Hey, Jock, tell your captain I'm doing a left hook back round the corner.'

'The captain's there behind ye, Sarge. Nae doot he'll tell anither platoon off to support ye's.'

2 Troop veered away to the left, over ditches and soggy pasture, leaving the tree obstacle to be investigated by later forces. The file of squadron tanks followed, very much like immense waddling ducks all in a line. Or, perhaps more vividly, like a procession of clumsy, trumpeting elephants, with their Black Watch attendants close about every tank except the lead Sherman.

The monotonous countryside, the continuing drizzle, the incessant rumbling of engines and tracks, the heady internal atmosphere of engine heat, body sweat, ammunition smells, reeking oil, and frequent urinating into topless empty ammo tins, all conspired to lull the crew into a kind of perplexed mesmerized state.

Down front, in the wide shared driving compartment, driver George Leach had little to do while driving across open farmland. And there was little to see in the tiny oblong of his periscope. His mind tended to drift off into fantasies about driving a sleek Rolls-Royce, with Sir Archibald Warren lolling back in the rear cushions and Len Moore as the footman. The co-driver, Len Moore, had even less to do, although he was one of the two soldiers in all the British Empire most up front and on the road to Berlin that afternoon.

Len, a West Country lad, was not impressed by the Dutch scenery and preferred to make plans for the first leave, whenever that might be, back home to Blighty. In the turret young Jack continually blinked his eyes as tiredness made the gun telescope play all kinds of cinematic tricks with the landscape. Wireless Operator, Harry Brown, found listening to the empty radio world as conducive to aural tricks as Jack's telescope was to optical illusions. Sitting there, a total non-soldier by nature, but nursing the huge 75 mm round which he would thrust into the opening breech the first time the big gun fired, Harry remembered Harry Graham's idea about the Christmas pantomime. Just two months to Christmas. They would write their carol parodies. Other troopers, like medieval clerks, would scribble ample copies so that the enlarged squadron audience could bawl out words somewhat less bawdy than 'Salome' or 'Peggy O'Neill'.

The trite words of the amended carol came back, trite but appropriate for the purpose. 'Sergeant Warren last looked out'. Although his own periscope offered no practical addition to the views constantly available to other crew members, Harry himself looked out. Through the trees distant houses appeared, which must be outskirts of Sint-Michielsgestel village. A tall, squared off, red brick church tower stood near the road forward. The Germans would be up there, on lookout.

Sergeant Warren's microphone clicked as he pressed the switch in it. 'Hello, Able 2. Code name Anne in sight. All looks clear. Able 2, over.'

Another verse, thought Harry. 'Sergeant Warren clicked his mike ... Said the war was over ....'

The afternoon exploded. The Van Dyke landscape of peaceful Dutch rural life disintegrated into a fury of fire, and blood, and terror, and whirling moments.

Fire slammed against the tank. White-hot light blinded eyeballs. Hurricane forces howled past ears. Steel rained out of the turret walls. Rained inwards. Thunder followed the flame. The tank shuddered and floundered like a dying elephant.

The 75 mm round in Harry's arms blazed into a blood-red furnace. Became a flaming, searing angel form grasping Harry within its arms in a dance of agony. Steel shards stabbed Warren's legs within the tank as he saw the distant flash and the sudden smoke-cloud around the tank. Sharp daggers and iron clubs dug and crashed at George, lacerating his whole body. Len's trouser legs spouted blood with no pain yet. Jack screamed, surrounded by shrilling demons and clashing echoes, but himself strangely immune.

Jack pushed the sergeant's legs upwards, hooked his fingers on the turret ring, hauled himself up, and out, and, in almost bird flight, soared over the turret top and down to the far ground. Warren, lying on the turret, saw what looked like a fiery angel surging up within the turret, stuck out a hand, grabbed a solid epaulette, and pulled Harry up and over. Len's arms were free enough to open his hatch, pull his body and tattered legs out of the compartment, and lend a hand to George who somehow emerged from the other driver's hatch. Both tumbled down the front of the Sherman.

Other tanks had come up level, vengeful, angry, firing wildly but effectively in the direction of the briefly-perceived distant flash, daring the enemy to fire again. The Troop Firefly, moving in haste too close, added its monstrous voice and, for a lightning moment, fiery chariots seemed to speed out on either side of it as its own muzzle flash scorched the sward beneath.

The same Black Watch captain, close behind, snapped into his radio, 'Medics, immediate! By the smoking tank! Stretcher-bearers. And fast, fast, fast!'

The Sherman did not 'brew' as so often, in a hundred-foot gusher of flame from pierced gasoline tanks. Only hesitant smoke betrayed its fate.

Warren leaped and hobbled. Grabbed a bedding roll from the side of the tank. Ripped off the lashings. Wrenched out a blanket. Flung it over Harry. Doused the flames. But not the stench of burning. 'Medical Orderly, here! Quick!'

An ordinary Black Watch private bent gently over Len, as a medical orderly dived on to his knees beside Harry. 'Don't bother about me. I can bandage myself,' said Len to the Scot. 'Look after my driver.'

'Too late, mate! Sorry, old pal!' said the Black Watch man, who was obviously, like so many, an English reinforcement. 'He's a goner. Never 'ad a chance. I saw it all. Reckon he was already dead when he climbed out. Muscles gone on working, like. I seen it before. Gi'me yer first dressing. I done first aid in the scouts.'

So the afternoon disintegrated, into action, anger, passion.

Harry Graham swung his turret so that the telescope was on the church tower. Fired. Adjusted sights. Watched flight of tracer. Red dust flowered from the tower. His loader, the other side of the gun, slapped him. Loaded again! Fire! Load! Check! Fire! Load! Fire-Load-Fire-Load .... 'Gunner, cease fire. Traverse right.'

Arthur Dwight, his face paler than ever, head erect over the turret, ordered his 17 pounder Sherman Firefly forward towards the houses. Two other Shermans raced alongside.

Turrets swinging. Guns firing without sighting. To scare the enemy.

The field towards the houses dipped into a tiny stream. The Firefly tilted down to the stream, braked hard, halted, shuddered. Its long protruding barrel, pointing downwards with the tank, had thrust its muzzle into the ground which sloped up beyond the minute stream, for all the world like an elephant's trunk nosing contentedly into prime fodder.

Arthur climbed down to inspect the damage. Bent down over his gun muzzle.

Shells shrieked. Fire bloomed. Thunder crashed again.

The corporal's body was flung back from the gun muzzle.

Tanks right and left fired madly, almost insanely. Sherman tracers raced across the field and between the houses, searching for the powerful enemy intruder.

A tank crew trooper grabbed at the shoulder of a Black Watch medic bending over the body of a Black Watch corporal. 'Leave him. Can't you see he's dead? Come for our corporal. He's still breathing. Lost his legs, I think. Maybe his eyes too. But still breathing.'

Harry Graham's tank crunched back on to the road, soon a street, angling to a sharp bend. Need to go forward and reverse. Driver edging around the narrow corner. Corporal Panter's tank close up behind. Too close, by textbook war. A small market-square ahead. A miniature town hall. Street to the left towards the bridge. Main street right.

The bridge! Over Dommel River! Wide river. Code name 'Bronte'.

Voice of Jack Ginns, Harry Graham's commander, 'Driver, advance left. Hurry! The bridge is the objective. Get it!'

Harry, thoughts of pantomimes long banished, angry at the bloody Hun and what happened to Arthur ... Harry squinting through the telescope for the huge shape of some enemy tank beyond the bridge.

A tiny German figure, without helmet, dashed out of bushes beyond the river, ran down the slope, jumped under the bridge.

'Get him, gunner!'

But the bridge became flame, bulged, heaved, splintered, rose a moment bodily in the air, then was flying timbers, stanchions, paving, shooting up into the shape of a tree fifty feet tall, and then slowly showering down, polluted rain, into the Dommel river so wide to cross.

'God almighty,' whispered big Jack Ginns into the intercom. 'I swear I saw bits of bloody German in that lot. Silly, brave sod!' Then, sweating hard and switching to 'A' set, 'Hello, Charlie. Hello, Charlie. Bronte now. Bronte clear. But Bronte blown. Sorry. Charlie, over.'

Panter's Sherman waddled importantly down the main street. Dutch eyes peering from cellar gratings. Mortar bombs flashing ahead. Waddled to a bend. Waited an eternity for death. Death desisted. So waddle to another bend. And another bend. And another eternity. In the automatic inglorious process of liberation. Until dusk said 'Halt!'

Back on the fatal fields the squadron debussed in stunned silence. Not many dead today. Not many horribly mutilated. Only pale-faced Arthur. And doggerel-composing Harry. And mechanic mates Len and George. And Balbo, almost a bunny for once, hopping madly about, refusing to quit, then calming down and becoming listless under Bill Fox's harsh but kindly tongue-lashing. 'Get back to bloody echelon for a day or two, you damned old fool!'

Squadron and regiment debussing, refuelling, cooking, eating, cleaning guns, squatting, sleeping. Or failing to sleep. Ginns' and Panter's tanks still out in the village streets on picket in a night haunted by periodic flashes and crashes; and continual fears.

Black Watch Captain, Charlie Robertson, a tank follower all day, was awake and alert with Panter and Ginns. And one or two, and then more, cautious Dutch civilians creeping out of cellars in the ever echoing, threatening night, bringing coffee and hoarded cigars to the troops.

In the gathering, uncertain darkness Charlie Robertson, Jack Wilson, and a number of Black Watch NCOs, crouched at the edge of the wide, deep, swift-flowing River Dommel. Only the heroic German engineer, who blew the bridge and himself to pieces, had yet appeared on the far bank, although gun and mortar crews did their best to spoil the Tommies' sleep from afar. Charlie carefully scanned every inch of the darker bank beyond the silvery river which mirrored back every distant mortar bomb flash.

'See those telephone wires, floating in the water, Jack? Haul them in! One Dutch Resistance man says they have hidden some very small boats upstream. He's fetching them now.'

'And so, if we, my platoon, can grab those wires,' agreed Jack, 'we can pull ourselves across like one of those old-fashioned river ferries you still see at home.'

'And we'll cover you. The pioneer platoon is on the way with a Class 9 bridge. The colonel will get the entire battalion across. And then the engineers will come up with the big stuff, the Class 40 bridging to take the tanks over in the morning.'

As darkness and renewed mists shrouded the village, ambulances groaned to the rear with the load of Arthurs and Harrys of Yeomanry, Black Watch and civilians as well, amazingly still breathing after their physical shattering. Both Arthur and Harry rode blessedly unconscious, not yet come back to conscious fight against deadlier enemies than the Fritzes: the pain of extreme mutilation and the subtle whisperings of death itself.

And Ginns' and Panter's crews watched, and stank in their iron dens, and drank war-soured coffee in dainty Dutch china cups. And hunched, improvised crews of Black Watch ferried themselves across the river, hand over hand along the vagrant telephone wires, the khaki shapes humped close to the water's surface like primeval water beasts in a Brontosaurus-haunted jungle gloom.

Yes, I command this Sherman tank. I give the orders. I dictate the game.

There are days when no shots are fired, when we cruise along the open roads or rumble into liberated villages. Then I fly, and pose, and strut a little, and condescend quite a lot, from my post of authority here nine feet above the paved way. And, although our speed officially may be nothing more than 25 miles an hour there is an equation, almost mathematical, whereby speed, plus weight, plus steel mass equals more than the real speed. So this, my steel leviathan of the roads, bears down on you with the impetuosity of a hundred miles an hour. And you do not stand to argue.

Friend or foe, you give me way! If you are a Norman living in a Normandy town, or a Dutchman living in a village of Brabant or Limburg, you rush into the streets, cheering my progress, waving your message of joy, breathing the newly-liberated air, trying to catch my eye: the eye of me, the Liberator. And you bring, if you're a man, a bottle of wine or Jong Ginever; if you're a boy, an allied flag or some apples; if you're a girl, a kiss; an older woman, flowers.

For I, here above, here in advance, am Liberation. And my crew unseen. And the infantry trudging on wearily behind. And the airmen swooping past, high beyond recognition. And the generals, away back in their caravans. And the factories which built the tanks, filled the shells. Peoples. Governments. Churchill. Roosevelt. Stalin. All back there. And I am here, only my head visible, but their ambassador, gathering the wine and the flags and the flowers and the kisses. And maybe condescending to let the crew peep out too.

But, though you're a friend, you step back from my churning, gouging, flailing tracks. And, if you're an enemy, you surrender or take cover. Hide or run. And hope that the anti-tank guns will come. The 88s. The Tigers ....

The Tigers, 'aye, there's the rub'. The mighty Tiger tanks, and the rumours of mightier Royal Tigers. And the 88 millimetre guns that can shoot down a plane at 10,000 feet, and mash our steel to cinders at 2,000 yards. And who like to lurk around that bend ahead, just 50 yards of range. Another equation. If the Tiger can 'brew' me at 2,000 yards, what will hell be like at 50 yards' range?

Because only my head moves all over this battlefield. Infantry in ditches; my crew deep within; my supporting tank back behind the bend; the enemy ensconsed in houses, up the church tower, under the bridge.

But only my head moves visible over this battlefield.

They say it's a quick end for commanders. Beheading by 88 millimetre shot. They say you won't know much about it. I'm not sure about that. I'm not sure about death. I have this horrific feeling that death is a fall over an endless precipice through screaming winds and raging flames, where the soul suffers the body's agonies for an entire eternity without rest. I'm not sure about this 'peace and light at the end of the tunnel' business. So, I stand in my tank, the great liberator: a human head with a 30 ton body of armoured steel. Nobody can see my feet of clay. Nor, in the bombardment, hear the furious beating of a faltering heart. Nor know the torment of my own awaited hell of unceasing torture.

So, I stand at the edge of a precipice which is bottomless. Yesterday I did not fall into that void. Days, weeks, months now since D-Day, I have evaded the fall. But *now* is *today*. And then there's tomorrow ....

And the griping fear of the bend in the road. And knowing that there are always bends beyond the bend beyond that bend in the road.

3   Those Blasted Bridges

By 03.00 hours, or 3 a.m., next morning, 24 October 1944, B Squadron, 1NY under Major Philip Wykeham, began to cross the bridge over the Dommel. This was the heavy bridge erected by the engineers and sufficient to carry 30 ton tanks. Charlie Robertson and most of the 7th Black Watch had already crossed during the night on the infantry's own temporary bridge. Panter and Ginns still stood point guard in their tanks in Sint-Michielsgestel. The crews in those tanks would be almost approaching asphyxiation after twenty-four hours of scarcely relieved incarceration within their tiny iron cells, of squalid, crushed habitation and dramatic excitement.

Even earlier than Major Wykeham's move the colonel had called his squadron leaders together. Whilst the colonel set out the general plans for action, in actual battle the squadron leaders had considerable scope for individual decision. In fact Colonel Doug Forster had been heard to comment that he often felt like Noah, releasing the raven and the dove out into the void and wondering if and how they would ever come back.

'Colonel Doug' was a large man, most resembling an outsize cuddly teddy bear, although renowned for his audacity and drive once aboard a horse and riding cross-country. Retired from a regular officer's career and then returning to duty for the outbreak of war, he was much older than anyone else except perhaps for RSM George Jelley, the boy soldier of the 1916 Somme battles. The colonel possessed that quiet charisma of thoughtfulness and understanding which attracted most Yeomen much more than the strident rantings of the war correspondents' favourites like Montgomery or Patton.

Now he stated dispassionately, 'We achieved the vital bridge yesterday, the bottleneck of Sint-Michielsgestel, even if the bridge was blown by some unknown hero in field grey. The Royal Engineers see to it that such a hindrance does not provide the enemy with too long a breathing space. If any. Now the three squadrons will diverge, each with a bridge as its objective. Get across those bridges, gentlemen, and we can cut the Tilburg road, one of the two best escape arteries left to the enemy south of the Maas.'

There was a murmur of muted enthusiasm from the majors, in spite of their overwhelming tiredness. This kind of action made good sense.

'So', concluded the colonel energetically, 'let's go capture those blasted bridges ... preferably before they are blasted!'

By 03.05 the first Sherman had rumbled and shook and bounced over the engineers' bridge with no problems from friend or foe. And in quick pursuit, Sergeant Jack's lighter Stuart raced across to take lead position on a day which was to pass into tradition as the episode not of Jack and the Beanstalk but of Jack and the elm tree.

Like Warren the day before, Jack decided to walk around a particularly nasty-looking bend, not far beyond the bridge and a little way beyond the infantry's most advanced post. Like Clague and Warren the day before he encountered a tree. An elm tree. Positioned, it seemed, by the same landscape artist as yesterday.

Beside the tree was a house. Jack decided to crawl through the house and reconnoitre. Unlike yesterday, as he emerged into the back garden he spotted a strategically placed sentry. In field grey. At thirty yards range Jack fired his pistol, with which he could guarantee to place one in every five shots on target at an extreme range of about five yards. The sentry ducked and ran.

It was as though the sergeant had fired a Very Light to a prearranged plan. Or had shouted 'Let battle commence'. His feeble, almost diffident pistol shot provoked a sudden cacophony of noise. Rifles, machine guns, mortars, howitzers, beating out fortissimo sound with orchestral precision. The Germans started it. The Yeomanry wasted no time in giving orders. Fire met fire. Noise rolled over noise. The dawn was brightened and accelerated a hundred times by the flashes of guns firing and shells exploding.

As the smoke of battle played imitation thunder-clouds among the trees, Sergeants Jack and Bamford decided that everyone was so intent on pyrotechnics that they would not notice a few bodies crawling up the very middle of the road. Together with Trooper Ovens they unhitched a tow-rope from the nearest Sherman. Then all three began to crawl up the road.

'Strike me if this isn't just like poaching in a neighbour's woods,' muttered Bamford.

'Keep your voice down. Jerry might hear,' grunted Jack, though noise like a thousand blacksmith's forges, all at full crash, would have made it impossible for ten thousand Welsh male voice choirs, all singing their fortissimo, to have been heard.

'My backside feels as high as the summit of Ben Nevis,' continued Bamford.

'Here, lad. Hook it on here,' said Jack to Ovens as they dragged the tow-rope under the branches of Jack's elm tree. No Wehrmacht bayonet, no ornamental SS dagger plunged out from amongst the leaves to impede them. No craftily tossed stick-grenade looped over the branches. They might just as well have been on a tiny desert island pounded on all sides by typhoon sea breakers.

A wave of Bamford's arms to the tank behind. A jerk from the distant Sherman. The tree began to move. To detach itself from the far hedge. To swing open and wide. Almost as though at that signal (as when the chaos commenced at the sound of Jack's pistol shot) the noise of battle ceased. Unbelievably ended. Probably because of the Germans' awkward but effective tactics of brief, hectic stands and quick, sudden retreats.

The road opened up and the squadron procession, still led by Jack's Stuart, closely followed by Bamford's Sherman, poured through the gap. 'God, if I didn't get shot in that lot, Jerry's never going to hit me,' breathed Bamford, his high, open eyrie of turret, normally a place of hazards and horrors, now seeming a place of refuge and solidity after the impetuous crawl along the lane.

Jack's saga was not yet at an end, though. Moving on foot between farm buildings he spotted a group of enemy infantry ahead, hidden from the road but exposed to the farmyard. They were spread out behind a hedgerow and armed with Spandau machine-guns, the fast guns whose firing sounded like ripping calico, and bazookas or panzerfausts, the bomb-projecting tube small enough to operate by hand but large enough to destroy a Sherman at a hundred yards range.

Jack pondered on wriggling back to his Stuart and sending a wireless message requesting an artillery 'stonk'. But that took time. And an old cartwheel standing against a barn wall gave his unorthodox Yeomanry mind an idea. The Stuart, smaller than the Sherman, would still not be able to manoeuvre into the narrow gap between barns from which the enemy could be surveyed.

'Ovens, lad,' he called.

'Here, Sarge.'

'Keep down! Keep down! Unscrew that big useless anti-aircraft machine-gun off the turret top. I've found a use for it at bloody last.'

Gathering up some old pieces of stinking rope from the farmyard, Kenny Jack resumed his crawling progress, pushing the cartwheel in front of him like a learner swimmer pushing a float, and grumbling to himself, 'I might as well have joined the blinking Black Watch as the tanks.' Ovens slithered behind him dragging the heavy 0.5 gun. Together they lashed it to the cartwheel which was lying flat.

'Ok, boy. You fire. I load. As many belts as you please. Give 'em hell!'

The cartwheel made an excellent firing base, traversing easily and tilting sufficiently. The 0.5 was a large machine-gun, somewhat slow in its rate of fire but delivering its load with impressive fury at a few yards range. Ovens was a competent gunner.

Field-grey figures toppled over, catapulted backwards, turned in dismay, ducked into ditches. In moments the enemy ambush had disappeared. Within a few moments more a piece of white rag waved above a ditch.

'Come out, you buggers. *Heraus! Kamerads!* Surrender! *Kaput!*' shouted Ovens in a delirium of triumph, jumping up and waving his arms.

'Get down, you idiot,' yelled Kenny Jack. But Fritzes were already responding to Ovens's signals. Another white rag raised. Bodies unfolding. Others lying eternally still. Others writhing on the ground. Prisoners surrendering. Trudging over the intervening cabbage patch with that odd mixture of resignation and relief that their war was ended.

'One, two, four, six, eight … ' counted Ovens.

And, out on the road, Wykeham, half a mile back, listening to Bamford's reports, ordered, 'Hello, Queen 4, take the lead towards Sunflower, Queen 4, over.'

Lieutenant Vaughan Green, 4 Troop Leader, flicked the wireless control switch to 'A' set, pressed the microphone switch, and 'Hello, Queen 4, moving through Daffodil now ...' Vaughan Green, wondering why, with the radio clatter in his ears, and explosion airwaves thumping on his skull from without, and the need to bring every brain cell to bear on that stretch of ominous Dutch lane, some vital sense far down within the mind, a kind of 'X' set, was sending up momentarily irrelevant messages like:

'This is Caesar in dusty triumph ....
We read all about it in History ....
How could we foresee it for us?'

Charlie Robertson with A Company, commanded by Major Small, of the 7th Black Watch, had shepherded the tanks towards Halder. They had trudged along at the steady pace designed to walk the thousand miles and more from El Alamein to Berlin. Now they hastened the step a little for the bridge, the objective, code-name Marigold, was ahead. And then, precise to the moment, a field-grey figure was visible for a moment in the far bushes, and ....

UP WENT THE BRIDGE! Apparently rising as an entire structure. Then as it twisted, disintegrating into wood and tarmac and mortar. And leaving that vital gaping hole over the next river to cross. 'Call for the Pioneer Platoon, bugger it!' Charlie heard on his set.

The Fritz was a crafty enemy, so the Black Watch spread out to search the apparently empty areas before the river. Charlie Robertson carried an American Tommy gun, which he had picked up in a German dugout at Le Havre, and which the Germans had somehow, somewhere, purloined from some American. Waving his Tommy gun in what he thought to be a menacing manner, Charlie was still surprised when a huge German emerged from what appeared to be a pigsty. The German was cowed, hands high, shouting, 'Kamerad! Kamerad!' Charlie grinned reassuringly at the man, but stood well aside. 'Right, then, good Kamerad! Let's go! Back the way I came is best.' The German leading, but glancing back apprehensively at the Tommy gun and the slight Highland captain with his fierce moustache; Charlie, dominant but still as apprehensive as any welterweight put in to face a superheavyweight. Towards the end of the trek through the bushes towards Company HQ, Charlie saw something square and metallic lying on the ground close to his outward-going boot prints. The loaded magazine of his Tommy gun!

Like a rugby winger in sudden sprint he swooped, whipped up the magazine, and jammed it into his gun. The German glanced around in a slow bovine stare. Then marched stolidly on. The Scot followed, cold shivers running down his spine, wondering if he was the only soldier in this man's war to have captured an awesome prisoner by waving what was, to a cool eye, obviously an unloaded gun?

Rex Jackson sat in Ken Snowdon's tank of 3 Troop, C Squadron, and, from his low co-driver spot, swung his telescope to watch the fires. A huge building, presumably a convent of sorts was spouting flames and smoke from several windows. Monks or priests in long robes were rushing out of the building carrying precious bundles and then fetching tiny buckets of unavailing water from a nearby well. Farther along some cottages were also blazing fiercely and setting off their own unmilitary smoke-screens to add to the confusion of battle. Artillery damage. Sad for the civilians. But deemed necessary, no doubt, thought Rex, to drive out enemy observers, snipers or even machine-gun nests.

Then his attention was caught by the sight of a large Dutch woman, her arms waving, her legs running, her lips opening, her words unheard amid the scream and blast of falling mortar bombs. She was inspiring small groups of peasantry to dash into the burning buildings, bringing out here the more valuable household possessions, there animals and poultry trapped in outhouses.

The tank radio was on intercom. Rex pressed switch and commented. 'Ken. That woman will get killed with all those Moaning Minnies falling all around. Can't you head her off? Tell her to get under cover until it's all over?'

'No chance,' replied commander Ken. 'She's saving her household, and that's more important to her than the chance of a shell splinter up the backside.'

'Makes you think though, don't it?' added Stan Hicken, the driver. 'Us sitting here, frigging frozen to our seats inside inches of armoured steel, when that poor woman's running around bareheaded and barefoot, without a thought for Moaning Minnies.'

'Makes sense, though,' said operator Tommy T., 'she

wants them chickens for Sunday dinners. Gawd, what I wouldn't give for a nice leg of chicken just now. 'Struth! Offer me the chicken or the wench, and I'd take the chicken just now.'

'Ok, lads, keep the chatter short,' said Snowdon, 'keep your eyes wide. No time for us to relax.'

As they waited in a routine traffic block of front line battle, for tanks and infantry and mine-clearing engineers to move ahead just up the road, another different figure swaggered into the view of Rex's periscope. A burly soldier in steel helmet, brown leather gaiters, and trench-coat, striding towards the very front of action. Oblivious to explosions he halted, waved at the tank, did the V sign, and, in a very brief silence, shouted what sounded like, '—ess you, boys!' before striding on.

'Who's that lunatic?' asked Rex.

'A padre. Army chaplain,' responded Tommy. 'What's he doing up here? No ferkin' church-parade in this lot, I hope.'

'Idiot!' exclaimed Stan. 'Padres only come up this far, either to give last rites to the dying, or to bury the definitely dead. Some poor beggar's bought it.'

Ex-schoolmaster 'Ratters' Rathbone was leading another half-squadron to secure the bridge over the Dommel at Hal. Stan Hilton, gunner on Sergeant Huitson's tank of 2 Troop, B Squadron, had the gunner's usual highly magnified view of the very narrow circle of land picked out by the telescope, alongside his wider view, lesser magnification periscope. After a pleasant, unhindered run along country lanes, Stan saw the bridge. Objective! Victory! Success! Keeping his fingers tight on the controls and his feet ready at the firing buttons on the turret floor, Stan watched as the bridge filled his vision. 'Two hundred yards,' he estimated.

The telescope lens blinked red, clouded black, whirled grey, brown, silver, red again. The tank halted, rocked, shuddered. Smoke filled the turret. Something like hail rattled down outside. Huitson ducked down behind Stan.

'Blast!'

'You can say that again!'

'Hello 2. You can see ... bridge blown ... bang on time ....'

BANG is right, thought Stan.

'Gunner, hose the bank, and those houses!'

Widely scattered Germans were making short dashes across the far bank and into houses over there. Stan trod on the trigger for his Browning machine-gun. This was mounted in the turret on the other side of the big gun and worked co-axially with the 75 mm, responding to the same telescope sights and hand controls. As the Browning spat fire, one out of every six rounds a tracer bullet, Stan adjusted the controls to move the continuous line of bullets along the bank and into the houses. As his operator slapped his thigh to indicate that the big gun was loaded Stan pressed the pedal trigger for the 75, and the large high-explosive shell raced across to open large holes in the walls of the houses.

There was a kind of fascination, even a thrill, amounting to an exhilaration, in sitting at the controls, sending out fan shapes of flame and death, pumping great charges of high explosive destruction across the wide river. And seeing dim shapes of enemies bolting like rabbits towards safer refuges. Furrows of turf bursting into fire. Walls tumbling. Windows widening. Doors shattering. Trees bowing under the gales of rounded lead and jagged iron.

A mile or two farther south, with C Squadron near Esch, Harry Graham turned his telescope on the second vital bridge in two days. Still that same damnable river which turned and twisted across country.

'Sarge! Bridge in sight. Suggest you creep up on this one unawares, sort of.'

'Ok, gunner. I see it. But no bloody unawares of it. Driver, speed up. Stick your foot down. A bit of Brooklands now.'

The Sherman surged forward. Other tanks in sight caught the mood. Dashed for the final bridge before Vught.

'Gunner, ready to fire on any movement by the bridge. God! There! Man lighting fuses. Fire, gunner, fire!'

Harry stamped on both firing buttons at once. Ill-directed or not. Scare the Jerries off. Which it didn't.

Slowly at first, like a mocking ghost, without a gusher of flame, the bridge took off in helicopter flight. Spun a little. Then a second explosion reached up flaming claws and tore the soaring bridge apart. The Sherman braked hard as, once more, an unwelcome, red-hot, dagger-sharp hail of shards began to fall on the tank. Sergeant Ginns dived for cover and slammed the turret flaps closed.

'Damn, damn, damn!' he shouted amid the continuing echoes of the far too powerful second blast.

'You seem to do things to bridges, Sarge!' chuckled Harry. 'Don't need dynamite with you around.'

'Hello, Charlie,' came the troop leader's voice over the 'A' set, audible even on the intercom set. 'Don't bother to report. I saw. And heard ....'

Way back, Charles Cathcart, Colonel of the 7th Black Watch was reporting to Brigadier James Oliver, who was CO in Africa: 'All three bridges blown!'

'Blasted bridges! We'll get the pioneer platoons and the RE's busy. Then tomorrow ....'

Tomorrow was 25 October, and B Squadron were again well positioned to move early. Lieutenant Margetts's 3 Troop, with Sergeant Bamford leading, was called urgently to cross the new bridge at Hal and attack a road block which had held up a cavalry regiment from the left flank.

'No crawling about today,' said Bamford to his crew, as they came in sight of the road block down a long straight road. 'Normal tank tactics. Brass up that road block and don't stop until I say.' Then switching to 'A' set to report.

The road thereabouts had no bends, or buildings, or woods in which to hide. A show of force was advisable. 3 Troop's other three tanks had followed closely to support Bamford. The artillery's observation tank was only yards behind. Highland infantry spread out on either side, leaping over the deep ditches which lined the road.

'Keep firing, gunner. Hello, Mike 3 Able. Am now in sight of ....'

Sergeant Bamford saw the pin-prick of red flash in faraway trees, and before thought could grapple with the flash, he saw the tornado of fire which billowed up from the turret in front of him, and he saw a lightning flash, a sudden brief sunset, and then black darkness. Eternal darkness.

He did not hear the thunder of the fiery strike on his own turret, or the distant thump of the enemy gun firing, or the howl of the round which had already struck. He felt nothing. He spoke no last heroic words. A curtain fell. Sudden. Swift. Total.

Behind him Sergeant Lloyd saw and heard and felt the blast, and knew. 'Driver, reverse. Left hand down. Quick! Move!'

Wally Tarrant thought, 'Stupid! That will put us in the ditch.' But discipline had linked Wally's hands to his brain and his brain to the word of command. While he was still thinking, his hands and feet had moved. The responsive Sherman shot backwards, slipped sideways, and cocked over into the ditch.

Another great 88 mm shot howled through the air where Sergeant Lloyd's head had been a fraction of a second before. The shot hit the artillery observation tank with such force as to slew it right across the road. All retreat was blocked. The 88 mm, distant in the woods but still lethal at the range, fired and fired again. Vehicles exploded. Men died. Impotent infantry ducked into the ditches. The lifeline to artillery was silent.

Young 'Reb' Reboles, caught in the storm of destruction along the road, saw a driver's hatch moving on a burning tank. A hand was trying to raise the hatch. Then he noticed that in the confusion and under the almighty power blows from the 88 shots, the tank in front of the burning tank, also sending up ominous thin trails of smoke, had crashed into the tank behind so that the two vehicles had become locked in such a way that the hatches would not open. And the turret was burning. And the escape hatch under the driver's seat was probably sealed by its position jammed across a ditch.

'Only one thing,' thought Reboles. 'Move the front tank! Simple!'

He ran across the road. Jumped into the driver's seat of the abandoned front tank. Found the engine still running. Engaged gear. Frightening grinding noises came from the engine at the rear. Reboles accelerated. The tank strained. Then crashed forward a few yards. Smoke wreathed Reboles and he vaulted out of the driver's seat, down the side of that tank, raced back to the second tank, helped raise the now freed driver's hatch, and clutched at a hand. The driver struggled up into the air. Behind him the co-driver, gasping and coughing and groaning, also pulled himself up. Fell over the side. Into the deep, welcoming ditch.

'Hello, 3 Charlie,' called Lloyd, from his tank still half-tilted into the same ditch, but sheltered by the shattered first tank in line, Bamford's. 'Hello, 3 Charlie. Am still intact and able to hold on. 3 Charlie, over.'

It was the squadron leader himself who replied. 'Hello, 3 Charlie. Well done. But you can come out now. Bring your crew. Over.'

'Hello, 3 Charlie. I'm not abandoning ship yet, sir. No danger of sinking. Our little friends happy to have me at the party. Off.'

Fifty yards behind Lloyd an infantry captain was saying to Reboles, 'Good show that, Corporal. But you could have had your balls blown off. Damn risky job. But lucky for those two fellows you did it.'

'Thank you, sir,' replied 'Reb', who was most un-'reb', unrebellious. 'If Jerry couldn't hit me that time, he won't have a better chance again. I'll see to that.'

Other troops and squadrons carefully outflanked the gun which had caused all the damage. Young Bobby McColl with C Squadron, listening to the battle reports, checked his map, calculated that the offending gun must be somewhere to his right. About 600 yards away. He ordered driver Don Foxley to swing right slowly and carefully. In moments, a squat, square outline, foreign to nature, appeared among the woods, beam end on to 3 Troop of C. 'Gunner, traverse right. On! 600 yards. AP. Fire!' And the single armour-piercing round from the Sherman provoked smoke, and flame, and escaping tank crew from the self-propelled 88 mm gun which had massacred Bamford and a few more.

'How's that then, sir?' asked Lieutenant McColl's gunner, justly pleased with his instant aim.

'Too good too late!' snapped McColl. 'That bastard got an entire troop of ours before you ended him.'

Explosions continued to reverberate around Bamford's desolated tank up front. But in a brewed Sherman the risk of incinerating engine fire was always worse than that of casual artillery fire outside. Corporal Houghton and Trooper Mudge, not yet exhilarating in survival, cautiously emerged from their potential death-trap, lifting the body of Bamford between them, hoping that a spark of life still remained in the commander, relying on the medics who were always close at hand, even in this prelude to Armageddon.

Still cautiously they crawled and dragged themselves along the lee side of the tank from the 88s, ducked in under the steel plates of the Sherman, cowered down sheltered by 30 tons of armour.

'Thank Christ. We're safe enough here for the moment. Is he still alive?'

Sergeant Lloyd, also cautious but undeterred in his self-imposed sentinel stint from his ditched tank, spotted movement in the ditch, forward of the tank. A solitary German, dragging himself along, waving, weeping, shouting useless sounds amid the din. No other figures followed.

Lloyd called Wally Tarrant and, armed with their frail, temperamental Sten guns, they jumped: tank to ground, ground to ditch.

The sergeant spoke good German. The enemy fugitive was only too anxious to surrender. But he was shouting that an English Tommy was lying in the road badly wounded. The tank men searched the German briefly, pointed him back towards their own infantry, then pursued a careful route along the deep ditch. Yes, there *was* a Tommy, a Jock. But, by this time, dead.

'Let's go look at Bamford's lot, then, Wally.'

The ditch made a safe approach through the trembling, burning earth. Bamford's tank stood high above it. Bamford's crew lay underneath the tank. 'God damn and curse bloody Hitler!' snarled Lloyd. Bamford's crew had been hit by a shell improbably bouncing *under* the tank. It was almost impossible to tell which was which in that ultimate comradeship of sudden, brutal death.

'Can't do a thing!' Can't do a ruddy, sodding, ferkin' thing,' groaned the sergeant. 'Let's get home and see if we can bash some bloody death down among those 88s.'

All this while, as McColl's troop completed their encircling move, Stan Hilton's tank was back, just across the water from where he had brassed up those houses yesterday. One or two Dutch people climbed among the ruins of their homes, searching, chattering. Stan's crew dismounted. A somewhat crestfallen Stan approached the nearest Dutchman to commiserate.

'Sorry about your house, friends. You see, the Germans were going to hide out there, so we had to fire. And it is difficult to fire at a house without damaging it.' And Stan said silently to himself, 'Yes, brother, and you enjoyed it while you were creating all those fireworks, yesterday.'

The Dutchman smiled unexpectedly. 'No go. We are enthusiast.'

'I beg your pardon. I don't understand.'

'We are all enthusiast. All Dutchmen enthusiast. You liberate us. Better you blow up our house two years, three years, four years ago. Then we have house and Germans. Now, no house and no Germans. Better no house and no Germans. *Ja*! We are all enthusiast. How are you?'

Big, avuncular RSM George Jelley had found himself taking a scout car into a village or town which he supposed must be Vught. Numbers of Dutch people were running out of houses towards him, obviously anxious to embrace him, impressed by his dignity and air of authority, holding back uncertainly. He became aware of an overpowering smell of rich female scent, and a cold, damp feeling on his neck. He swung around, a parade-ground bawling-out on the tip of his tongue. An elderly Dutch woman was spraying him with perfume. 'I have been keeping this for the first British soldier. I have been keeping this for years,' the woman cried.

'I ought to have brought my wife,' chuckled George. Encouraged, a pallid, hungry-looking man lifted up a little boy and said, in English, 'Kiss the good English soldier, my son. This is our special day. Kiss him.' But the son appeared to be as unwilling to kiss the burly RSM as one of George's own troopers might have been. The father looked disappointed.

'Don't worry, father,' commanded George. 'Just a minute.' He leaned back and searched in the scout car, found a bar of chocolate, offered it to the child. The child winced and shrugged away, as though from a venomous reptile.

'It's good chocolate. Shokola. Chocoolat-ee,' soothed the RSM, running through the British soldier's normal repertoire of what a foreign word must sound like. 'ChO-cOl-lAte!'

'Not understand,' responded the father. 'Never see chocolate all his knowing time. No chocolate with Huns. Here, look.' He took the bar himself, bit off a corner and chewed. A glorious look of contentment came to his face. He offered a square to his son, who tasted it nervously. He handed more squares to other children standing by, who handled, fondled, tasted and then masticated the strange substance, faces lighting up for this premature Father Christmas in khaki.

'Right! Surrender your chocolate ration, driver,' smirked the RSM. 'All in the cause of allied solidarity, Trooper.'

Another discontented soul was Geordie Johnny Byrne. A tiny driver with a big heart, Johnny had looked out through his periscope as he eased his tank up to the captured river-bank. There might still be anti-tank guns or bazookas about, of course. You never could be sure. He was delighted when he saw a white cloth waving on the end of a stick on the far bank. A couple of Germans began to climb out of a ditch. Several more peered fearfully towards the British tanks. Then a machine-gun opened up from the British side of the river. Several Germans fell or threw themselves down in panic. Immediately the evening came alive and alight with frenetic firing from both sides. Artillery joined in. Highland infantry moved up beside the tanks. Johnny saw a Highlander stagger and collapse.

It was an hour or more before the desperate German resistance died down, before the weight of tank and mortar and artillery fire had ploughed every square yard of the enemy positions, before the tanks and Highlanders could move forward and occupy the now scorched and devastated patch of land.

At the hour of twilight Johnny was free to go out through his driver's hatch and stretch his cramped limbs. He walked among the pitiful little holes in which the surrendering Germans had tried to hide themselves. He counted up to 40 bodies strewn like the proverbial rag-dolls across the tiny battlepatch, not large enough to be termed a battlefield. And, central to it all, three – only three – Germans sat on the ground, unkempt in their baggy uniforms, and all three weeping the grief of bereavement, betrayal and dereliction.

Johnny turned to a Black Watch lieutenant standing nearby. Troopers did not normally address infantry officers unless invited. But honest Geordie Johnny saw no other confidant at hand. 'The man who pulled the trigger of that bloody gun when they were surrendering ought to be shot himself.'

'Itchy fingers,' replied the officer soothingly. 'It happens in war.'

'I'd chop the bloody fingers off so that they wouldn't itch any more, I would,' and Johnny turned away to his tank, forgetting even to salute an officer of another unit. The Scot shrugged his shoulders and called to a corporal to move the prisoners along.

If Johnny Byrne was discontented his emotions were less complex and infinitely less sad than a small group of Cameron Highlanders and Yeomanry who stood at the open gates of a large camp near Vught. Military police in their red caps were already debussing from several trucks, and hurrying into the camp. Two of them barred the way against Camerons and tankers.

'Now, lads. You can't go in there. You don't need to go in there,' said the MP sergeant, gruffly but more kindly than the way MPs were accustomed to speak to sundry other units. 'Fact, you ain't going in there!'

'Christ almighty, what a stink!' uttered a Yeomanry corporal. 'Worse than a tank turret the night after the night before. Is that the local slaughterhouse, Sarge?'

'You might just call it that, Corporal.' The sergeant, seized of tidings beyond his normal comprehension, gathered the group close to him, lowered his head, and said in a whispered undertone, 'I'm not supposed to say anything. You'll find out anyway. The whole world has got to know. The whole bloody world. It's ... it's monstrous.'

He was finding difficulty in stating the ultimate horror. The group gathered closer and almost ceased breathing, lest he should awaken to the fact that he was a Military Police sergeant, and that they'd no right to loiter there.

'Concentration camp it was. Dutch. And Belgians. Civilians. Thousands of 'em. SS guards tried to shoot the lot of 'em before we arrived. Shot thousands. Against that wall there. You can still see bodies.'

'Shit! That's not piles of cast-off clothing by that wall,' exclaimed the Yeomanry corporal. 'That's piles of bodies. In rags. But they're too small, too thin to be people. Children, must be.'

'No, grown-ups,' sniffed the MP sergeant, suspiciously near to tears. 'Starving bloody humans. Small as monkeys. Thousands of 'em shot. And that smell is not them as died yesterday or this week. That's years of death and torture, or so the locals say. But the SS ran out of time. You lads made it here too quick. Most of the Dutchies and the Belgies survived. The SS slung their hooks. We're still fishing frightened Dutchies and Belgies out of shithouses and holes in the woods and ....'

A slow hesitant group emerged from behind dark trees. An erect Dutchman wearing the orange armband, a somewhat dishevelled British MP and, between them, a bowed, slight, shuffling figure in rags.

'One of 'em,' grunted the MP sergeant.

'Dutch?' asked a Highlander. The escorting MP shook his head.

'*Belge*?' said the Yeomanry corporal, in French.

The central figure looked up. A face haggard, wasted and scarred. '*Vous-êtes Belge*?' he asked, in a cracked voice as of an old gramophone record.

'*Non. Nous sommes anglais*,' said the Yeoman.

The man shook himself free from his escort and stumbled forward croaking, '*Anglais? Anglais? Les liberateurs? Mes amis!* Ah, *Dieu vous benisse! Dieu vous ...* ' and he threw himself down, kneeling, trying to kiss the Yeoman's muddy boots.

I am the gunner in this Sherman tank. I am power personified. I sit, cheek by jowl with this massive 75 mm gun, which, at a prod on my foot-trigger, can destroy a German Mark IV tank at 500 yards, or an armoured troop carrier at 1,000. And in the Bocage our normal fighting range could be only 50 yards. At that range I could shoot a particular leaf off a tree, and hole out on the periscope of the enemy tank. His eye.

A touch of my hand on the traverse lever, so! And tons of metal, the entire turret with three of us in it, sweeps left or right, at my command, and the mighty gun probing for the target. Another smooth pull of my other hand, so, raises or depresses the gun, for a shot at a mile range, or to send my Browning machine-gun spattering hordes of flaming bullets at the meadow in front of our tracks.

Oh, yes, I know that the 75 is small fry compared with those massive 14 inch guns that battleships carry. Our shells are small compared with the 1,000 pounder bombs which the Lancasters send down from the sky. Our tank is slow compared with the Typhoon plane diving towards earth with its rockets firing. But, unlike them, I sit here, behind a hedge, and pry through the leaves, picking my spot from the length of a football pitch away. And seeing my victim close. Staying to watch his death throes. Our tank tossed and tormented by the blasts and gusts of battle. Sensing the primeval thrill of the evil beast lurking in the undergrowth. Me! Power personified.

Yet running scared or sitting paralysed. Because only the gun is metal impervious. Me? I'm a welter of blood, bones, nerve-ends, imaginations, harsh memories, poised to disintegrate into screams of horror and pain.

And I'll tell you why: because I sit behind the gun, because I have this power, my German foe and comrade in terror, wants me dead. Me, especially. Because if he can hit me, hit my gun, cause this huge outward-exploding weapon to implode back on me with fire and shards of steel, my tank is no longer a jungle menace in his path, but only a clumsy, bumbling metal dinosaur – there to be annihilated by the advancing Tiger or Panther, without haste or greater risk.

So he wants me first. Sets his sights first on my gun, my periscope, my brain. My brain shrieking silently now, because it's fifty-fifty: I see him first or he sees me first. And he won't waste that first vital shot. He's out there now. I cannot see him. But I can feel this, my body exposed, even through my inches of steel protection at the turret front. I can feel this body exposed like a nude swimmer to the bite of a blizzard.

So I strut and sweat, I swank and slump; between heady pride in the power of my guns … and griping paroxysms of peril. In a dark, silent, treacherous night which is the reality of battle, even at midday.

4 Lunacy on the Sands

It was not in the nature of David Bevan to raise his voice. Instead his voice tended to chill over, so that the words snapped out like machine-gun bullets. And in the heat of battle all commanders experienced moments of anger or frustration.

In the case of Hank's second-in-command, Bill Fox, irritation did cause the voice to soar, and the hands to jerk, and the face to become mottled and bloodshot. Michael Hunt had been sent back to rescue the tank in which Corporal Dwight had been knocked out. Now, bringing the tank up through the crowded streets of Vught, crowded with jubilant, rejoicing citizens, he encountered the energetic figure of Captain Bill, making hurrying motions. The din of the tank engine and the carolling of the civilians made it impossible to hear. Mike stopped the tank and climbed down to receive orders.

'There's an emergency up front. Another Boche roadblock. Get that tank up that road to the left, full speed ahead. We need every gun we can lay hands on to break through. As fast as you can, Corporal.'

'Yes, sir. But we have a problem. The gun is bent.'

'What's that you say?'

'Gun is bent. I think when Corporal Dwight was wounded the end of the gun split slightly, and has twisted the barrel.'

'Stuff and bloody nonsense, man. I can see the thing from here. It's as straight as any gun ever is. You're dreaming, man. That tank is needed. Now! Get going. That's an order.'

'But, sir. If we fire this gun it will explode and possibly kill everybody in the turret.'

'An order, I said, Corporal. I'm not standing here listening to such nonsense. Who ever heard of a gun bending? Go, Corporal! Or I put you under arrest on the spot.'

'At least, sir, let the armourer see it. His wagon is just

down the road. It won't take a moment. You don't really think I would try to tell *you*, of all people, some kind of idiot's yarn, do you, sir?'

'There's a bloody crisis up that road. You can't ... oh, well. Go, get the armourer. But you've got two minutes only. Then it's advance or be put under arrest. Hurry!'

The armourer was indeed just down the road. He came along the street at the stately pace of all such practitioners and officials: doctors, policemen, sanitary inspectors, fitters, armourers. He examined the gun, looking at it from afar, and then, producing the instruments of his trade, fussed around it like a vet examining a docile elephant's trunk. 'Come on, man. Come on. The bloody war will be over ....'

At last he delivered his opinion. 'Was the corporal going to take this tank into action, sir? Ought to be arrested on the spot for rank carelessness. That barrel is bent, sir. Degrees out of true. And, see there! Only a split or two like paper cuts on your fingers. But fire that gun, sir, and your whole flaming turret crew will be remembered on Poppy Day for ever more!'

The captain paced up and down rapidly for a moment or two, then halted and grinned at Mike. 'You win, Hunt. Good man. Don't be bullied by damn stupid, ignorant, cock-sure captains. Get it into workshops. I'll go and win the battle myself if you're not available,' and he strode away.

The armourer winked at Mike. 'Good sort, under all that Wild Bill Hickok disguise, is our Captain Bill.'

Snowy's tank was already in action again. Down in the front compartment co-driver Rex Jackson was surveying the empty landscape and pondering on the ingratitude of fate, the fickleness of glory. Perhaps Hank should not have taken that abandoning of the tank so seriously. On the other hand another commander might have viewed it even more seriously and savagely. Rex wondered what a Guards major would have done about it, for Yeomen always believed that regular regiments were much more harsh in their discipline.

Because little Bobby McColl was such a good troop leader his troop caught quite a lot of sticky tasks. And, as Bobby's troop corporal, Snowy naturally inherited more than a fair share of the lead tank jobs. There was that horrific little first battle in the Normandy Bocage. Then first tank into Caen that blackest of midnights. Then through the orchards. First tank into the streets of fortress Le Havre although it wasn't his turn. Now Holland. Rex and Snowy, as well as Hickie and Tommy had been together all that way. Now, thought Rex, 'I wouldn't be a bit surprised if Snowy suddenly went bomb happy, jumped out of the stupid tank, and went bombing along for home. Anyway, what would I have done? One decision I'll never have to take. Not enough war left for me to be promoted commander!'

Tommy T., with his gift for perverting any name, had seen the map markings pointing to Loon-op-Zand and immediately christened it 'Lunacy on the Sands'. Indeed the battle was slowly reaching across an area of inland sand dunes, a freakish place that would become ghoulish. On the unstable terrain the tanks slid and bounced. Drivers were finding it difficult to execute tight turns or sudden changes of speed, necessary to evade the enemy. Gunners were unable to maintain a steady sighting of the gun towards possible targets. They had bumped and bucked over some uncomfortable country between the beaches and Holland, but this was some of the most perplexing. And, no doubt, the Germans would be solidly dug in at select points under good cover with open fields of fire, ready to devastate the first tank in line, and maybe a few behind it too.

'Driver, slowly left through that opening in the trees. Through that break in the bank,' ordered Snowy. 'Then you'll need right stick again to keep under cover. Gunner, keep alert as we break into the open. Everybody, close watch now.'

'Lunacy on the sands!' intoned Tommy, swivelling his periscope slowly. 'And don't I ferkin' wish it was Brighton sands ....' Which might almost have been his last wish ever.

As the Sherman thrust through the bank, and before the crew could see clearly, a howl, and a crash, and a screaming of metal splinters, and boiling flame, and a hardly-heard far-off thud, paralysed the crew for a moment. Blast ripped and ricocheted round the confined space like a screeching, whirling dervish trying to escape. Flame slithered through the turret ring. Periscopes were wrenched out of sockets in front of eyes pummelled within their own sockets. Tank overalls, discarded by Tommy in the turret fug, took fire between his legs whilst bullets hanging in the belt from the Browning beside him began to incinerate and explode. Assailed and seared at the focus of manhood, he yelled wordlessly, driven by primeval fears and urges, and flung himself over the gun, up into the commander's aperture, and out through impossibly restricted space, past Snowy who was still shouting into the microphone, 'Bale out! Bale out!'

Nightmares of Shermans seen so frequently spouting cremation fire up into the heavens sent Rex wrenching, colliding, leaping and sliding out of the tank. Vaguely he saw others jumping and running. The bank was only feet from the co-driver's side and he threw himself down there, under the trees. There were cosy firing positions cut into the bank but Rex realized suddenly that they, and he, were on the wrong side, the enemy side of the bank. He crawled frantically in what might be the home direction.

The nightmares continued, and changed form. He was crawling straight into enemy positions, and whichever way he moved it was always towards the German lines. Tanks and infantry were all directing their fire at one tiny little British soldier crawling hopelessly about between the two armies. The real storm of battle overhead lent substance to the nightmares. Storm was the appropriate word. Man-made lightning flashes, followed by man-made thunder, inducing a man-made hail of jagged metal, and a man-made terror which was far more imminent than any fear of remote, invisible, incomprehensible gods.

4 Troop of C Squadron were trying to find gaps in the same barricade of banks and trees. 20 year old Ron West, operator in the Firefly tank, code 4 Charlie, watched his troop leader, Lieutenant Skipper, trying to work his tank across the sandy slopes at awkward angles. The tank appeared to jolt, slither and spin, then circle round aimlessly within its own length. The long coil of immense iron track from its on side detached itself, looped backwards, reared and struck at the air like an angry serpent. It was only the equivalent of a puncture on a wheeled vehicle but infinitely heavier, more complicated and time-consuming to rectify. And not to be attempted while that battle storm still raged and while the tank sat, hardly shielded by trees, under the jowls of the enemy guns.

'Right! Our turn, lads,' ordered Percy Sumner, Ron West's commander, an older and very calm man from Sheffield. 'Advance, Larry. And all of you keep your eyes skinned.'

Gunner Jackie Skinner and Ron himself could see Rex's tank in front, still smouldering. They could estimate roughly the angle of the shot which had brewed that tank. So too could Percy. And they were all looking intently in the correct direction when there was a brief, bright flash beyond the trees. Percy ducked instinctively and the space where his head had been crashed and roared with impact, explosion, flame and shattering fittings. An explosion at that range is not seen. It is experienced from within a welter of lightnings, like dwelling in the midst of a thunderhead. The mounting for an anti-aircraft gun, unused, on the turret top took the full force of the shot and, while the blue lightning still flared, ball-bearings and splinters of metal from the mounting peppered the tank top and bounced into the turret.

Again a crew, an entire group, was stunned for the moment. Larry, the driver down below, recovered first. 'Is there anybody alive upstairs? Was that a misfire of our gun? Did you fire the ferkin' gun, Jackie?'

'I don't know. I don't think … It was a great bang. Perhaps we've been hit. My periscope's gone. My telescope's gone. We've been hit. That's it! We've been hit.'

'Hey, Percy! You OK?' persisted Larry. 'We ought to bale out. Hello! Who's in charge up there?'

'I am,' came Percy's voice at last. Ron peered over the gun to where Percy had collapsed in a tight heap behind the gunner's seat. The commander looked as though his face had been ravaged by a grizzly bear. 'I'm coming to. A bit dizzy. Yes, bale out. Bale out, all of you. You ought to have gone. Without me. Get out! Get out!'

There was a wild scramble from the confined dangers of the smouldering tank into the noisier but more widely spread calamities of the sand-dunes. Middle distance explosions still had enough force to buffet the tank. Dismounting was a perilous business with red-hot splinters still scattered far and wide. As co-driver Les Carr measured his leap to the ground the tank swayed violently and Les tumbled frantically, an ankle cracking under him as he landed. Stumbling, shuffling and cursing, the group sought shelter in the nearest angle of the bank of trees.

Coming through the trees, still disorientated, Rex encountered field-grey uniforms. In the moment before he turned to run, he realized that there were Seaforth Highlanders there too, holding a reasonably amicable conversation with the Germans. It was the Seaforths who had the guns. And it was the Panzergrenadiers who were clasping hands tightly on their heads. They must have been prisoners for some minutes because no cautious Highlander would permit a prisoner to put his hands on his head until it was certain that the prisoner had no hand-grenades to hide in those hands. Until then it was 'Hands right up! Palms wide open, *Kamerad*!'

'Which is the quickest way back?' Rex enquired.

'We were just discussing that,' said the Seaforth corporal. 'Are you going back, laddie? Can you take these prisoners with you?'

'Can you lend me a gun, then? I've just baled out of a burning tank.'

'Sorry, laddie. No spare guns here. We'll have to take these prisoners back ourselves when the fun dies down.'

Still somewhat befuddled Rex trudged on. Saw a Sherman. Stopped to look. Smoke, thin smoke issued from the turret. Its engine was still running. He moved closer. The gap in the bank. The trees. It was his own tank.

'I must have walked in a circle,' thought Rex. 'They say you do in the desert. Might be a desert here, all this sand. She's not gone on fire, anyway. And engine still running. Did Stan get out? I thought everybody got out. But it was all confusion. Might still be somebody inside, unable to move. She might still go up. Never can tell with Shermans.'

Stan or somebody else might be inside. Old pals of the long months of journeying, camping, fighting, sustaining each other in the worst moments, sharing the frivolities of the waiting times. And that scarred old Sherman was a friend too. A veteran of battles. Not to be further injured by some lurking Panzergrenadier with his bazooka. Or an 88 mm gunner anxious to finish off non-blazing targets. An arsonist from Berlin? Rex climbed carefully on to the tank.

Nobody in the driver's compartment. Nobody in the turret. A fire extinguisher hanging there suggesting sensible precautions. Rex squirted the foam lavishly in all directions. Engine still running. So as not to emerge again into the battle outside, he squeezed through the gap in the turret cage, down into the driver's seat. Fiddled with the gears. Seemed to be working. Now for the final call of the cards. If she moves, and if that 88 mm gunner is still watching, and if he is a psychotic arsonist from Berlin, then look out, Rex! Look out, old Sherman! Reverse gear ... gentle pedal ... ease her back ... sundry bangs and shakings still afflicting this neck of the sands ... lunacy on the sands, Tommy says ... well, all war is lunacy ... come on, then, old girl ... foot right down ... right hand stick hard back ... spin in a circle ... and, home James! ... we're going to make it ....

'Stat me,' exclaimed Ron West from their hideout where they had been wiping the blood from Percy's face. 'Rex is getting back into his tank.'

'They'll brew him up good and proper if he moves it from that gap,' groaned Percy, not yet able to see through layers of misplaced first-aid dressings. 'Stop him. Shout to him, somebody.'

'No good, in this,' observed Ron. 'Like a thousand demons banging tin cans. Can't hear yourself speak.'

'Tank's moving,' shouted Les. 'He's got the flamer moving.'

'Hope it's not a flamer. He's circling. Coming back.'

'They'll massacre the lunatic,' yelled Percy, the normally calm Yorkshire Sunday school teacher, tearing at the dressings in order to watch.

'No, he's OK. Fifty yards to go. Twenty. Ten. Goal! Home! Hip hip!'

The excited group jumped up and cheered, until a random shell threw sand house-high a few yards away. At least the sand damped down the force of whirling, spreading shrapnel and grit. They ducked down again.

'Tell you what,' growled Les. 'If one single Rex can get his tank back ...? Our old corned beef tin has had it. But we could put the track back on the Lieutenant's tank and save that from the nasty little Fritzes. Get ourselves a mention in despatches. Or, more like, seven days pay stopped.' So the troop leader's tank was repaired and ridden back to safer pastures by the battered and limping crew of the troop corporal's tank.

All this time Stan Hilton's tank in B Squadron had been sitting in reserve in a green field. Stan lay enjoying the luxurious bed of soft grass, dry for once under a pleasant sun.

'Many happy returns, Stan,' said a sergeant passing by.

'Is it the bugger's birthday?' asked another voice.

'Yes. 21 today,' laughed Stan. 'Key of the door. Except there ain't any door in this field. But, just what the doctor ordered, sunshine, and woodlands, and liberty, and peace.'

'Call that peace? Up there, look, in your bloody blue sky?'

Stan had been lying with eyes closed. Now he opened

them wide. Long, pure white vapour trails, like flowing scarves of wool, pointed from east to west against the clean blue sky.

'Rockets. German V2 rockets. Aimed at Antwerp,' the sergeant informed him. 'And pity the poor Belgies and Dutchies those fall on. They say 50 per cent cut out and come straight down en route to target. So keep looking up, lads. Father Christmas might be coming a bit early.'

'You've just spoiled my 21st birthday party,' complained Stan, snuggling into the grass for a few more moments before some squadron leader or troop leader or corps commander realized that there was a trooper down here with nothing to occupy his hands.

It was no birthday party for Spud Taylor and A Squadron, out among the dunes. The Camerons were busy firing off all their mortars, and the squadron was expecting to move off in the direction in which the Camerons had been firing. Having checked his gun for the umpteenth time Spud climbed out of the tank for a last breath of fresh air. He saw his commander, Mike Tansley, busy digging a hole. He wandered across to Mike.

'What are you doing? Can I help?'

'I'm digging a hole to bury you in, Spud.' Mike was burying ration tins, empty meat and veg. tins, in keeping with strict squadron orders that all detritus, material and human, was to be buried where at all possible. 'Don't say that, Mike. It's tempting fate. You would never forgive yourself if ....'

'Don't worry, lad. I'll see all you lot safely to Berlin.'

Spud was worried. Something had to happen when such a statement had been flung in the face of fate, as it were. And, as the squadron began to advance, Spud handled his Browning machine-gun with even more care and concentration than normally. The turret machine-gun fired at trees to the left whilst Spud, down in the co-driver's seat on the right of the driver, brassed up ditches and woods to the right, giving no opportunity for close-hunting bazooka-toting enemy to lift their heads.

'Misfire, co-ax!' The chill words sounded over the intercom. Tank crews hated misfires in the close quarters of the turret. It might mean clearing the struck but unexploded round out of the breech by hand. The column of tanks had halted. Firing ceased. Spud leaned back and squinted up through the turret cage to see what was happening.

All other remedies having failed Norman Sidwell was loosening the co-axially mounted Browning machine-gun from its mounting. Withdrawing it most delicately. Handling it more sensitively than a nurse with a premature baby. Pulling it on to his knee for better balance.

'Steady, the Buffs!' he intoned the traditional army watchword.

The bullet, cooked in the hot barrel, exploded. Shot out of the gun. Hit the curving turret wall. Screamed through a pattern of ricochets, back and forward, up and down, the crew ducking senselessly as the fatal busy bee buzz rocketed around the tiny turret, pinged through the cage, subsided exhausted on the floor beside Spud.

'God, I'm hit,' yelped Norman, pulling up his trouser leg.

'Fatal, that!' scoffed the driver, gazing at Norman's leg which was on a level with driver's and co-driver's eyes. Gazing at the slightest weal, the merest scratch grazed by the erratic bullet through the coarse denim trousers.

'Up yours, too, mate!' gritted Norman. 'It's OK for some.'

'Right, lads. We survived. Good work, Norman. Get that co-ax. firing, boy. And pronto.'

'I knew something would happen,' thought Spud, not sharing his thoughts. 'Pray God that's all for today.'

As Elijah of old said to the prophets of Baal, 'Maybe your god wasn't listening'. The column started up again. One Sherman in the lead on the left of the road. Corporal Tansley, Spud and crew in the second tank, on the right. So Spud had a clear view. Seconds only to wait. He had a clear view. A flash at 500 yards. A red tracer spark coming straight at him. The world standing still. Time frozen. Spud dead to all thought. Except for the view. A red tracer spark deliberately, unhurriedly, irresistibly heading towards him. Straight at him. A clear, precise, indisputable view. An armour-piercing shot. Sparking off shreds of crimson fire. Growing larger. Bang on target!

CLANG! Like a mighty hammer clanging on Wayland's smithy, the shot crashed into the moulded steel beside Spud's ear and gouged its way along the side of the tank, whining, grinding and spattering fire. The impact plunged Spud into silence and darkness.

'Spud! Spud! Are you there? Are you alright?' Mike Tansley's anxious voice. Spud shook his head and decided that it was still on his shoulders. The tank smelled too foul for it to be heaven. His limbs were too frozen for it to be hell.

'No bad news, lads. All good news!' – their always cheerful commander. 'That shot only grazed us. And Bill up front has knocked out the gun. It's all over. Lucky that wasn't the one that grazed your leg, Norman?'

'Well, that should be it for today,' thought Spud, still seeing bright lights and hearing rhythmic thuds. 'Second graze with fate. Third time lucky. It's got to be, whatever the third time is.'

'Do me a favour, Spud. Hose down those trees, right, two o'clock. Snipers reported. Nasty people. In your own time.'

If turret crews hated misfires within their tight, iron cells, tank commanders hated the report of snipers when it was so much more efficient for the commander to keep his head out of the turret, rather than closing down the flaps and relying on the restricted field of periscope vision. Spud set to work again, trigger tightly pressed, the co-driver using a finger trigger mechanism on his hand-controlled machine-gun. Tightly pressed. Right through a long belt of bullets. Sighting on the intermittent tracer rounds to direct the stream of solid bullets in a hosing motion much as if he were manipulating a water hose. So simple. The motion of hosing. The flare of tracers. The pounding, regular impact of the gun on his flesh. The almost musical drumming of the stout Browning gun. It became a rhythm. A ballet of fire. An art. A fascination. A thrilling emotion of power and skill and domination over opposing forces, man and nature both. Spud became a mechanical extension of his gun, and then, in that marriage, the gun became a joyous, obedient, throbbing extension of his flesh. A longer arm. A more powerful fist. A strident, dictating voice.

'Good shooting, Spud,' chirped Corporal Mike Tansley. And died.

Was it a finger touch of fate which made Spud turn from the fun-filled shooting gallery in front of him to the ghastly carousel spinning behind him? The commander's body, now a dead weight in the worst sense of the phrase, had collapsed out of the turret aperture and fallen across gunner Titch Crawshaw, forcing the little man down into the tiny space in front of his seat. There his arms were jammed against the control of the power traverse and the turret was caused to spin round and round with no way of stopping it.

At each revolution the mangled and still bleeding face of

the corporal glared unseeing at Spud as the gunner's seat swung past again and again. Only inches, through the thin metal grille of the turret cage, separated the petrified, static co-driver and his mate from the spinning obscenity of cheerful life transformed into brutish cadaver in an instant, by a bullet in the brain.

Reporting feverishly, reacting immediately to an order to withdraw, reversing urgently down the road, the crew tried to lift the fallen body to the turret, to the ground outside, in case medical aid could revive the stalled heart and seal the gaping hole in the skull. The corporal, a cold mortal, habitually wore a greatcoat. As the crew strained to lever the heavy load up through the narrow turret opening, time and again the sagging body slid down inside the greatcoat, and back to the turret floor. Sweating, swearing, daring God to blast them with lightning, the slight youths grabbed again with bloodstained hands to inflict more indignities upon the remains of one who, only moments ago, had been the epitome of activity, authority and immortality.

Mortality exerted itself in another, and almost as grievous a way for Bill Higham, riding on Sergeant Ray Eley's tank farther north. Their route took them along a solid road raised so high above the surrounding land that every moment they expected, and awaited, that fateful clang of armour-piercing shot penetrating the Sherman's brittle skin. They scanned the countryside ahead for movement, or unnatural squared shapes, or flashes, or spirals of dust.

But nothing. The village objective lay ahead. Just a few houses strung along one or two gentle bends in the road. All innocence. Objective captured. At the first house an infantry officer appeared from beside the building, unexpected and unexplained. Bill's tank was supposed to be the spearhead of the army on that road. The officer waved to Eley, motioning him to descend. The sergeant stopped the tank, waved on the second tank in the file, and vaulted off the tank, giving the officer a sketchy salute. It was politic sometimes to salute unknown officers even at the spearhead point.

Bill climbed on to the turret to obtain a clear view and keep watch. He watched the second tank squeeze past. He watched the commander give the 'V' sign. He watched the tank swing into the bend there. He saw flame belch out of the front of that turret. He saw black objects spinning into the air. He saw the entire tank crunch backwards. He saw milling human figures on the turret top. He saw one pause to jump, and go cartwheeling back across the tank. He saw another hit the ground, start running, and go on running for, it seemed, seconds after his head had been smashed like pulp. And he saw the infernal furnace-pillaring of fire that only the Sherman, the 'Tommy cooker', the roaster and griller of Tommys to black charcoal shapes, could produce.

And, as Ray Eley turned from the officer, scrambled to his turret, stared at the screen of flames and smoke which blanked out the village street, Bill, phlegmatic Scouse though he was, felt himself go green, gulped and swallowed as his stomach revolted, gripped the turret flaps until they cut into the palms of his hands.

'Bloody hell!' said both of them in almost one voice, 'if it hadn't been for that officer ... who shouldn't have been anywhere near here ... THAT would have been US.'

Way back and at eventide Michael Hunt was challenging another of Bill Fox's orders.

'I'll be alright, sir. Really it's nothing. Nothing at all.'

'Boloney, man! Silly twaddle! You've damn well been hit and you're staggering and bleary-eyed. You need at least to take a standing count. Get back and see the MO. At least check you for concussion. That's an order. And don't suggest sending for the bloody armourer.'

'Just for a check up then, sir.'

'Yes, and if you don't I'll knock you on the head myself and chuck you in the meat wagon. Off you go!'

In something of a daze Mike found his way to the MO. Other Yeomen were sitting or moving about in various stages of light wounding or injury. The serious cases had long gone down the fastest road towards specialist care. Mike saw another corporal from his squadron being helped into an ambulance. 'Hello, Ken. Where are you going in that?'

'I've got a slight case of elephant's leg, Mike. But they don't have any vets here.'

'I thought all MOs were vets,' said Mike irreverently.

'Kind of you to say so,' said the MO behind him. 'Horrible man! Come on in. Let me look at that head.'

'You won't send me off in that ambulance, will you?'

'I don't think you will need prolonged treatment, Corporal. Your friend there won't be back for a month or two at the earliest.'

'You know, sir, we rarely hear what happens to our wounded. One supposes they get sent out of contact very quickly. But it would be nice to know sometimes. Especially when you have pulled somebody out of a burning tank and tried to put the pieces back together on the spot.'

'Who were you thinking of particularly? Hold still a moment, please.'

'Did you know Corporal Dwight, at Sint-Michielsgestel the other day? It seems years ago already.'

'Yes, I remember. Bad case that. But the Black Watch orderly got to him quickly. Lost one leg. The other doubtful. Eyes affected. But he was a big lad. He should win through. But it will be a long pull ....'

'And Trooper Brown, at the same place.'

'Ah! Severe, that is to say, extreme multiple burns. Touch and go. Now that *will* be a long job. But the last I heard they were coping ....'

'And Sergeant Warren. Older man. Not with us in England. Looks like a little farmer.'

'Oh, him! You'll never keep him down. Hopping around and cursing all quacks and minions under authority. We'll be letting him loose on the unfortunate Fritzes in a day or two. Now hold still again, young man, just briefly.'

'Hello, Able 2 Baker ....' Yes, I'm the wireless operator, and gun loader in the turret of the Sherman tank. I don't think I like being an operator. Perhaps next time round I'll be a gunner. Or even a commander. Certainly a co-driver. Back in Blighty they paid you more for your trade test as a wireless operator. Something of an honour to wear the sparks badge on your arm. Not an oily-fingered mechanic like the driver.

But they didn't tell you what it would be like in action, in a Sherman turret. There is only one escape hatch, where the commander perches behind the gunner's seat. Between them and me ... more importantly, between the hatch and me is this almighty gun, blocking the way out. Even in normal times it takes a deal of squeezing and squirming to get under the gun and into my seat – a fairly roomy seat once you get here. But no place for a person with arthritis.

That's in normal times. In the instant of time, the flash of reality, when a tank blazes into multiple explosions – engine, petrol tank, donkey engine, ammunition all going off like ten volcanoes and a thousand firework displays – there are obstructions beyond the normal. Under the gun hangs a huge bag which catches the empty cases as the big gun fires. There is a heap of battle rubbish and thrown-off personal clothes or boots. And maybe a fourteen-stone corpse mixed up among it. And I will have to crawl and tunnel through that lot – while the tank goes BIG BANG and bang again, BEFORE I can even begin to leap towards the light. Even if the way is visible through the thunder-clouds of smoke and fire.

So, who cares about trade tests and an extra shilling a day? But I do have one advantage. I am the ears, and often the voice of the tank. I sit here like an open-legged, ungainly mother nursing a new-born baby – except that my baby is a lethal load of shell-case joined to armour-piercing shot joined to detonator. I sit here waiting to load my next round into the gun after it fires. And, over the wireless network I hear the battle. The commander scans the fields and gives orders. The gunner swings his gun and focuses his sights. The driver pulls on his sticks and treads on his pedals. The co-driver nurses the second machine-gun and keeps a front lookout. I sit out of general sight and mainly listen. And respond. I listen in on the real battle beyond these hedgerows.

I hear the next tank along when my commander cannot see him. I catch the troop leader's first words. I hear the squadron leader himself intervene. I hear messages handed down from the colonel, from the brigadier, even the c-in-c 'says' .... And beyond the known voices the more distant messages, from allies, from remote and dimly heard foes, from static and jamming, and maybe from witnesses of the air which none of us yet understand. The dead of other battles trying to warn us? I have time to imagine.

And I have time to visualize the battle. Like someone sitting alongside a sports commentator and viewing the wider game which ordinary listeners can only partly comprehend. I hear commanders whoop in triumph and gurgle in death. And then the message, 'We're brewing ... ' sometimes ended with a code-sign all regimental and proper. Sometimes ending with a whimper, or a scream. Sometimes, worst of all, ending in mid-word, with a silence. An echoing silence. An interminable echoing silence.

I have found that silences are worse than heard sounds. Heard sounds may echo, but the echo diminishes, and dies away, and can be forgotten. Silences go on echoing for ever and cannot diminish. Noises may interrupt, but the silences are there for ever. And in the silences I imagine the battle approaching. I hear the messages of frantic fear and composed fate. And I wait. And I begin to compose my own message. Because I must be next. The messages come nearer. The silences will not be overcome. I have my message ready. There will be no way out ....

Bravely. Clearly. Regimentally. 'Hello, Able 2 Baker ....'

5 Raamsdonk 1 – Catastrophe

30 October, and life was kinder to Spud Taylor. With a new unknown commander in the turret, a Jimmy Somebody, an old steady soldier and obviously a Liverpudlian. As their Sherman pounded along a decent road towards the hamlet of Capelle, a Dutch boy came running excitedly to meet them, waving a Union Jack, signalling them to stop.

'Slow right down. Let's see what the kid wants. But keep your eyes skinned, and ready to move or shoot,' commanded the new corporal.

Clambering up the tank as it continued in slow motion, the boy shouted wildly in surprisingly good English. The corporal took his earphones off to catch the words. 'The Germans are going. They're running away. The war is over. Long live Churchill!'

'Where did you get that flag, kiddo?' asked the commander.

The boy paused for breath and then laughed gaily. 'A German soldier running away, took it out of his pack. Said to his comrade, "I was keeping this for the invasion of England. For our victory parade in London. But we are never going to need it now".'

'And did he say that in English, kiddo?' asked Jimmy Somebody, a little cynically.

'Of course not! I speak German, and English, and French, and Dutch. I shall be an ambassador one day.'

'You're doing pretty well already, young 'un.' But further conversation was made unnecessary because the little ambassador was followed by a host of young boys and girls, some on bicycles, some running, come to escort the Liberators into Capelle. And so the battered, filthy old Sherman squared off behind the bicycles and Spud had his own victory parade into the tiny Dutch hamlet. Older civilians danced, shouted, and waved ecstatically. The stolid

Dutch citizens were behaving with all the exhilarating fervour and delight of a Spanish fiesta. Until some remote German mortar commander, sensing the slight upon his race, opened up with the familiar batches of six Moaning Minnies, screaming, regimented clusters of bombs descending like Mongol hordes from the far steppes, to drive rejoicing citizens back to the safety of bricks and the other kind of mortar.

Colonel Doug had been explaining the situation to his squadron leaders.

'Just one more push is needed. Our 33rd Armoured Brigade and the Highland Division have circled right behind the German army in North Brabant, via Sint-Michielsgestel, Vught and Loon-op-Zand. Now we must capture Raamsdonk from where we shall dominate that last bridge over the Maas. Once we have Raamsdonk the trap will have snapped shut.'

'That sounds just a little too easy, sir,' commented someone.

'I agree. The Germans will be as aware as we are. Intelligence believe large enemy reinforcements, infantry and tanks are moving in to prevent us. And the roads up to Raamsdonk are exposed for miles around. There is no question of outflanking the place before we take it. So it must be straight up the direct roads into the hornets' nest.'

'And that sounds like a useful way of saying "right into hell", sir.'

'Again I agree. But we've handled this sort of thing before, and we'll handle it this time. B Squadron will push on today. If they cannot clear Raamsdonk completely, C Squadron will go in tomorrow.'

Which meant that Lieutenant Wall was forming up 1 Troop of B, accompanied by a cohort of Argyll and Sutherland Highlanders. Because of casualties 1 Troop was down to using two lance-corporals as commanders. The order of march was to be Lance-Corporal Reboles's tank, followed by Lieutenant Wall in close touch, then Sergeant Falconer and, bringing up the rear, Lance-Corporal Knoth, who was so new to the task that he had not even been issued with binoculars.

Seen from the distance Raamsdonk was just another small gathering of modest but substantial houses strung along the elevated road that ran through marshy ground, much of it actually waterlogged. Seen from the distance it appeared innocuous, peaceful, too insignificant to be the focus of desperate strife. But Reb Reboles knew by now that the enemy would let them come on, perhaps into the very heart of his trap, without giving the slightest hint of his existence.

Some commanders dealt with this moment by counting up all the eventualities of catastrophe and then working back towards reassurance, as a purge for fear. Others slammed the door on predictive thought, driving fear back down into the subconscious where he, frustrated demon, would await his day. A few commanders considered the permutations of chance to be an essential element in the great heroic adventure in which they considered themselves to be engaged. Again, a few older time-serving veterans had insufficient imagination to see beyond the next bend.

Reboles was an imaginative lad, as his brave actions in recent days had clearly demonstrated. He saw his only sensible response to fear to be an evaluation of all the sordid aspects of the worst scenario, and then reassurance that such a chain of events happened only to a small minority. He had considered the sequence of a total brewing of the Tommy-cooking Sherman.

No written report could ever truly describe that horror because it all happened so suddenly and so fast, before you could even say the brief word 'Fate'. And it would happen unheralded at any split second of the hundreds of thousands of split seconds which made up a day of battle. Say 'Fate!' and it could already have happened, and ceased. In bitter wounding. Or the darkness of death.

Neither could any cine film adequately portray the entire episode, because the battle landscape was so vast, and the passage of shells was so fast, and the lacerations of flesh so tiny, and the pandemonium of noise so demented. And there was always the smell, acrid smoke, rotting animals in the fields, sweat and stale urine, roasting human flesh.

Counting the stages of the catastrophe of a tank brewing totally, they followed on, merged, overlapped like this: first, a bright flash at a distance; second, a world-embracing flash, blotting out your entire seen world; third, the dark blur of disintegrating objects; fourth, the shock of irresistible shot colliding with solid, immovable armour; fifth, the wrenching at eye-sockets and nostrils, the bursting of eardrums, the ripping apart of lips, the sucking of fluid out of the lungs by invisible blast; sixth, the flaming into searing fire of the homelite, the petrol-driven battery-charger in the turret itself; seventh, the crash upon crash of heard noises; eighth, the even more intense flaring of gasoline in the engine and storage tanks; ninth, the beginning of the horror as the mind begins to realize what is happening; tenth, the strait-jacket restraint of immobility, wounding, paralytic fear, charring of muscles; eleventh, the overwhelming martyr's pain of death by burning at the stake, but a martyrdom whose entire sensations are compressed into a moment: twelfth, the struggle of the spirit to rip itself free from the tortured body, and from the hell of life into the clear new day of death; and thirteenth, if life lasts long enough, that smell, of burning, of me, mingling with those last sensations – loved ones lost, grieving – youth wasted – life spilling – indescribable agonies – the final indignity of collapsing bowels ....

All done, known, experienced, accomplished within the saying of the brief word 'Fate', that is if blackened lips, seared tongue, choked throat and shredded lungs could emit, could utter a word.

Knowing this, but knowing also the power of his guns, and the willingness of his crew, the young man led the small attacking group, choosing, like so many other commanders, to keep head well above the level line of turret, and risk immediate decapitation as an insurance against becoming trapped within the incinerating turret.

Reboles, Wall, Falconer, Knoth and their crews, and their infantry escort plodding behind, leading towards the blank, silent, empty bend in the road where the first ominous houses began.

Into the bend. And the first tank churning on the near track, the outside track accelerating, the whole vast towering machine slithering into the bend. And round the bend. And out of sight of its followers. And the second tank moving into the bend. Supporting the first. Hurrying to keep in sight. To watch. To see. In time to see ....

Fate!

'God, get me!'

The whole street seemed to burst into flame and noise and smoke. The first tank was out of sight, but the second tank, speeding on, was engulfed in the same torrential outburst of explosions, from enemy guns, from random bursts, and from the funeral pyre tanks themselves as they were pulverized from without and within.

To the tanks behind, the entire scene looked like a forbidding Turner seascape, perhaps called 'Storm at sea with fireships': as a frame to the action, an outline of dark, rolling, menacing clouds behind and within which lightning played; below the clouds a wild, fiery torment which no mind could understand; at the central point, a focus of ruddy, oscillating anger; and into this inferno the two stark, brilliant fireships sail. Destroyed, the two tanks continued slowly to advance in mechanical momentum as though trying, without human aid, to seek out their unseen destroyer.

Back from the angle of road Stan Hilton and the other gunners launched into a mad fury of firing without sighting, seeing no enemy but intent on causing such commotion and destruction that the enemy might be hindered or deterred in his intentions. At the edge of the village, beside the dwelling houses, were farm buildings and haystacks. Suddenly the haystacks, set blazing by the tank guns, seemed to lift off and climb skywards like misshapen aircraft with jet flames streaming from them. In mid-flight, mid-extinction, they glowed even more fiercely. Then exploded, exploded and exploded, again and again, with repetitious force that sent the tanks rocking as on a typhoon-swept sea.

'Loving Jesus!' said a voice on Stan's tank, 'what in hell or earth was that?'

'It looks as though those so-called haystacks,' replied the sergeant, trying vainly to sound calmer than he felt, 'were really ammunition dumps. This is worse than a London pea-soup fog. Can you see anything down below, driver, co-driver?'

Behind them, Knoth's tank was able to see some distance through the smoke, and Bert Moreland, one of the crew, called to Knoth that there was what appeared to be an anti-tank gun moving at the far extent of vision. Having no binoculars the young commander screwed up his eyes, stared, wiped his eyes, stared again and then pronounced.

'It's only some civvies with a pram.'

'Ferk that,' muttered Bert. 'If I was a civvy in this, I'd be twelve foot deep down the nearest cellar. Under a load of coal.'

Alerted by the attention the rear tank was paying to the

movements of the 'civvies with a pram', and unaware of Paul Knoth's definition of that phenomenon, operator Phil Swaby on Stan Hilton's tank swung his periscope in that direction. Yelled,

'It's a gun! Stan! Three o'clock! Anti-tank. Lining up on us.'

Dutch farm lad, Piet de Bont, was worried about the animals. Every human head was ducked low in farm ditches. The animals had been shut up. But guns were firing, haystacks exploding, houses burning, barns tumbling. Piet de Bont hoisted himself up and went to inspect. Farmers were like that. Back near the Seine in Normandy an old farmer had stopped the battle by walking across between our guns and Jerry's guns to rescue an old milch cow tethered Normandy-fashion at the end of a long rope in the middle of the open field that was no-man's-land.

Piet de Bont was scared but intrigued by the sound of metallic jangling, guttural voices and thudding boots around the corner of the farmhouse. He crept forward to look. A German crew was hauling a massive gun on its mounting to point towards a Sherman tank which had appeared in a break in the houses on the road about two hundred yards away. Piet was appalled. Waved his arms. It was too far to hear a shout in that holocaust of explosions, with the stored ammunition in the haystacks still cooking, sending off aerial displays of dazzling light, and rattling, banging and reverberating close at hand.

But Phil Swaby's exclamation had alerted Stan, and, even as Sergeant Falconer snapped out the order, Stan was traversing the gun. A touch on the hand grip and the smooth Westinghouse system swung the huge turret through a complete circle of traverse in under thirteen seconds. Not that far! Looking through his telescope Stan saw a square black shape, static amid the wheeling green and grey landscape. His telescope's graded sighting lines swept over the shape and along the side of the farmhouse. Too far! Quick brain pulses identified the shape; a gun traversing towards them, just as they were traversing towards *it*. But more advanced in its traverse. Yet not as swift as the Westinghouse system. Too far!

Hurriedly Stan pulled the grip to reverse direction. The efficient electric system responded and again was travelling too fast. Too far! Too fast! TOO FAR! Desperately, as brain identified enemy gun lined up precisely to obliterate Sherman, Stan trod his trigger. The turret gun breathed fire, smoke, raging sound from its mouth, and its rear breech end hurtled back into the turret, empty shell case shooting out of the breech and into the bag under the gun, the great gun itself sinking back into the embrace of the buffer system, the gun breech smoking defiant anger to the enemy but meekly open to receive from operator Phil the next solid round to be fired, if needed.

Piet de Bont stood in an agony of indecision as the two guns, the German gun here and the Sherman gun distantly, vectored in towards each other like long lost lovers reaching out to embrace. The Sherman gun swifter, but overshooting the mark. The German gun on. The Sherman faltering, halting, traversing back. Fire – from the Sherman. A black spot in the centre of the red flower at the Sherman gun's mouth. A black spot, blob, bolt, howling missile, straight, true, smashing into the German gun, splaying it, dashing it to jagged splinters, flinging its undercarriage like a child's toy away across the farmyard. And the crew: some of them falling, writhing, crawling, running away, dragging comrades with them. And Piet diving back to his ditch, vowing never to watch another battle, and 'Let the animals take their chance!'

One German gun gone and haystacks exposed, exploding. Two burning Shermans somewhere amid the increasing clouds of smoke. Falconer and Knoth crawled tentatively forward with their consoling group of Argylls beside them. Sight was virtually impossible. Hearing was battered and ravished. Smell became the dominant sense, and gathered and communicated all the obscene messages of battle. The two tanks continued to fire precautionary shots, machine-guns hosing down buildings, big gun blasting out high explosive warnings. Highland men threw grenades and added slighter sounds of Bren and Sten gun bursts into the dark, mid-afternoon void.

'Hold fire,' gabbled Stan into his microphone, as much ordering his own fingers and feet off the controls as conveying a message. 'Somebody out there in the smoke. Khaki. Black beret. Crew. Hammond. Corporal Hammond. Alive and moving. Wounded. Legs not working.'

'Right, I see him,' – Falconer. 'Driver, move on as now. Gunner, fire over his head.'

'German medical orderly,' reported another voice. 'Helping Hammond. Christ, no he ain't. The bugger's trying to drag Hammond away, Stan. Shoot the so-and-so.'

'Careful, Stan' – Falconer again. 'The Browning's not that accurate. Over their heads, boy. Over their heads.'

Stan urgently, mistakenly, providentially, trod the wrong button. The 75 millimetre cannon, massive to a non-tank man at close range, bellowed sound, belched fire and propelled a shrieking shot over the orderly's head.

Again, the orderly wildly tried to drag the injured corporal back into nether smoke, with some most unmedical idea of taking him prisoner. 'Driver, speed up. Gunner, play hell! Go!' The orderly looked up from the struggling, unwilling tank man, saw a thirty ton Sherman grinding grit out of the road surface, slamming straight at him. Rivers of machine-gun tracer lashing over his head from two tank machine-guns. Frantic, he jumped up, threw both arms into the air in abject surrender, then, just as intently started to drag Corporal Hammond towards infantrymen running along beside Falconer's Sherman.

Incensed, Falconer leaped nine feet down from the tank turret. Saw Argyll people holding the medical orderly and another German, badly wounded in the face and obviously a member of the anti-tank gun crew. He waved his revolver furiously, finger on trigger.

'You bastards. You bloody unscrupulous bastards. I'll kill you! Get back, Corporal' (to the Argyll NCO).

'*Kamerad*!' cried the orderly. 'Me medic. Me no combat. Me Red Cross. See!' tapping his armband.

'You yellow bastard. You combat, see! You try take Corporal Hammond prisoner. That not no combat, see! You bastard. Me firing squad. This revolver. So say your bloody prayers. And God help you.'

'Can't do that, Sarge. We're not ferkin' SS. We Argylls are bad enough. Look at my load of scruffs. But we're not SS. Either give him a gun and make it the OK Corral all over again, or let *us* deal with the bugger. Nice and gentle like. A nice soft Highland boot up his balls to cure him of rape tendencies. Come on, Sarge. Get back in your tank. We haven't won the war yet.'

Falconer grinned sheepishly. 'Lost my temper. Thanks, Corp. Is our corporal OK? Hammond?'

'We'll see to him, Sarge. And really gently for him. Now

where's that bleeding Boche medic that thought he was
playing at real soldiers, huh?'

Soon the dark blankets of torrid, stench-ridden, all-
pervading smoke intervened between German and Britisher
as effectively as a military umpire. And down night came to
reinforce the blackness. Dutch civilians crouched lower into
ditches or cellars. Highland infantry sought demarcation pits
in which to set up Bren guns at the new, most forward line of
liberation. And Major Wykeham's voice ordered B Squadron
back for replenishment, cleaning of guns, and binding of
wounds.

'An oily-handed mechanic!' That's what those blokes
up in the turret call me. So what? I drive this 30 ton
monster as though it were an Austin 7. I miss corners by
inches as we swing, slide and jerk on the braking
system which slows or halts the tracks. And there are
only inches to spare on most street corners when a tank
trundles round.

It's almost like sitting in the chest of an elephant, or a
buffalo, or perhaps a whale, and looking out through a
tiny eye, and steering this immense body with not
much more effort than playing a set of jazz drums. And
I talk with the engine. That is like the trumpet voice of
an elephant or the booming call of a whale. And I
understand that language: know in an instant if there is
a sickness, a tiredness, a lack of energy in that voice. I
understand its sound. None of those arrogant wallahs
in the turret can catch those meanings.

And I'm not really a fighting man. I am a driver. A
mechanic. A technician. A taxi-driver from London to
Berlin. I don't want anything to do with fighting. Not
like those blokes upstairs who seem to get a kind of a
chilly thrill out of targeting and being targeted. Out of
shooting and being shot at.

Somewhere over there is a driver, a Fritz from
Hamburg or Cologne, who equally does not want to
shoot me. He is only a bus driver going the opposite
route, Berlin to London. We would wave as we passed
by, if it wasn't for the turret crews. Or we would stop.
Share a pint of beer or schnapps. Talk about engines.
End the bloody war before we had finished our
sandwiches.

No, I'm no fighting man. But I'm a fought man. You've heard of the cavalry being the right of the line. Well, I'm the first of the line. Because: what part of the tank comes into sight first? Look at this Sherman. Look. There! The driver's little cabin sticks out in front, well in front of the turret. Right under the big gun.

There are two ways a tank usually shows itself. Either front on, coming barging through a hedge. Or side and front forward, edging round a bend. Either way you see the tracks, then the nose, then the driver's cabin under the gun. But no turret yet!

So what is Fritz the Gunner going to do? – who *is* a fighting man, unlike me or Fritz the Driver? Although he may think that our 75 gun is a pop-gun alongside his 88, Fritz the Gunner is not going to mildly wait while the turret barges through the hedge or crawls up to the corner. Fritz is going to belt an 88 shot right through the nose. Through the driver's cabin. Knock me out and the tank grinds to a halt or swerves madly into a ditch.

And then there are the mines. Fritz is not going to leave us nice open autobahns along which our Shermans can race his Panthers. He digs nasty little mines into the road and covers them up. Nasty BIG mines, carefully camouflaged. And not to shoot up the turret. Just to explode under the tracks, under the nose, under the driver's cabin. And up we go again!

'Hello, Squadron Headquarters. Send up another oily-handed mechanic. Ours is spattered all over his little cabin.'

So they put me in uniform, not because I'm a fighting man, but so that Fritz can have a legit. target. So, what can I do? Just listen to the voice of the engine saying, 'I won't let you down, brother. I won't let you down ....'

6   Raamsdonk 2 – Chaos Triumphant

'Just a seven furlong sprint down the straight. A good hard gallop. Then we're home and dry,' said Captain Bill Fox. 'But, of course, it won't be the straight at Epsom or Ascot. Yesterday, B Squadron found Raamsdonk thick with nasties. B only made it halfway. No reason why today should be any easier. The Hun will not give up sight of his last bolthole without a fight. So not so much a gallop, lads, as a good day's stalking.'

Out of the immediate battle, officers had the advantage of a little extra kit, a few additional supplies – to be paid for – and a servant to keep up the mess routines. Now, with 3 Troop scheduled to lead again, little Bobby McColl thanked his batman as superfluous kit was packed away.

'Thank you for all you've done. Not easy, trying to keep kit decent in this filth. Must be away! May not need you again.'

'Don't say that, sir. It's tempting fate.'

'You're a betting man, Mac. You know about odds. How many times has 3 Troop taken lead role into terrifying towns and nasty little villages?'

'You can bet the odds on gee-gees, sir. But you can't live by them. Every day is a new day. That's what I say, sir. Couldn't live this war by any other reading of the tea leaves.'

'A wise commander still calculates the odds. Thank you anyway … just in case ….' He mounted his tank which bore the Northants name of Helmdon.

Along the road, inspired for the moment by the mighty momentum of this full tide of tumultuous, booming tanks, each capable of crushing concrete walls under its tracks or devastating solid houses with shellfire at a mile range, 3 Troop advanced; 3 Troop, C Squadron, 1NY, 33rd Armoured Brigade. Sergeant Thompson, just returned from hospital after severe wounding in Normandy, now insisting on the lead position. Lieutenant McColl commanding immediately behind. Two Black Watch Kangaroos, with Lieutenant Donaldson commanding the infantry. Then Jack Ginns in the Firefly with its outsize gun, manned today by Corporal McKenzie, he who had dressed up in SS uniform during a lull in Normandy, and had almost been shot by a comrade who was unaware of the crazy joke. Rear guard came Corporal Ossie Porter, a tall, gangling youth whose most warlike ambition was to qualify as a dentist. Ossie's tank had been co-opted into 3, because Snowy, Rex, Hickie and Tommy T. were still way back fetching a replacement tank.

Inviolate, the column rumbled and crunched into the first critical bend, and round the bend, and into the straight that led to the church, which meant victory, and relief, and another day to live. Beyond the bend.

Flash! Gunner saw. Fired. Thompson saw, ordered. Shot in the air. 'Gunner, fire.' Self-propelled gun. Shot's tracer racing. Gun by church. Flash, again. SP garlanded with flames. 'SP by church.' Thompson still ordering. Sherman gun reloaded. Panzer 1 bites the dust. McColl still prying through dust and smoke to see. See. See! So important to be able to see.

'Hello, Jig 3 Able. SP by church. Now brewing nicely. 3 Able, over.' – Thompson reporting.

'3 Able.' Troop leader using the lower commander's call-sign in the normal manner. 'Good shooting. Take care. Off.'

Down in the front of McColl's tank, Don Foxley, driver, strict Baptist, hesitant soldier, murmured, most sincerely, 'Thank God for that.'

'Slowly forward, driver,' ordered Thompson to Dick Oborn. 'Great shooting, Bowden, you hit that SP before I finished speaking.'

'Correction, Sarge. Hit him three times. You'll find three little holes, all inside a dartboard size, when you go to look. I can see them through the telescope.'

'Forget him, then. Watch for the next. Driver, squeeze past that SP. Careful, the road is tight there. I can see a big ditch, driver. A big ....'

Dick Oborn stared through the tiny oblong of periscope, at the vast, looming SP, and piles of rubble from a destroyed house, and the yawning ditch; twitching the hand-held sticks at either side of his knees, swerving, reversing, judging, peering; something crumbled under a track; the

tank tilted, yawed, slid into the ditch. Angled sideways. A
ship blown over by the hurricane, the bridge touching the
waves. Or the turret almost level with the pavement. But the
guns still pointing hopefully forward.

'Damn!' said the sergeant without emphasis. 'Have to get
a tow. Driver, see if ... SP!!! Gunner, another! Two o'clock.
Fire if you can.'

Bowden pulled the traverse, sighted while swinging, saw
massive steel slopes of armour, great gun moving towards
them, feet away. Trod. Waited to be blown to hell. By our
own gun. Fired at such an angle. From a ditch. Flaming
round might cook inside the gun. Blow us all to ....

The Sherman gun belched. Outwards. Before thought,
belching flame answered out of the SP. Flame from our
round's impact. The two wraiths of fire and smoke meeting,
kissing, embracing, dancing together, a mad, barbarous fling
encircling the two vehicles. Killer and killed.

'Able, SP brewed. Am ditched but OK, over.'

'Able, can see. Coming past. Hold firm. Off.'

Bobby McColl switched to intercom. 'Steady forward,
driver. See if you can get through. Everybody, eyes peeled.
Bloody smoke!'

Don Foxley muttered another prayer. Automatically. All
mind, eyes, hands, feet concentrated on the road, the ruins,
the burning tanks, the Sherman upset in the ditch, the
lowering smoke clouds. Carefully he controlled sticks and
pedals. Sherman steady on the road. Heavy on road. Tracks
reacting to brakes. Drive wheels responding to pedals. Until
a sensation of crumbling, and slipping, and falling,
neutralized the brakes, rendered pedals impotent. And Don
clung to the brake handles for balance as that tank, too,
toppled into the vast ditch.

Black Watch Donaldson, Lieutenant Donaldson, in the
Kangaroo saw the second SP loom through the black haze.
Knew the Kangaroo to be the eunuch of armoured warfare, a
gunless, empty, Sherman body. Saw the most terrifying of
enemy weapons, anti-aircraft, anti-tank, anti-personnel, the
imperious 88 millimetre projecting from the gloom yards
away. Gave the order to charge. A Kangaroo tilting at a
rampant rhinoceros. Charged. Smashed into the great
enemy vehicle. Two wrecked leviathans slaughtered
together. Never knew then that the SP had already brewed.

Turmoil raged all around. Calamity, cacophony and chaos.

Tides of smoke and floating embers lashed and swirled between the tanks, smothering and suffocating commanders in their turrets. SPs blazed and spewed forth more carbon fog. Shermans ditched, Shermans prowling, seeking passage. Infantry splashing in flooded ditches. Germans in that house. Black Watch in this. Germans and Black Watch in others. Supporting artillery pumping more death into the street. Machine-guns casting random nets of sparkling danger across the scene. And always the hanging veils of blackening smog, the repulsive vapours of cordite fumes and rotting flesh. The steady, dogmatic side-drum beat of the Brownings, the faster, irritated rattle of the Brens, and the sinister, ripping-calico crackle of the Spandaus.

Bobby McColl surveyed the chaos about him. Reported back to Hank Bevan. Instructed Thompson, Ginns, Porter to stand fast. Seeing no infantry officer within the narrow prospect of the embattled corner of the street, he told the operator to come up and watch. Co-driver to take over loading. Gunner ready for the next SP to show.

Lithe, athletic, bounding with energy, he pushed himself out of the turret opening, rather like a skier pushing off for the high jump. Went down the front of the tank hand over hand. Past Don Foxley's periscope. Hit the road running. Aiming himself through the blind oblivion, premature night, towards where the infantry might be.

It was an unaimed, careless, probing burst of Spandau fire which took him. Killed him as he was folded, flayed, flung backwards by the succession, the torrent, the Mach speed of bullets; sharp, solid bullets scything the flesh and gouging the living organs; exploding tracer bullets setting the clothing alight and grilling the mortal remains. He died under the welter of indiscriminate bullets as a heavy shell, equally heedlessly despatched, crashed into the turret of his tank.

Porter's tank weaved in and out of the maze of vehicles. Ossie, exceptionally tall, head perilously high out of the turret, thus was the first to see three enemy vehicles. Crawling unsighted towards them. Unsighted as yet. Smaller guns. Not 88s. But fatal at ten yards range. Ossie bawled into his microphone, 'Gunner, right. Right, right, right. On! SP! Fire!' Double deafening blasts. Gun firing, shell exploding in a second split a thousand times. Boom-crash! 'Gunner, gunner, right again. On! Fire!'

Boom-crash! 'Right again, gunner. Another. On! Fire!'
Boom-crash! One, two, three. Three SPs alight, above them
incendiary red mouths bellowing echoing curses, adding to
the chaos of light blazing into darkness, and noise deafening
into silence, and knowledge of enemy moving like invicible
dragons, more and more reinforcing the dead. Hydra-
headed armoured serpents, three springing when one was
amputated. Death-dealing traffic jammed into a narrow
street, keeled over into ditches, splashing through floods,
hiding under crumbling houses.

Don Foxley, in a silence that was not silence but only his
own loneliness, peered over his shoulder into the turret, and
saw glowing, ruddy fury. Reached up. Pushed open the
hatch. Climbed up. Roasting heat from the oven where the
turret had been. Hurled himself into the sooty darkness
ahead.

The incredible storm penetrated into cellars where old
men, women and children were sheltering. Shrapnel, broken
bricks, glass shards, smoke, gruesome almost tangible
smells. They huddled tighter in cellars, adult bodies covering
children. Only one young curious boy moved. Or *at least* one
young curious boy. Warned by his mother, 'There's a battle
outside. Do not go up those steps. Keep down.' But little Jan
had never seen a battle. Watching for the moments when the
adults cowered in the utter straits of terror, he crept along
the cellar floor, quietly up the steps, onto ground level,
scared by the juddering and rattling of doors and windows.
Gingerly grasped a corner of curtain. Looked out into the
world.

A tall, majestic tank stood outside. Not a flat-topped ugly
machine like the German tanks. A smooth, high, rounded
tank. British. Liberators. The Tommies had come. The men in
the sandy-brown uniforms. Liberation. He didn't know quite
what the word meant. It sounded good. When the adults
whispered it, 'Liberation' sounded glorious. But the British
tank was on fire. From the top of it rushed fires such as the
preacher described in church. Fires to burn up sinners.
Burning up the sins but never consuming. The tank was not
consumed. But the burning went on burning, right up into
the sky.

A lid midway down the front of the tank opened. There
climbed out a bedraggled soldier, young enough to be a
schoolboy hero, thin enough to seem a ghost. Out of that

furnace machine. The young hero poised on the front of the tank. Jumped down. Ran. Stopped. Picked up an abandoned German rifle. Raced towards the church. The untimely dusk of battle wrapped itself about him like filthy grave-clothes. And he was no more. The little Dutch boy was afraid. Ducked down. Turned. Stumbled and fell down the cellar steps. Snuggled close to his mother. The woman, face downwards, reached out an arm and drew him closer.

Don Foxley, hesitant soldier, hesitated no longer. Jumped off the tank. Headed for the church, the only object bigger than the prevailing chaos. Ran. Saw a jettisoned German rifle. Stopped. Picked it up. Ran again. To the church door. Pushed it open. Fell inside. Fell through the church door. Crawled to a pew. Don Foxley, strict Baptist, not seeking some kind of divine protection. Simply the refuge of solid walls. As had wounded Black Watch infantrymen, stretched out on pews. Tank men in black berets crouched under the pews. Even Germans in their field grey, stooping and scowling at the far end of the huge building. Not peace, for enmity still intervened. Not quiet, for the battle still screeched and travailed outside. But, for the moment at least, sanctuary.

Sergeant Ginns urged his Sherman forward. The projecting 17 pounder gun made it more difficult for the Firefly to turn. The traffic block seemed total. Ginns urged his driver forward. The long-suffering bank above the ditch shuddered and subsided. The Firefly slid into strangely poised immobility. Ossie Porter pushed forward and reversed. Seeking a way. Endeavouring to see. Urgent to end the stalemate. Sergeant Thompson, up front, his tank stuck, jammed tight stuck, but amazingly immune from brewing, kept wireless control. The only true, stable elements in the disaster area: Porter's tank patrolling, Thompson's voice controlling, and more of Charlie Robertson's Black Watch splashing along the incomprehensible network of deep ditches.

Alf Rushton, the 'Coon', who thought more of scoring football goals than of hitting gun targets, saw it. An SP. Another SP. Moving. Its huge gun poised. Massive armour of steel plates about the omnipotent 88 gun. An SP. Coming from behind. Alf exclaiming 'SP! Behind us! Behind us!' Gunner Harper ripping at the controls, trying to wheel the turret through 180 degrees. Trying. Too slow. Ossie turning.

Staring at the SP. No use giving orders. Just stare him out. Stare. Die, if you must.

McKenzie in Ginns's tank seeing the same SP. Slapping Ginns's shin. Gesticulating. Ginns staring. 'Can you get the gun to bear?' Their tank skewed and slanted in the ditch. The German panzer commander, seeing Ginns's tank in the ditch. Discounting it. Discounting the skeletons of ditched Shermans, blazing SPs, Ginns's tank askew. Leaving the gunner to line up the slow SP traverse on Ossie's tank. The slow SP traverse. Not like the slick Westinghouse system.

McKenzie, his gun disabled. A round partly wedged into the breech. Immobile. Immovable. No way prescribed but 'send for the armourer' Send for God! McKenzie grabbing another massive shell, using it as a hammer. Bashing the wedged round into the breech. Not done! Fatal! Both rounds will explode. Once, twice, thrice, bashing the wedged round. A dozen times. McKenzie should be a dozen times dead. The wedged round shifts, jams, moves, bangs into the breech bringing the breech block slamming behind it. And aloft, the SPs slow traverse achieving the thin segment of circle faster than Ossie's traverse sweeping the 180 degrees needed. The SP lined on Ossie's tank. Inches away. Ossie almost smelling the commander's breath. Staring into his blank, robotic eyes. McKenzie, at the incredible tilted angle, moving the 17 pounder handle. Armour plate in sight. SP gun in sight. Arrogant commander in sight. McKenzie fires.

The muzzle blast from McKenzie's gun almost blinds, almost braises, almost shatters Ossie's facial bones. Between them, hell again opens up its bright red fountains, and the stark, square, intruding SP becomes a white-hot beacon of devilish glory.

Total traffic jam. Total obscurity. Total chaos.

Thompson reporting to Hank Bevan, 'Hello, Jig 3 Able. Stalemate. Road occupied up to church. But no movement possible. Some houses still held by enemy. Can you reinforce? 3 Able, over.'

3 Troop of C Squadron holding the last bottle-neck before the last bridge. But, equally, stuck in that bottle-neck! 3 Troop of B Squadron to go to their support. The doughty Sergeant Lloyd to lead.

Sergeant Lloyd reported to his troop leader. Operator out of action. Operator down with severe fever. Medics say flu. Impossible to take lead role without an operator.

'Take this new lad, Williams I think his name is,' said the troop leader, 'rather than disrupting another crew.'

'Over here, boy,' shouted Sergeant Lloyd to a forlorn, pale, new arrival, still loaded with kit. 'Shove your kit up on the back of the tank. Williams, is it? What's that? Tom! How old are you, boy? You look as though you should still be at school.'

'Say that to me,' laughed driver Wally Tarrant, 'and I'll bugger off back to school now, all the way to Chippenham.'

'Get in your cab, Wally. We're late. Now, boy, Tom isn't it? You're operator. Know what to do? More or less? How old do you say you are?'

'Nineteen, Sarge.'

'Gawd help us. Monty's into baby-snatching now. Don't worry, kid. We'll look after you. We're all old sweats here. At least I'm old and Wally there sweats. Just do what I say and no harm will come to you today. We're only going to support C Squadron. Mount up, then.'

Lloyd's tank, Nan 3 Able, bowled boisterously along the road towards Raamsdonk. Without pause. Without interference. Without fear. All the interference was now concentrated in the few yards leading up to the large church on a slight eminence, at the far end of Raamsdonk's main street. Lloyd's map was carefully marked. Round a bend and then round another bend and there you will find Jig 3. Porter's tank covering the rear, they said. Behind Lloyd, and encouraging him on, came the pageant of spare troops of B Squadron, more Black Watch, sundry aid and recovery vehicles. 'Only needs the ice-cream truck and the dustcart now, and we could escort the dear old Lord Mayor of London to his mansion house,' he commented to his crew on the intercom, the crew being already battened down for action.

Nineteen years old, young what's his name? Williams? Pale faced. Hardly out of nappies. Didn't they know this was a job for men? 30 year olds. Even 40 or 50 year olds would suffer this kind of battle better than schoolkids. And sod your myths about Hitler Youth! Bloody abandoned martyrs, they were. So Lloyd chatted to himself as Raamsdonk grew more discernible within its shroud of battle murk.

Round a bend. And round a bend. And ....

Shermans ahead! Blast wrenching at Lloyd's face. A bright whirring projectile boring through the turret wall, smashing the homelite, setting its petrol on fire, spraying young what's-his-name eighteen or nineteen years old with flame, splinters, blast, axe-blow death. And silence.

The wireless set had shattered. Sergeant Lloyd bent down inside the turret and shouted in gunner A. Hilton's ear, 'Any hope ... the young ...?'

'Nope ... goner ....'

'Let's get ... shout to drivers ... bail!'

The two of them levered themselves up past the rising flames, jumped, bounced on the engine covers, hit the ground, went to earth. Down in the drivers' seats Les Redgrove and Wally Tarrant rose together, like a circus duo, lifted the flaps, catapulted themselves on to the tank front, caught a glimpse of the turret burning, another glimpse of the street ahead, and dived back into the brewing tank. An outsize Panzergrenadier was standing in front of their tank wielding a lethal Schmeiser machine-pistol.

'Did you see that, Les? Blinking Goliath in person.'

'We're safer in here, mate. Closed down.'

'Yeah, until this tank blows itself and us halfway to the flooding clouds in half a minute flat.'

'What are we going to do, Wally? I can feel the flames warming my ass.'

'You've got a machine-gun there, Les. Scare the great bugger away.'

Les looked at the Browning as though realizing for the first time that it was there. Grabbed the butt. Pulled the trigger. Held it tight while the gun festooned a brewed-up SP ahead with crimson splashes.

Carefully they opened the hatches again. Cautiously they climbed out into the air. Soft, sibilant whispers sped past their cheeks. Hard, splintering thuds rocked the roadway. They stepped off the burning tank like small boys pushing tentative toes into frozen water.

'That door's open over there, Les. At the double.'

Together they plunged across the street. A German stick-grenade, mallet-shaped, hand-thrown, planed through the smoke towards them. Hit Les on the head. Did not explode. Tapped Wally on the shoulder in a friendly way. Did not explode. Seemed to follow in their footsteps, bouncing along like a friendly toy dog at their heels.

'Who flung dung?' gasped Les as they hurtled through the doorway and flung themselves breathless on the hard stone floor. 'Here we are, and here we stay. For the duration if necessary,' responded Wally.

Still way ahead in the church, Don Foxley said, 'It's getting dark. If we want to go, now is the time.' Two or three voices replied with unenthusiastic agreement. Others shook their heads and crawled deeper under pews. 'I'm going,' said Don, no longer hesitant. Explosions had forced the big church door open again. Don and the others pushed through. Ran. Bullets buzzed and flickered about them. A grey arm behind a wall hurled a stick-grenade. It hit a wrecked vehicle and exploded harmlessly. Another grey arm swung over the wall.

'Jokers!' grumbled Don. He stopped, crouched down, aimed his German rifle at the wall, pulled the trigger. Pieces flew off a chimney-pot.

'Don't do that again, Don,' pleaded Dick Oborn as they ran on. 'You'll kill me with laughing. Aims at the bloody Hun. Hits a ruddy chimney-pot. More practice on the ranges when we get home, buddy!'

'Let's get home first, you idiot.' But Don threw his captured German rifle into the nearest ditch.

Sergeant Thompson was going home. Hank had ordered him out. For hours the Thompson tank, call sign today Jig 3 Able, had stood immobilized at the head of the traffic block, unmolested because the enemy had obviously considered it destroyed. Inside the sergeant had controlled the moving traffic via his wireless. Ossie Porter was continuing his traffic policeman role, back and forwards, luckily without becoming ditched. Charlie Robertson's Highlanders had waded through their ditches and established a new tidemark of the British advance. The enemy had been unable to save their Raamsdonk outpost. Other troops were safely bypassing Raamsdonk, bereft of its 88s; and the bridge, the last bolthole from the south, was in sight.

A German commander beyond the bridge saw the approaching tanks and Kangaroos, ordered the blowing of the bridge, consigned his comrades in North Brabant to British prisoner of war cages. Or common graves.

Sergeant Thompson was going home on the back of Ossie Porter's tank. Don Foxley, Dick Oborn and others were going too. Ginns and McKenzie hoped to go. Wally Tarrant and his mate would have wanted to, as well. Ginns and McKenzie rushed into the street. A fresh blizzard of enemy

machine-pistol fire and hand-grenades drove them back to
the house. And made the escapers on the back of the Porter
tank shrug deep into the bedding rolls strapped there. Wally
and Les did not even distinguish the noise of the mobile tank
moving amid the surrounding din.

There was no way at that moment, in the twilight and in
the continuing crossfire, of casually exploring the street to
find survivors. Black Watch medics would find the
wounded. The other survivors could fend for themselves.
Wal and Les settled down, Les with a swelling lump on his
head, Wally also with a supreme headache and singed hair,
to spend the night, at least, under shelter.

Ginns and McKenzie were lodging farther down the
street, on the ground floor of a partially damaged house.
Literally on the floor. Gunfire persisted. Beating out warning
messages from one army to the other, and back again, rather
than aiming directly to kill. As the night darkened, voices
were heard. Cries in the street. Stumbling movements
upstairs. Then, nearer midnight Ginns and McKenzie heard
a voice from above, like a haunting spirit in the loft.

'Hello, Tommy. Tommy, hello. Is that Tommy from the
Tommy Cooker tank?'

'What the hell's that?' gasped McKenzie.

'Hey, Tommy, speak! I speak English. I lived in your
London. Are you Englishman, bloody Englishman down
there?'

'No, I'm a bloody Scotsman down here,' shouted Mac.

'You are my prisoner, then, Mister Scotsman.'

'Not on your fanny. We're winning the bloody war. So
you're my prisoner. We'll take you in tomorrow morning,
when we can see you.'

'Alright, Tommy Scotsman. I have bedroom. Best room in
house. So we make peace treaty tonight? All sleep tight? Not
let buggers bite?'

'What's your treaty, Mac?'

'This not Mac. This is Franz. From Hamburg. Tomorrow,
you win, you take me prisoner and I go back to lovely
London, to lovely fat Maria down the Old Kent Road.
Tomorrow, we win, I take you prisoner. Adolph give me the
Iron Cross. Is good?'

'Is good!' interrupted Ginns in his lusty voice. 'Now go to
bloody sleep, Fritz or Franz or Fanny Fannakerpants,
whoever you are. I've got a lump of shrapnel in one arm, and

what feels like an 88 shell exploding every two minutes in me head. And if you don't ruddy well shut up I'll come up those stairs, even in the dark, and throttle you with me bare hands.'

'Oh, you're so nice to know,' laughed Mac. Then loudly, 'OK, Fritzie Franz. It's a deal. Lights out now!'

But it was difficult to sleep, even with the assurance of a peace pact with the unknown Franz upstairs, when every snore, and snort, and rolling over of uncomfortable Germans upstairs echoed and rattled menacingly in the downstairs room. Which also opened into the street, still alive with spooky apparitions from the dying flickers of fire in abandoned vehicles. And from which street some prowling enemy might at any moment creep in.

'Thank God for the ruddy Black Watch out there in the ditches,' groaned Mac, trying to adjust his weary bones to the unyielding floor.

Come morning, it was Franz who must surrender, together with some four hundred more Fritzes around the perimeter of Raamsdonk. And later, Hughie McGranahan and his operator sat at ease on the top of their turret, their guns vaguely pointed at the mass of prisoners marching past, with half a dozen Highlanders to shepherd them.

'The price of victory,' sighed Hughie. 'Who would win a battle?'

'What do you mean, Hughie?'

'See those smiling beggars. They're off to demob. Finished. Their war is ended. Nice comfortable billets in England. Plenty of grub. Routine duties. No more killing or dying for them. No more wondering what's round the next bend.'

'I suppose you're right.'

'The price of victory. What do *we* get? A rise of pay? A kiss on the cheek from little Georgie boy? An earlier release from this man's army? Like hell we do. What I shall get is "Right, now, Corporal. Stand up nice and straight in the turret so that the Boche can see clearly to shoot your bloody head off".'

'You're right. I wouldn't be a commander if they paid me.'

'That's just it. They don't pay you. They don't pay anybody. I'd get a bigger bonus for making the tea in an aircraft factory. Roll on demob! What's for dinner?'

Don't ask me what's going on out there. Yes, there's a battle going on out there. But don't ask me what's happening. Yes, I am the co-driver of the Sherman. But I can't see anything. I can't hear anything. I can't feel anything ... yet! And I don't want to feel what I think I *might* feel ....

Down here in the driver's cabin, alongside the driver, I can't see anything: that is, except a thick, blank patch of hedgerow jammed against my tiny periscope lens. I can't hear anything: that is, except the continual thunder rumble of battle and the incessant indecipherable radio background bickering when the commander's not giving orders. I can't feel anything: that is, except the continual shocks of explosions, far and near, too near, which cause the tank to roll like a rowboat on a flurry of tide currents.

And I can't do anything. That is the worst. The commander can order, the gunner aim his gun, the operator slam another round up the breech of the 75, the driver pull on his brake sticks and tread on his pedal. I sit here nursing the butt end of the second Browning machine-gun, but what good can I do when I can't see a thing?

It's logical, isn't it? The commander up top is not going to let any of the tank show over the ridge. Only his own eyebrows. That is called 'turret down'. If there is a target, then he will let the gunner have sight of it by moving up a bit, ordering the driver to advance a yard or so until the gun is clear of the ridge. That is called 'hull down'. Or it might be a hedge rather than a ridge behind which we are sheltering. Either way, all I can see is a mass of hedgerow or a mound of earth.

The rest of the crew will tell you that the waiting and the silences and the uncertainty are the worst. They're almost glad when Fritz opens fire. Then it's all action. Commander commanding, gunner gunning, operator loading, driver advancing or reversing like mad. Me? – looking at my patch of hedge or mound of earth which grows a bit or dwindles a bit. No action release for me. I twiddle my thumbs, and rub the butt end of the Browning, and check the belt full of unfired bullets, and think.

Think of home, of Blighty, of leave, of girls in the woods. But it doesn't work. The other ghosts rouse up. Ghosts of paining and screaming and bleeding and dying. And worse. Worse is when one of the others gets 'his'. And the commander snaps, 'Co-driver, take over driving!' Or 'Co-driver, come up and gun!' Or the operator commands, 'Co-driver, I'm commanding now. Come up and load. And mind the commander's head rolling loose under the 75!'

Yes, that's my oftentimes release in action. I'm the crew-man that takes over. From the dead, or the dying, or the horribly wounded, or the bundle of bloody rags which is one of the three.

God! Sometimes I think I'd rather die myself. It's nearly always too late to do anything very much for my pal who's fading away into a gruesome waxwork beside me.

Lean over, and lift him, pull him, in one piece or in pieces, out of the way. And climb over, sit in the puddle of blood, wetting myself and automatically reacting to the commander's commands. Or crawl through into the turret, wrestling with a heavy sack of stiffening flesh jammed into coffin space. Fight him viciously aside so as to get to the gun controls or the loading seat before Fritz fires again. The final shot!

No time for niceties, or sympathy, or sensitivity. But still moments and seconds and minutes that seem like months and years in which to gulp down my horror of the gashed meat, and the gushing blood, and the ultimate stench of bowels relaxing in death ... and only a moment ago we were laughing together at some stupid joke.

7 Guy Fawkes Bang!

Schoolmasterly 'Ratters' was the kind of intermediate officer that colonels prayed for. Unflappable, intelligent, militarily unambitious, likeable, he could operate equally well as Major or Captain Rathbone, as squadron leader or supernumerary. Having led B Squadron in that epic street fight through the sacred city of Lisieux, and commanded half of B Squadron across the Dommel river, he now expected another move in the hierarchy.

New senior officers had arrived. Lord George Montague-Douglas-Scott (a regular officer), Sandy Saunders (like Michael Rathbone a former NY Trooper), and others had come on from the disbanded Second NY and other regiments which had suffered inordinately in Normandy. Tom Boardman (another ex-trooper), leader of the August Night March, was due back from hospital. So there would be a shuffle in leadership. 'Ratters' would not go into a flap about that.

Vaughan Green was the kind of junior officer majors prayed for. Of the same schoolmasterly cut as Rathbone, he was mature, thought long and hard about every problem, but was amenable to discipline. And was exceptionally respected by his troopers. He and Rathbone were good friends and able to exchange the kind of profound, very private thoughts which many soldiers had to keep secret.

'Cuppa char?' offered little Ray Ager, Green's driver. 'Ah, thanks Ray. Are you chef today?' Then scribbling down in his notebook for future use: 'For we saw the bridges we'd broken ... where ... the ... leaf-green river bends; and our tracks raised the dust of ... our passing? – shelling? – bombing? ... from the shattered houses ... of ... FRIENDS!!!'

Captain Tom Boardman jumped from the jeep which had brought him up the line. Slim, athletic, mid-twenties, he seemed no worse for his earlier wounding although, like so

many others coming straight from home, he looked like a
lonely paleface among a tribe of rough Red Indians. He
waved to known faces and headed for the colonel's modest
headquarters in a barn bearing ominous burn scars. Tom was
rather relieved to see that no immediate belligerent action
was signalled by NCOs and troopers sitting eating, squatting
chatting, or leaning against tanks and smoking pipes or
cigarettes.

Ken Quail met an old friend, Ray Ager, whilst wandering
through the lines of tanks. 'I see Tom Boardman is back, Ray.
You were his driver on the Night March, weren't you?'

'Yes. He just shouted to me as he went by, "Are you still
seeing green?" '

'Aye, that blessed green tracer they fired overhead to give
us a directional guide. I was his driver, too, you know, for
that particular bit of fun.'

'How could you have been? I was driving his tank that
night. August 7th. Never forget. Up front of all the regiment
and all the Black Watch.'

'And of the entire Canadian Army which we were in at the
time, remember? Yes, I drove Tom Boardman before you –
but in the scout car. Didn't you ever hear the famous story:
how I disobeyed orders, and got Tom the Military Cross?'

'I thought *I* did that,' argued Ray. 'But go on! I'll buy it.'

'They sent Tom up in the dark to recce the route.
Remember they said it was the Germans' strongest defence
line of the war.'

'They always say that. Just to make us feel important,
idiots that we are.'

'He ordered me to drive out way in front of the British
lines. On and on. I thought, "I hope this milord knows his
way better than some other posh officers I've driven for".
But he seemed pretty sure. On and on. I thought we must
have reached the Germans' front line, spaced out as it was.
Later I came to believe that we had. We were right in among
the Jerries.'

'Don't I know the feeling. Even with a regiment behind
you it gives you the heebie-jeebies, mate.'

'Anyway, we stop by a railway bank and the Captain takes
his field glasses and mapboard. Oh, and his revolver. Made
me laugh. Jerry sitting up there with his dozens of 88s, and
Tom goes off to war with his little pistol. He says to me,
"Wait 20 minutes. If I'm not back, go straight to RHQ and

report me missing. 20 minutes. No longer. And that's an order, Quail''.'

'Must have been scary. Not my scene.'

'Scary? Wait for this! When my eyes got used to the dark I see, propped up with their backs against that railway bank, three blessed Jerries laughing their heads off at me. "Ken, you twirp, you won't see Torquay again for long enough", I said to myself.'

'But what could you do?'

'Nothing. After a minute I saw they were dead. And that didn't really make me feel any better, sitting there staring at their ugly, grinning skulls. And realizing Tom had been gone 20 minutes. He had said, "Get the hell out of it, Quail. Go back on your own tracks because of mines. We've been lucky coming ... ". I swear those dead Germans were laughing and heckling me. 21 minutes. 22 minutes. I'd never disobeyed an order in my life before. 23 minutes. Tom must have had it. 24 minutes. If you don't get swept up into a Jerry prisoner of war camp, you get British cells for disobedience, Quail.'

'But the Captain turned up?'

'Right on 25 minutes. Never said anything about the 20 minutes. Was glad to see useless young disobedient Quail, I suppose. "Let's get out of here!" he shouted. And, as though they heard him up on the top of Bourguebus Ridge, the Jerries suddenly let fly with all they had. Right on top of where we had been. But we weren't there. You've heard of Sir Malcolm Campbell and Bluebird and 300 miles an hour. We topped that going back, aided by a few Jerry shell blasts up our backside.'

Meanwhile Colonel Doug was greeting the returning officer warmly, but also with a glint in his eye that spelled sinister intentions. 'Good to see you, Tom. Take over the reins of the old job. Lots of command moves you'll need to learn about later. Do you know Lord George? Now, Tom, you will be wanting a little activity to get you back into fighting fitness. How are your mathematics?'

'How long do I have for revision?'

'You don't. We are scheduled for another indirect shoot. Remember Le Havre when we were used as artillery? Out of sight and hitting the Boche from beyond the horizon, as it were? We are to do a repeat order of the same menu. Line up all fifty tanks by the compass. Range them one by one by means of a forward observer. Then, on a single order, all fire at a large island in the Maas. The infantry will be going in to mop up when we have blasted every Boche eardrum on the place.'

'And you want me as forward observer, sir?'

'No. Much more complicated than that. Your job is to line up all fifty tanks on the correct compass bearing. Which you will calculate. There will obviously be a variation between the tank on the extreme left and that on the extreme right. Work it out carefully. We don't want to waste too many rounds on ranging. Oh, and Tom, I don't know how your geography or astronomy or whatever it is matches your mathematics. But don't forget to allow the variation off for the difference between magnetic north and true north.'

'When is this barrage due, sir?'

'When could it happen, but November 5th? And what code-name could they give it, but Operation Guy Fawkes? Get those fireworks lined up, Tom.'

C Squadron did not have an official knocker-up. No trumpets sounded reveille in the line of battle. Night guards might bang their guns on sleeping tanks, if instructed, to rouse crews at an early hour. But, as a rule, each troop was responsible for getting its personnel on duty according to the requirements of the day. After the last hectic days in Raamsdonk and elsewhere the requirements of this day were few. Except for one unfortunate class of tank crewman. Operators were still expected to adjust their sets on a daily basis. It was big Ken Squires, operator on Hank's tank and squadron signals corporal, who came round, brimming with ill-accepted humour at an early hour to call operators, while other crew snuggled into the damp grass and slept on.

'Come on, you lazy scamps. You dozy operators. Netting in ten minutes. Open netting today on my call sign. Rouse ye! Rouse ye!'

The inevitable chorus of 'Ferk off! Up yours!' was an idle protest. Operators rolled out of their blankets and climbed into turrets. At the appointed time Ken Squires would send out a signal on the appropriate frequencies, and operators would tune in precisely to the two frequencies which their set enabled them to lock on to. In battle it was theoretically possible to switch from one frequency to the other on the pronouncement of a codeword. This was in case Jerry was listening. In fact this danger was so disregarded that the squadron had never used the switching drill in actual battle, just as they had never used the Morse so assiduously practised at training regiments. Conceding to the concept of secrecy, if the squadron was in battle or moving imminently into action, the signals corporal would send out a silent signal, which transmuted into a netting whistle on the receiving sets. When out of action the signal could be spoken by the signals corporal, thus giving the impression of important wireless activity, where there was no real action, to any German who might be eavesdropping. So today it was:

'Hello, all stations William. Report my signals' – Ken Squires on the squadron leader's tank. 'All stations William, over.'

'Hello, William Able,' (the 2-in-c's tank), 'OK, over.'

'Hello, William Baker,' (the second captain's operator), 'OK, over.'

'Hello, William I,' (1 Troop Leader's tank), 'OK, over.'

'Hello, William 1 Able,' (1 Troop Sergeant), 'OK, over.'

'Hello, William 1 Baker,' (1 Troop Corporal), 'OK, over.'

'Hello, William 1 Charlie,' (1 Troop Firefly), 'Strength 3, over.' (Something wrong with his set or his netting technique, for strengths ran from 1 to 5.)

Of course, 1 Troop Leader might be a sergeant these days, and 1 Troop Sergeant might be a corporal. And the second captain might be a sergeant-major or even a lance-corporal.

To the north, nearer the River Maas, was Balaclava. That might sound like a geographical conundrum. But with the Northamptonshire Yeomanry system of naming tanks after Northamptonshire, American or Russian place names, Balaclava was only another tank. A passing medical orderly was speaking to the crew as they relaxed.

'You chaps lost your gunner?'

'Yeah. Doug Gardner. Went sick. Any news?'

'Sure. The MO sent him back to a casualty clearing station because of an ingrowing toe-nail. Guess what they did?'

'Sent him back to his tank? Chopped his whole leg off?'

'Not quite. The doc said to him, "You're not serious enough for us. We could chop your leg off, which you don't quite want. But anything less than that is beyond us. We're sending you to Brussels".'

'So the lucky blighter's gone to big, bright Brussels.'

'Better than that. They said that even there it was not serious enough to do on the spot. So they're sending him back to England.'

'No! You must be joking. You're taking the mickey. Surely?'

'Wait and ask him when he gets back. 'Bye!'

Major Hank Bevan was sitting on his camp-stool, indulging in the only release he permitted himself from military duties, which was sketching scenes of everyday tank life.

'Are you really taking that up after the war, David,' asked Bill Fox, helping himself to a small tot of Calvados still remaining from their odyssey through the region of Calvados and Camembert. 'Do you really favour being a full-time artist?'

'Certainly not back to that deadening stockbroker's round, trains to the City, pin-stripe suits, bowler hats. No thank you.'

'You're not actually putting much on that paper this morning. You're worrying about something?'

'Oh, it's an excuse really, that drawing-paper,' tossing away his sketch-book. 'I was only postponing the inevitable. I should be writing the "England damn well regrets" letter to poor Bobby McColl's father.'

'I think that boy saw it coming.'

'What do you say to the man? And he said to me, "Even if you cannot bring my son back, at least bring me something to remember him by". As though he knew. But what is there left to send after that bloody shambles?'

'Not even his shattered wrist-watch that I could find. And God knows I searched hard enough.'

'One can't write to a father and send him rags of charred and bloody clothing and say, "This is all that's left of your only son".'

'Shall I try writing that letter? I'm less involved.'

'No thanks, Bill. You can wait until you're writing home about me, one fine day. And that will solve the whole damn stockbroking question.'

Troop by troop, and squadron by squadron, some 48 available tanks of 1NY lined up near Helvoirt, to range on the long island of land which lay between the Maas itself and the Aftwatering Canal. This area had been a refuge for Resistance fighters and the legendary guerilla 'Sam' had made himself known to the colonel. But German units were making a last stand on the island. The big Firefly 17 pounders would have to range up to 3,500 yards in unseen firing.

Tom Boardman checked his figures for the fifth or sixth time, and began his tedious liaison with the OP up near the island. Each tank would have to find its line, set the range and then fire proving shots, initially at unintended targets. That is to say, the ranging targets would not be the true targets destined to feel the full weight of the barrage. The first tanks, carefully and in their own time, fired the first shots.

The wireless link with the OP was crackly, but clear enough to detect a note of consternation in the observer's distant voice.

'Hello William William. I did not, repeat did NOT see fall of those shots. Try again. Over.'

The moment of puzzlement was soon past for there were another 45 tanks still to shoot and surely the idiot at the OP would see one or two of the impacts? More trial rounds sped their way towards the feint targets.

'Hello William William. I do not believe this. Your unintended targets are even more unintended than you imagine. You are averaging up to twelve degrees error. I say again, twelve degrees error. That is not one gun but all guns. Over.'

'What the hell has gone wrong?' mused the colonel. 'I could understand one careless gunner mixing up his north with his south. But every single gun?'

Tom Boardman added up his figures again, looking for a reason for variation from the true aim .... Variation? True aim? Magnetic variation! 'My God,' he said, turning rather paler, 'I've got my magnetic north the wrong side of the true north!'

To his surprise Colonel Doug barked a hearty laugh. 'Get it right, then, Tom. Get it right. And quickly. But good that you spotted it before all 48 tanks put 200 rounds each of expensive government property into the depths of the Aftwatering Canal. Come to think of it we might have got ourselves a few fish for breakfast,' and the colonel wandered away, chuckling to himself.

Snowy and Rex Jackson, Hickie and the crew of 3 Baker had acquired another tank in time for the Guy Fawkes shoot. An endless belt of service corps lorries was dumping loads of 75 mm and 17 pounder ammunition behind the tanks, as the quantities to be used were too great to be stored inside the turrets. Commander, gunner and operator-cum-loader would be hard at work firing the long series of shots. Driver and co-driver, in the case of 3 Baker Hickie and Rex would be out back handing up more ammunition, and helping dispose of the multitude of empties which would otherwise fill the

restricted turret space. A wireless headset hung down on a
loose lead beside the tank so that Rex and Hickie could
converse with the inside crew. The ammunition was coming
up in boxes of three. Rex and Hickie were struggling to rip
boxes open and stack rounds conveniently.

A sound, like the whistle of an old-time servants' hall voice
pipe, came from the suspended headset. It was followed by
Snowy's voice. 'Listen in lads. Everything is ready for the
start. The colonel will give the single order for the whole
regiment to start firing.'

It was astonishing how silent 48 tanks and some four
hundred men could be. A family of badgers might have
passed along the regimental lines without being frightened
off by one abrupt movement or one indiscreet murmur.
Human silence was total, although the mechanical heart of
the regiment continued to beat in a regular, unhurried
manner.

'Hello, all stations William. Ready? All stations William …
200 rounds … FIRE!'

If silence had been total, noise was an overwhelming
sensation. All in a flicker of an eyelid. Noise, a living, moving
thing that hammered at eardrums and thudded on skulls so
that within seconds of the colonel's abrupt 'Fire!' ears were
again listening to total silence. Ears deafened. Giving reason
to the order not to give orders. After that one word 'Fire!' no
other orders would have been heard until the long-suffering
flesh adjusted its sensitive organs to begin to perceive and
distinguish between the thunder-beyond-thunder of the
guns and the quiet radio-borne words of commanders.

And the fire, the actual flaming fire, which greeted the
word 'Fire!' was such that even tank crew who had escaped
through the furnaces of burning Sherman turrets experienced a new intensity of light, a more painful searing of the
optic nerves, a far more brilliant ghost-play of the blue and
green and purple flashes in the brain which the reds and
yellows and intolerable oranges became through the saving
kindness of the eye's mechanism.

And the heat from the gun muzzles. The temperature of
the open air in front of the tanks rose several degrees within
seconds. And continued to rise. And smoke there was, the
usual terror-bearing cumulo-nimbus clouds of black,
semi-solid particles. Yet the firing was so intense that the
flame bore through the smoke so that even the battle's own

clouds could not dull the stupefying, blinding light of the untimely day created by the guns. It was as though a whole range of volcanoes had turned horizontal and were gusting their molten lava across the waters. And, a mile away, and two miles away, a lesser shimmer of red answered the gun muzzles. A curtain of intensifying scarlet, gold and carmine, broken from time to time by a sudden violent answering volcano, spouting vertically and dying into black clouds.

Something like a ballet of living fire danced back and forward, here and there, left and right, as gun muzzles poured out flash upon flash. Commanders sat on turrets mesmerized by the recurrent and prodigious commotion they themselves had provoked. Gunners moved like automatons, firing, staring at an empty world, adjusting, aligning, firing again, hands tight on controls, most like coxswains of embattled ships, dashed and wrapped about by fearful tropical storms. Operators slammed huge rounds into narrow breeches, tapped gunners' thighs, grabbed fresh rounds, breathed foul smoke from the reopening breeches, loaded again, developing what Ken Squires had forecast as 'the strongest right arms in the West, and not from drinking Guiness'. There was no time for refreshment, for respite, even for wiping sweating brows.

Behind the tanks, as the fiery ballet continued to its strumming wild flamenco rhythms of echoing drums, little firelit goblins hopped and twisted: the Rexs and Hickies of the regiment, limned in crimson against a purple backdrop of night, bending, swinging, lifting, thrusting ever more fuel into the vast cauldron in front of them, these flickering figures most like stokers in the grimy stokehole of an early coal-burning iron ship, heaping on the fuel at furnace doors amid raging incandescence.

As the blinding, battering barrage continued, the ear became slowly adjusted to the faint, pathetic human syllables issuing from earphones. Then, at an uncalculated midpoint in the despatch of their hundreds of shells, Rex heard from inside the turret a word that chilled a tank man more than the advent of a Tiger tank at 500 yards.

'Misfire! 75!'

Whereas the invicible Tiger tank might be in sight, might be bringing its gun to bear, might be about to propel that awesome armour-piercing shot into the Sherman turret, 'misfire!' meant that the operator was opening their own breech on to a fired 75 round which had not exploded. But could explode at any moment. Filled with lethal propellants and designed to disintegrate into a thousand decapitating shards. Could explode now within the close turret walls. And the operator, failing a second attempt to fire the thing, would be drawing the misfire out of the breech, into the turret, through the turret, to the commander. 'For what we are about to receive ....' And might explode here or there. Regulations prescribed a period of waiting with the aberrant round still inside the closed breech. Waiting to see if it would cook in the hot barrel. And explode spontaneously. But tonight there was no time for that. So hand it up to the commander. And then out to Rex.

'There you are, boy. See what you can do with that!' And Tommy was already loading another round. Gun ready.

What to do. Suicide to leave the round at the rear of the tank amid dozens of live rounds. In front of the tank there was a small depression in the ground. Unpopulated. Leave the shell there. Roll it gently into the dip. Run back behind the tank.

'One good thing,' chortled Hickie, looking extremely relieved. 'You won't get more than one misfire in a battle. Unlucky if you even get one.' They set to work again on the diminishing store of heavy shells to be lifted to the top of the high turret.

'Misfire! 75!' The snapped comment from the headset. 'You must be joking! Just our sodding luck!'

Once again Rex accepted the perilously heavy and slippery struck round from Snowy. Hastened to take it to the depression in the ground. Rolled it with infinite care, not to disturb the sleep of the other misfire. Ran back even faster. Again, Hickie breathed consolation.

'Misfire! 75!'

Snowy's voice, irritated, 'You can't be cocking properly.'

Tommy's voice, exasperated. 'Don't tell *me* about cocking. I'm an expert at that.'

Stan's retort, from down below, 'You're the regimental ferking expert on that.'

But the bawdy humour, usually a salve for moments of high dudgeon in impending peril, was a weak straw of human effort washed away immediately in the night's flood tides of noise, flame and personal danger. Again the struck round emerged to be cuddled by Rex.

'You won't get more than one ... ' Hickie had said, working on a reasonable law of averages. 3 Baker suffered another Six. An unprecedented horrific total of nine in all, ejected, nursed, passed from hand to hand, laid gently side by side in the dip in the ground. As gunners and operators stepped up their actions, anxious to end the intolerable succession of sights and sounds, as the man-made tempest swelled to even more sweeping gales of speeding, heavy projectiles, more frequent bolts of lightning, more tremendous bursts of interconnected thunder, Rex ran back and forward, lifted, hurled, caught and deposited, until his mind was a seething fantasy of imaginings, horror, shock and eventually weariness.

It was said that when the barrage eventually died away, with a few irregular belated bangs of tardy guns, nobody spoke, nobody moved, nobody reported by wireless, for an indefinite period whose duration went unrecorded by the colonel, or the intelligence officer, or Tom Boardman, or the squadron leaders. As often happened, the eventual silence, and darkness, and absence of movement was, in some ways, almost more shocking and hurtful than the barrage itself.

A time passed in which tanks rumbled back to laager, crews for once left guns uncleaned, engines untended, petrol tanks unfilled, rations untasted, letters from home unopened, bedding rolls untouched. Crews slept. Some angled into turrets like recently buried Beaker Folk, knees up to chin. Or on the chill, dank soil. Or on top of the bedding rolls upon the warm engine covers.

A time passed during which wits returned, natural functions made their demands, discipline reasserted its grip. Another urgent colonel's conference was followed by squadron conferences. While the squadron conference was still in progress, old, lovable Dick Bates, Hank's driver, senior sergeant, and an inveterate eavesdropper, came down the squadron lines whispering urgently the amazing news.

'It's going to be "ready to move". We're on the move. We're going to bombard again. But this time it's Germany. Believe it or not. You'll get it soon from troop leaders. It's Germany this time. Blinking Hitler's own perishing Bocheland!'

I don't drive a tank, although I could if I had to. And I might have to soon, the rate we are losing drivers. But I drive the ammo lorry. No, not the MO's lorry. Ammo!

Ammunition. Loads of it. Load up. Drive up the line. Replenish the tanks. Drive back. Load up again. Drive up again to a different map reference .... Back and forward, like a bloomin' pendulum. Up and down again, like a flamin' yo-yo.

Or perhaps I shouldn't use that word 'flaming'. It's tempting fate. For I am sitting atop the finest, biggest, noisiest, blazingest Guy Fawkes bonfire you ever saw. And no problems about lighting it even on the dirtiest night of the year.

I've got 75 millimetre cannon, and the even bigger 17 pounder stuff. Armour-piercing and high explosive. Thousands of Browning machine-gun rounds, hundreds of them fiery tracers. Hand-grenades, yes, even in tanks, and Sten gun ammo. Smoke bombs and Very Lights. The whole flaming caboodle. All neatly stacked and snugged up to my backside in the truck.

And when that lot goes up it'll be like hell reaching up to heaven and singeing Saint Peter's balls at the Pearly Gates. You've heard of ... seen, perhaps, what happens when a Sherman goes up. One Sherman and a hundred foot spurt of roaring flame. Well, every day, I replenish nineteen Shermans. A whole squadron at least. So, on the bright day when I go up ....

Oh, no, of course, I'm not front line troops. Normally at night the tank lads come back a mile or so and we move up to replenish them. Not just me. There's the petrol lorry as well. He makes a pretty sight when he explodes, all in one fireball eruption. And there's the SQMS's lorry with lots of flammable stores. And the water truck. Not likely to burn so easily, that one. But spare a thought for poor old Jack Aris in the water truck. Never still. Back and forward all day long, for troopers are thirsty, but their tanks are even more thirsty and won't wait to be given drink, like horses might.

So it's normally at night that we appear. But sometimes the tank lads have to hang on, right bang in the front line. Then I drive what they call my 'soft-skinned' vehicle up under Jerry's nose. And if a Tiger tank can blow a Sherman to hell and back at a mile range, what is he going to do to my 'soft-skinned' Bedford at two hundred yards? Not a nice thought, I can tell you.

And then, of course, in this war we don't have us nice neat rows of unbroken front-line trenches like in the last lot. Nor a no-man's-land where trespassers are persecuted. These days the line is shifting all the time. And there are gaps. And arrow-points of advance. And aeroplanes that wander both sides of the line.

Back near Caen we were two miles behind our tanks, but they were five miles ahead of the old front line. That made US three miles beyond where we had no business to be. And the lads up above could only see smoke and mist. Couldn't see the white stars painted on our vehicles. So a single Jerry fighter-bomber came over first. Riddles us with machine-gun bullets. The RAF decide to go one better. Send over a squadron with thousand pounder bombs to straddle us innocents. Then the Yanks MUST do better than that. Came over in droves with what must have been ten-ton bombs.

When the smoke cleared there were the remains of 'soft-skinned' vehicles splattered all over the fields. And a good many of their soft-skinned drivers splattered among them. That's why sometimes I sit on top of my lovely load of primed incendiaries, and think, 'It might not be so bad after all if, one of these days, they have to stick me in a good old "Tommy Cooker" Sherman as a spare driver.'

8 Misery in the Mud

It wasn't actually Germany yet.

Dick Bates had not listened closely enough. It was indeed a long-distance move. A long distance by the standards of tank movement in war. From a river site close to the North Sea, to an area of Limburg on the opposite side of Holland. And as near to Germany as British troops could yet attain. But still ground to be won, villages to be liberated, 88 millimetre guns and mines to be suffered, days to be endured.

And the ground was sodden, swamped, awash from incessant rains. A vast sump of mud across the entire region of the regiment's ordained plan of advance. November was cold. November was damp. November was dark. November was deadly.

Michael Rathbone was the innocent listener-in to a conversation of his superiors. The B Squadron Leader, Philip Wykeham, was ardently discussing with a colonel of the Argyll and Sutherland Highlanders a move to examine demolished lock gates in the mist-wreathed village of Hulzen. And to find a way to push tanks and infantry through the obstacle. The regimental second-in-command stood listening and nodding. 'Ratters' knew that he was nominated for the job. Not the sort of thing he was particularly keen on.

'No, Major,' declaimed the Highland colonel. 'That is not a job for a captain. I would not even send a lieutenant to do that. Is there no capable NCO tank commander who can go up there and look-see?'

'We have capable NCOs, of course.'

'Then send one. Obviously, I cannot insist. I can only suggest. But if we are to work in harness we should be using compatible ranks. My first man up will be a sergeant.'

'Oh, well,' muttered the squadron leader, undecided and

uncomfortable. 'Oh, well ... what do you think, Michael? Should I keep you back and push Huitson up? He's a cool customer.'

'That's your decision, Philip. I'm ready to go. But perhaps what the colonel says makes tactical sense.'

'Of course, man. Waste a sergeant rather than a captain, if there is to be waste. Which, pray God ....'

So three stripes on the arm replaced three stars on the shoulder, and Sergeant Huitson drove his tank towards the lock, more boldly than he himself felt. That brought his troop leader, Vaughan Green, up in close support. By this time engineers had appeared on the scene with emergency bridging equipment, suitable for both foot passengers and tanks. Beyond the lock, a quarter of a mile away, was another dike with a small bridge over it, apparently undamaged.

As the engineers were still completing erection of the first bridge, Huitson clambered across on foot, and began to stroll towards the second bridge, for all the world like a casual hiker crossing by a public footpath.

'Careful of Schu mines,' shouted Lieutenant Green. 'Mines, Huitson! Watch your feet!'

Pausing only to wave, Huitson continued on through the mists in his rather spectral adventure.

'Damme if I'd want to be out there walking,' said Ray Ager to Ken Lyke, who had just joined him in the driver's compartment of Green's tank. 'Mines. And Jerry guns behind that bank. And even if Jerry doesn't get him, there's all these dikes and swamps to fall into. Catch me out there?'

But Ray's presentiments were unfounded. Huitson walked to the second bridge. Waved encouragement. Walked back. Tanks and infantry rushed over the engineers' temporary structure. The second bridge became a highway. The Argylls marched forward as if on a training scheme, for once unchallenged by the resourceful enemy. 4 Troop stayed to see them dug in, before moving back to the village where the squadron was being briefed for another advance on the morrow.

4 Troop rumbled back to their appointed laager with the troop leader's tank in the lead. 'What the heck's that?' yelped gunner Shorty Coleman, taking advantage of the gunner's longer view through the gun sights. 'Flipping Hollywood come to Holland? Straighten your backs, chaps. Polish your

brasses. And empty that ammo tin of what ain't whisky. I think we are going to be filmed.'

'No such luck, Shorty,' laughed Lieutenant Green. 'It looks to me like a big still camera. No moving pictures.'

'Ah, well. I didn't quite see myself as Errol Flynn,' answered Shorty. 'And after being stuck down here with cramp all day I don't think I could manage a Keystone Cops performance. Ken might. He's a rugby player.'

'Break the camera, my mug will,' grinned Ken.

The official war photographer was waiting for them. He had asked for a crew which had been in action that day. Green's troop had been pointed out to him. Now he wanted Green's crew, and Huitson's, to pose like this. And like that. Leaning on the tank grinning. Posed looking out of their hatches with serious, war-like faces. Shorty expostulated, 'Here! How many more? I want my flipping tea. And we were last in, at that.' Vaughan Green agreed. 'And I have a squadron conference to attend. This must be the last pose.'

'They tell me you are a poet, sir. Could I have one of you, say, reading a book, if you have one? Seated on the tank.'

'Oh, I don't think that would be helpful at all. I'll stay for one more with the entire crew.'

As the flash flicked for the last time, and everyone said 'Cheese', Ray Ager shouted, 'Can we get copies of those photos?'

'Yes, eventually,' said the photographer. 'They'll be filed by the Imperial War Museum. And you can order as many as you like. But I can't get prints back to you now. I don't know where you will be.'

'Neither do we,' said Green.

'Well, there you are, sir,' observed Shorty, 'you'll be able to have a photo of us, all looking heroic-like, to stand on your grand piano, for your grandchildren to look at when you're an old gent.'

In the gathering dusk and haze, they slung a large tank sheet from the side of the vehicle to form the customary bivouac. Shorty lit a stub of candle to give a comforting glow to the tiny shelter. 'Get some tea now, sir. At least Jerry has gone home for the day.'

'Good show! I must be off to the conference now. Squadron HQ is in the school building over there. Keep a mug of tea for me, Shorty.'

He picked up his map case and began to walk across the

school yard. In the schoolroom Captain Sandy Saunders looked through the window to see if Vaughan Green was coming. He heard the whoosh, as of a high speed railway train.

Shorty Coleman, in the bivouac, saw the candle flicker and go out.

Vaughan Green, striding across the yard, saw something drop between his feet, as a football might. The world turned red. Unbearable light. A massive sledgehammer shape of flame, edged with hard, sharp daggers, thrashed up from the ground, hewed and bludgeoned through the soft flesh, and smashed the delicate brain.

Shorty looked out of the bivouac. Saw a torso flung to the ground. Screamed. 'Ken, get out here. Vaughan … Vaughan Green, it must be … 's had it … bugger the bloody Boche,' as he himself was running without thinking, bending down without comprehending, recoiling without wishing to. Ken Lyke, a quick mover, was inches behind him.

'Stay here, Ken. See what you can do,' knowing the statement was ridiculous already. 'I'll go find somebody to tell.'

'Much good will it do,' exclaimed Ken, mind working feverishly, but limbs totally refusing to move, even if ordered. As though the chance shell had deprived him too of the means to go from that place.

Sandy Saunders came at the gallop, shouting, 'Oh, my God! Oh, my God!' as though he were on a parade-ground and God was a soldier standing at attention. 'Oh, my God! Get a blanket, somebody, and cover him. Cover what you can. Why Vaughan? I'll have to go and tell Captain Rathbone. He'll be devastated. They are almost like brothers … *were* …!'

But, after a moment of silence and 'Poor Vaughan', Michael Rathbone did not express surprise. 'He knew. I believe he knew. 1935. That's how long ago. We joined the same school staff. Had so much in common. He knew. When John Margetts went off on that course to England, Vaughan said, "Goodbye, John, you won't be seeing me again". And when we were in Antwerp last week, Vaughan and I, the place he wanted to go was the cathedral. He knelt so devoutly … something I had not realized ….'

'But why that one single shell?' enquired Sandy of the empty air. 'Why? Today was all over. Nothing happening.

Then one single shell. He was late for the conference. Out of character. And that shell ....'

'Now, I remember, we were in the first batch of volunteers. We were anti-war. But knew Hitler must be stopped. And as the war started he told me he wouldn't survive it. I laughed at the time ....'

'A single bloody shell.'

'And a poet. He remembered that Wilfred Owen went just before the last. Just before the 1918 advance into Germany. It was like destiny. Just a day's hike to the German border. But light years away.'

The crew were quietly putting together those few things which a tank soldier can bring into his cramped space. A hand touched a notebook fallen under the gun.

'Look, this was what he was writing this morning. Poetry it looks like. Should we give this to Ratters or Sandy? Might be important.'

'What does it say?'

Hardened tank crew are slow to tears. But it was difficult to read the scrawled words, for more reasons than the handwriting jarred by a tank's motion, and the attempts at novel scansion.

> *They were young and happy and foolish*
> *and how could we tell they would be*
> *Unwilling perhaps and unthinking:*
> *yet still of a world made anew.*
> *Founders, endowers, rebuilders,*
> *and ever unresting till we*
> *Shall have made it come true.*

Dawn, the next day, shed tears. But they were the ethereal tears of mist and rain which seemed to have been damping and flooding this land for an eternity. Landmarks merged into an inconstant murk. Measured advances might have been impossible but for the aid of local Dutch Resistance members, who appeared as immune to the weather as they had been to the frenzied hunting of them by German soldiers over all the years of occupation.

Bill Fox, renowned for his interpretation of foreign names, looked at the map, looked up at David Bevan, and grinned. 'I'm lucky today,' jabbing a finger at the name 'Heitheuzen': 'I would have got that yesterday. How does one pronounce

such damnable words? But today it's this. Near. Not far,' and
ran his finger under the name Neer. Never ready to concede
easy defeat the Germans had counter-attacked and
recaptured Neer from another unit.

'Warren is back in action. Chafing at the bit. I'll take him,'
said Bill, who was to command a half-squadron advance.

Balbo Warren was indeed back as a troop leader. A man
with the build of a beaver and the aggression of an angry
buffalo, he was again ready to be pointed in the general
direction of Berlin. And go! Which was the order from
Captain Fox. Warren's troop motored at speed, all guns
blazing, like some reincarnated Wild West posse. And the
Germans, ever elusive, decided that honour was satisfied.
Retreated to somewhere 'not so near', as Bill Fox reported.
Concentrated on dropping odd shells and clusters of bombs
on places where troops might be in bivouac or lieutenants
might be walking to conferences.

As the sodden days continued and the NY forced a route
through towards Helden, everyone from colonel down made
frequent efforts to raise morale, especially by the use of
wireless witticisms at times when the entire active regiment
might be listening in.

Sergeant Jack, once more up front, radioed in, 'Hello,
Sugar 6. I have made contact with the chief of the
Underground,' one of his tasks being to achieve an early
rendezvous with members of the Dutch Resistance.

'Good!' replied the headquarters operator. 'Take a ticket
for Victoria on the Circle Line.' That kind of impromptu
jollity helped cheer another weary mile through the rain.

Wally Tarrant and Les Redgrove were still nursing the
bumps they had received from flying hand-grenades in
Raamsdonk. And every time they fingered those bruises
they thanked their lucky stars, believing that the grenades
must have been assembled by unwilling slave labourers in
some German munitions factory. Wally and Les were
touching wood, when they could find it, and calculating that
they had had their share of narrow escapes for this war.
Sometimes a succession of such evasions of fate gave a front
line soldier the idea that his ration of danger had been used
up, and that from now on some kind of immunity
surrounded him. Wally and Les were tending to believe
something along those lines. Meanwhile Ernie Sprittles,
whose illness had necessitated the hurried recruitment, and

resulted in the subsequent death of young Williams at Raamsdonk, had now returned after a series of mishaps.

Sergeant Lloyd was an efficient and thoughtful commander. So when Wally and Les and Ernie found themselves in the lead position, and creeping along the edge of a wood in thick mist and driving rain, they were not unduly worried.

'If we can't see those buggers, the odds are they can't see us,' commented Wally into the intercom.

'We still need all eyes searching as hard as you can, lads,' called Lloyd. 'No reports of Jerries yet, but when you do get reports it's usually already too late. So keep those eyes skinned.'

Each periscope on the tank was turning and probing, whilst Lloyd peered through binoculars which alternately misted up and then became splashed with drizzle. They scanned the line of trees, and the fields beyond, and the ditches at panzerfaust range, looking always for the shape or movement which did not belong to nature. Where they did NOT look was where the infantry always DID look. If you were a footslogger you watched your feet, and where you trod, and what you were likely to tread on. The mine dug in beneath its tiny but strong trigger could blow off your foot up to your knee if you trod on the spring trigger. There were also anti-tank mines. But those were usually dug in on roads or more obvious tank advance lines. On footpaths tanks did not look too closely at the ground beneath. There was too much else to look at.

Wally drove the tank slowly along behind the trees whilst the commander looked for an opportunity to break through them.

The tank seemed to jump in the air, and something like a huge wave of fire and smoke gushed up from the ground even before the mighty grumble of explosion reached their ears. Wally and Les were, as they put it, 'kicked solidly up the ass' and lifted off their seats. The 30 ton tank shivered and shuddered so that the crew were flung about as though in a cocktail shaker. Sharp steel edges acted as scalpels and rounded iron corners served for bludgeons. With a crunch that almost turned the body to jelly the tank settled back on solid earth. Stopped. Exuded smoke.

'What in hell ...?' shouted someone.

Wally looked down at the floor. Two wide fissures had appeared as though someone with a power saw had been trying to saw away the floor beneath his seat. Multicoloured snakes of flame and smuts slithered through the cracks.

'Driver, halt,' ordered Lloyd.

'I am halted, and I can't get her started,' reported Wally.

'Just precautionary. Sit tight for a minute everybody. I think the fire is burning grass and camouflage. But we seem to have wandered right into a dump of Teller mines and run over a couple at least, I should think. Everybody OK?'

'Ernie's passed out,' said the gunner, squinting under the big gun.

'Let's get him out for a moment,' said Lloyd, after reporting the disaster, and watching another tank take over the lead. 'The infantry are moving past us now. But watch where you are treading. Those are anti-tank mines but your weight might be enough to set one off and blow us all to glory.'

'Or wherever we are heading,' added Wally, opening his hatch and taking a sudden, violent fit of shaking as he saw the vicious-looking, squat, round mines spread along the edge of the trees almost as though accidentally jettisoned from a vehicle. 'How are we going to walk through that lot? It'll be like those Indian magicians that walk on hot coals or jagged glass.'

Grass under the tank continued to burn, but not with enough intensity to reach and prime the petrol tanks. The crew tiptoed daintily around the tank as the turret people lowered unconscious Ernie Sprittles to the ground.

'Poor old sod,' said Les. 'Just gets back from illness and then injury. And now has knocked himself out with the whiplash from that explosion. Bashed his jolly head against the turret wall, I don't doubt.'

'That turret wall packs a punch worse than Len Harvey,' agreed the gunner, climbing down with a water-bottle. They dashed water into Ernie's face, patted his cheeks, opened his collar, and massaged his hands until at last his eyelids began to flutter.

'He'll live,' said Wally. 'A tough one that lad. Take more than bloody Hitler and Teller together to knock him out for keeps.'

There was almost a pattern with some reinforcements, in that they were in greatest danger in their first twenty-four hours in action. Vaughan Green's discouraged crew had inherited a new commander. This was Corporal Dave Bucke who had, as it were, travelled thousands of miles and spent more than six months in coming up to reinforce 1NY. Dave had served with the Royal Tank Regiment through much of the deadly desert fighting against Rommel. Eventually he had completed the tour of time regarded as being the maximum a soldier could endure in battle conditions in the Middle East. Under the Python scheme he was returned to England and given six months leave before returning to a regiment. At the end of his leave he received marching orders for Holland. Through the jolting processes of the reinforcement system he moved from England to Holland, from army to corps reserve, from corps to division, and eventually down to a regiment, 1NY. Arriving at RHQ just as Lieutenant Green was so tragically killed, he was directed to take over the lieutenant's crew.

'You'll find us a helpful lot,' said Shorty Coleman, as they briefly shook hands all round. 'When you've been here a bit you'll find this is a good regiment. And a good troop. Most important of all, a good crew.'

'I'll take your word for it, Shorty – can I call you that? But let's mount up. We're due to move up straight away.'

Ray Ager started up the engine and, with its new commander aloft, the Sherman moved off. Five minutes along the road, and it was evident that this day was to be no walk-over. There would be enemy resistance. Mortar bombs began to fall among the infantry. Shells roared overhead.

Ten minutes along the road, a black, sharp missile rushed across the fields, slammed into the tank, and brewed the usual blast furnace out of the Sherman's front armour. 'Bale out!' and Dave Bucke was crouching with the others, fortunately with hardly an injury, behind the tank as the conflagration at the front of it sent out heat sufficient to make them back away and crawl towards a convenient ditch.

'Bugger that,' complained Dave. 'Six bloody months to get here. One sodding day in command. Ten flaming minutes of battle. And then it really is a flaming, blasted-open Sherman. Would you credit it?'

As C Squadron waited in reserve, listening to the wireless reports, feeling the impact of the distant gunfire, and shrugging deep into their ineffectual gas capes to keep off the rain, Hughie McGranahan waxed somewhat philosophical. 'You know, when they formed the Tank Corps, that's the RTR, in the last lot, they chose the colours red, brown, and green, because, they said, the tanks go through blood and mud to the green fields beyond. I can see the rotten mud. I've seen my share of the damned blood. But I don't see any of the ferkin' green fields beyond, do you?'

Tommy T. was first to respond. 'Makes you think. They put us in the Royal Armoured Corps, so we wear red and yellow flashes. D'you think that stands for blood and diarrhoea: red and yellow? Because in this man's army, sitting in those blasted stupid sardine tins of Shermans, being brewed up right, left and centre by those almighty 88 millimetres, mate, you're either spurting blood if you're injured, or you're shitting yourself with fear if you're not.'

Tall, even-tempered Jack Pentelow of A Squadron was one of the Yeomen who had been 'unhorsed' by the stiff German defence. A hand-held bazooka had blown up the tank, causing a scurry of the crew for the nearest ditch, not merely because of the danger of the expected Sherman incinerator performance, but also because a bazooka or panzerfaust was indeed hand–held and meant enemy infantry within 50 yards – or 5 seconds' reach for a top sprinter. Jack and crew sprinted the other way.

Tank crew were not trained in evasion tactics for the frequent tank disasters which necessitated bailing out. They were left to their own initiative. At the sharp end of a new salient deep into German lines-in this case almost three miles – it was difficult on a misty day to decide which was north and which was south. Few tank crews had been Boy Scouts trained to observe the moss on tree-trunks. There were no signposts, no policemen from whom to ask a direction, and unfamiliar maps could be misleading. It was possible for a tank man to wander round in circles as though he were stranded in a remote sandy desert, as Rex Jackson did in the nearer sands of Loon.

'I'm not sure exactly which direction we should take,' said Jack. 'But the bazooka came from over there. So we start walking in the opposite direction. Keeping our eyes open. And our ears close to the ground. So close that we can dive into a ditch at a moment's notice. Or quicker. Come on then, lads. Let's get home for supper.'

Taking advantage of every bit of cover they trudged along with no indication of direction. Even the battle had gone silent for the moment, otherwise the firing might have given some guidance. As they pushed through a belt of trees merging with untended undergrowth, they almost bumped into two men walking towards them. Germans! Before Jack could touch his Smith and Wesson revolver, the Germans had casually raised their hands, turned around, and fallen into step with the tank men. No words spoken. Almost without breaking step.

'Speak English?' asked Jack, shrugging his shoulders but drawing his unused revolver. There was no reply. Obviously 'No speak English!'

'Cripes! Have you ever seen two such scarecrows in uniform. They must have joined while Hitler was still a corporal. Plenty of medals too. Watch 'em, lads. But they seem to want to go in the bag.'

The tank crew stared at their new companions as they walked. Older men, the Germans had a swing of the shoulders and a relaxed pace which, in spite of their bedraggled state, suggested that they were not older men called up recently and hurriedly in an attempt to staunch the drain on Hitler's armies. Rather they seemed men who had aged in military combat. Probably veterans of the Russian Front. Unimpressed by Jack's puny pistol. But not unfriendly. Watching for sinister moves, the tank lads were still caught cold.

Without warning the two Fritzes jumped into the nearest ditch. Jack jerked his revolver up level with his waist. Tearing, shrieking bombs, horrid Moaning Minnies, hurtled out of the rain-clouds and spewed up mud, splinters, flame, noise. Jack jumped on top of the Germans. Other bodies slammed on top of him. Breathless. Pounded. But alive. Relieved. Struggling apart. Crawling up to ground level again. Peering into the mists. Standing, dripping liquid ooze.

'Jesus,' said the gunner. 'Those buggers knew. They must have signalled.'

'Don't think so,' – Jack. 'Maybe they heard what we didn't hear. Long before we didn't hear it.'

Still unspeaking the Germans arose, looked cautiously around, and waited for the Tommies to march again. The march made another precious two hundred yards of progress towards a meat and veg. supper. The Germans dived for cover.

Jack saw, thought for a split second, moved. 'Dive, lads. Down!' And he had time to look, think, shout, dive, and watch his pals dive, before the sound of express trains again tormented the skies and molten death sprayed far and wide a little way back down the retreat route.

'Artillery searching. Accidental. Those chaps heard it. Long before us. We'll use them like gun dogs, lads. Down when they go down. That's what they are, poor sods. A couple of tired old stray dogs.' He then essayed the usual kind of international patter which passes for communication when the curse of Babel prevails. 'Ruskies? Russia? You! *Wehrmacht*? Ruskie-land. Stalin – boom-boom?' and acted out soldiers leaping for cover. The Germans nodded, faces wizened, gaunt, filthy, expressionless. One held up three fingers.

'*Ja! Russland! Drei! Drei Jahren! Hitler kaput!*'

'*Ja*, old boy. Hitler will be. Hitler *kaput*.'

And that was the extent of their conversation for over an hour. Other attempts to communicate failed. And the raising of three tired fingers, three tired, grubby, scarred fingers was the only movement, except for the plod, plod, plod of feet. And, four times more, a quick cocking of the ear and a swift, smooth dive to the nearest refuge. Each time the tank men descended as though attached to the Germans by the links of a prison chain.

Figures through the mist. A crossing of remote country lanes. Khaki figures. A colonel among them. Jack saluted smartly, a reaction remembered from some remote age away back in Aldershot and Bovington. 'Prisoners, sir. May I hand them over, please?'

'No, Corporal, you may not. What you may do is shoot the buggers. Give this man a Sten gun. Look at our dead there. My men are in no mood to give quarter to bloody Nazis. Shoot 'em I say.'

'I'm sorry, sir. I can't do that. And, with respect, you can't order me to do that.'

The two Germans twitched, turned, jumped into a ditch. Thought processes preternaturally speeded up. Down! Must get down! But there was just time to say: 'Down, Colonel. Get your men down!' (Thinking: this is a raw unit; gaping, goofy men; hidebound colonel.)

'Shoot those escaping Huns,' shouted the colonel. 'Sergeant, get a ....'

Tank men again piling on top of, and beside the two Germans. A colonel waving wildly. Tornadoes of death out of the skies. Gawky infantrymen stunned, scattered, shredded, flung about the crossroads, over the verges, head-high pieces of body hurtling like further bombs, fire, blood, slaughter. Silence.

'Come on, lads. Let's get out of here. Before that so-and-so shoots us as well.' But the tank men were not noticed as they hurried off along the side lane, followed by their two enemy appendages. And leaving the raw infantry yelling, squirming, staggering, standing fixed in shock, while a sergeant bellowed orders to try to restore discipline.

Some painful minutes down the side lane, at another insignificant crossing of lanes or paths, more infantry. This time known Highlanders. A major. Jack saluted again. Offered his prisoners somewhat nervously.

'By all means, Corporal,' smiled the major. 'As long as we can count them on our score today. A bit behind the other companies in prisoners you know. Luck of the draw. Your B Squadron have tanks just around that bend. Good luck.'

Jack saluted again, relieved. Turned away. Then spoke over his shoulder to the infantryman. 'By the way, sir. If those Jerries disappear into a ditch it means Moaning Minnies are on the way. They can hear them half an hour before us. Must have sound amplifiers or electric sensors where most folk have eardrums. Veterans from the Russian front they are.'

'Advice heard and will be heeded, laddie. They look seasoned troops. But, about hearing the Moaning Minnies, did nobody ever tell you that tanks make you deaf?'

Colonel Doug was momentarily deaf. His Intelligence Officer, Lieutenant A.J. Owen was temporarily bereft of all his senses. They had driven over a German mine charged to destroy a 30 ton tank. They were in a scout car. The car was hurled into the air and fell yards away, a ruin of scrap metal. The colonel and lieutenant were flung bodily away from the car, arms flailing, to land on sodden earth. The regiment paused in awe at the news that the colonel had been hit again. Remembering that awful day, 8 August 1944, battle of Saint-Aignan. Night March accomplished. Code-name 'Fly by Night' attained on time. Tom Boardman's navigation immaculate. The regiment now five miles up the infamous Bourguebus ridge. Deep within the German's massive defences. Under the maws of the 88s. Menaced by the reserves of invincible (until that day) Tiger tanks and German ace commanders. Only a tenuous trail, the herd trail of 1NY, like a cattle-drive track on the Oregon trail, through enemy country linking the regiment, and the Black Watch beside them, with the main allied armies. Saint-Aignan assaulted and captured. The squadrons disposed in a tight laager circle, awaiting the inevitable, furious, last-ditch German onslaught to keep the British and Canadians from linking with the Americans at Falaise.

At that dire, ominous, historic moment, the wireless crackled: Colonel Doug and Major Brassey both badly wounded. It was as though an electric cable, bare, and charged with high voltage horror, linked every tank in the regiment. The colonel badly wounded and even now conveyed on an open-topped half-track back down that desolate, perilous Oregon trail surrounded by an enemy far more potent than Red Indians.

But here, in Holland, the regiment suddenly blessed the rain. The sodden, seeping, saddening, insistent rain which seemed synonymous with Limburg. For the colonel had landed at jet speed, with the full force of his big-muscled body … on sodden ground. And Owen too.

The MO, Captain MacIntyre, himself experienced in suffering wounds, tried to persuade the colonel to go back down the line for a day or two, but, 'No, Mac, I'll be alright. Don't send me down. I'll obey doctor's orders and let George carry on, if you let me stay.' (Lord George Scott was his 2-in-C.)

The adjutant, Captain 'Lew' Llewellyn, another of the schoolmaster breed of Yeomanry officers, called RSM George Jelley out of the RHQ barn. 'I've got a special job for you, George. The colonel's going to be OK. Mac says a couple of days will see him fit and hearty again. But Mac says also that depression could set in. And Doug has lost his favourite pipe.'

'That's right, George. Now, be a good chap. Go and have a scout around – forgive the pun – where that scout car is indeed strewn all around. And see if you can spot that precious pipe for him. It won't win you a VC, but Mac says it might make the difference. It was a bad head blow.'

Lew lifted a map, drew a rough circle, and said, 'Somewhere there.'

'But surely that's about four square miles? And way up front?'

'Correct! When they set out they were prospecting, as you

might say, ready to take alternative routes. And when they got back, they were stunned, incapable of reading a map. The Highland corporal who picked them up wasn't too sure. And it wasn't important at the time, judging from the corporal's description of what was left of the scout car.'

Burly George Jelley, more the stature of a rugby lock than a soccer referee, called his driver and issued the vague instructions available. 'Up that way, Bill. Then turn left, right or centre. We don't know. I think we'll be driving by smell rather than sight.'

They swanned around, taking side lanes and paths, heading always further out beyond the seemingly scant and precarious foxholes of the main infantry positions. It was nearly dark when, swinging his field glasses almost hopelessly for a last glance, George shouted, 'There she is, Bill. Foot down, boy.' They buzzed along the narrow lane. A Highland sergeant sprang into the path. Bill slammed on the brakes. The RSM grabbed steel plating to stop himself falling. 'What the blazes, Sergeant?'

'Sorry, sir. RSM Jelley, isn't it? You can't go any farther.'

'Hitler, Goering, and who else says I can't, brother,' roared George.

'Just take a look,' said the Jock, pointing at a large pile of anti-tank mines which had been extracted from the ground. 'We can't guarantee that we have got them all up. Waiting for the engineers, sir.'

'That's alright, Sergeant. I outrank you. So I'm going up. On foot. Anti-tank mines won't blow me up.'

'With respect, Sarn't-Major. You're heavy enough to set one off.'

'I didn't know that, did I, Sergeant? And I didn't hear that? We get a little deaf in the tanks,' and grinned that boyish grin which, from time to time, reminded fearful troopers that the awesome RSM George Jelley had falsified his age as a boy soldier to fight in that previous war.

He strode, parade-ground fashion, along the lane. The Scots sergeant thought to himself 'as though none of those bloody mines DARE go off!' He pushed and picked among a miscellany of refuse left by the explosion at the precise spot. Looked dubiously at the wreck of the scout car, continued to ferret around at the explosion site. No pipe. Almost automatically and without particular purpose he went for a quick look at the metal carcass of the little squashed vehicle.

One broken outline of one seat was still discernible. And on the seat lay the colonel's pipe. Intact. Waiting patiently, as pipes in a rack do, to be smoked.

RSM Jelley picked up his colonel's pipe, tested it, smiled. Then as he passed the Scots sergeant, said, 'I'll need a sworn statement from you. Nobody, but nobody is ever going to believe this story when I tell it at post-war reunions. Look. Undamaged.'

It was not the unhorsing of Jack Pentelow which brought A Squadron to a halt. It was the mud which led to no green fields as yet. Ken Ward, driving a leading tank just as he had done up the main street of Helden, surveyed the sea of brown paste ahead. Nobody, no tank man particularly liked driving into a town, with all the perils of street fighting. But he wished he could be back in dangerous Helden streets, with proper roads under his tracks, and houses to guide him, and, of course, Dutch citizens venturing out with flowers, wine, cheese and kisses. Not in this limitless, directionless, uninhabited wilderness where, through this level mess, the tank continually dipped and swayed, as though about to tip and sink into bottomless depths. Tanks had been known to sink. One crew had been lost in Normandy because of violent rains working on unstable soil.

Flail tanks, the sure deliverers from the mines which the Germans seemed to possess in superabundance, were ahead, sunk into the earth, their great rusty chains still beating unsuccessfully at the yielding ground, their tracks churning and driving the heavy vehicles deeper and deeper into clinging, all-conquering mud. To one side, the squadron recovery tank had come up to tow another Sherman out of a bad slough. Now the recovery vehicle was slowly sinking. Both seemed to be down beyond where a Plimsoll mark would be if tanks had that security provision.

'Halt!' said Ken's commander. Unnecessarily. More potent conditions had ordered halt. Silence reigned for a moment across the fields. Engines had been switched off to listen for any enemy sounds. There were none. Only the wireless crackled and whispered. The loud voice came from Squadron HQ, suddenly, critically, jovially.

'Hello, all stations Yoke. Stay put. But your guns are now pointing into Germany. Anywhere beyond 2,000 yards is Deutschland. You are welcome to fire at random in your own time ten rounds 75 each. At Hitler's country. And give 'em hell. Good shooting, gentlemen. Yoke, off.'

No, I'm not a male nurse. Or a medical student. Though I do work under the sign of the Red Cross. I'm just a medical orderly. With a bag of bandages. A little knowledge. And a lot of hope. A medic.

No, I am not RAMC, the real medical corps – although your blasphemous ranker soldier will even insult them. 'Rob All My Comrades', they call them. No, I'm a member of the regiment and trained to drive a tank. But things happen like this in the army. Fred Karno's Army always!

You know the old chestnut: Sarn't-Major comes on parade. 'Anybody 'ere play the piano?' Four lads step forward. 'Right! You four! Carry that piano from the NAAFI to the Sergeants' Mess.' Well, it happens. Came on parade one day. 'Anybody here been in the Red Cross? No? Anybody in St John's Ambulance? No? Let's try something else. Anybody been in the Boy Scouts?'

Well, I didn't connect the two, or three. I thought maybe there is a job to do with scouting, fieldcraft, map-reading or such. Things I like. I'd been a Scout with an armful of badges. So I stepped forward. But the sarn't-major laughs: 'Good lad! Boy Scout? No doubt you got your first-aid badge. We're making you medical orderly.' And that was about that. A little training. A lot of forms to fill in. And then mainly trying to turn people away from the MO's door on wet or frosty mornings.

It wasn't too bad in training. No sleeping out with the Bren carriers on Salisbury Plain. No sitting in freezing tanks in the snow on Thetford Heath. No weary waiting on the shooting ranges at Linney Head down in Wales. Or Titchwell up on the Norfolk coast. Always a warm medical hut. Or a decent clean ambulance. Plenty of hot water. Towels. Kind boss. Good doctor. No parades. No shithouse fatigues, excuse the French!

It was in Normandy that the truth hit home. I wished I'd never been in the Scouts. Or never stepped forward like an imbecile. No, I don't advance up front in the leading tank, nor the lead troop, nor the front reserves. But when somebody is hit, wounded, injured, killed, blown to recognizable bits of human butcher's joints – then I *do* go up front. Then I *am* first. Or maybe the supporting tank crew get there first. Or the infantry. But I'm always a good second. And, except for the odd, sad, concerned pal off the same tank who's less badly wounded, they leave me alone with the bloody mess. That's what it often is. No longer Bill or Taffy, Jock or Paddy, Corporal This or Captain That.

Our sarn't-major, for instance, who caught me out with the Scout trick: when I got to him in Normandy, the biggest remnant I could find was half an arm in a bit of sleeve with a wreath and crown on it. I didn't stand to attention to THAT. I ran to the nearest ditch and heaved. It was the worst I'd seen. Come to think of it I don't know why I heaved into the ditch because there was worse all around for yards, miles. Humans, cows, horses, soldiers, civilians, Tommies, Jerries. Much of the time you didn't know which was which.

NO! Wearing a Red Cross may give immunity from some things, like kipping in the frozen mud or cookhouse fatigues. But it doesn't give you immunity from ordinary human feelings when God's creation, some mother's son, your old barrack-room mate lies there, gushing his life away in red torrents. And you haven't got the skills to save him. And he looks into your eyes ....

Battlefield death is not like a hospital ward or a comfortable bedroom at home. If you don't think a nice, clean, daily washed-down butcher's slab is artistic or glorious, then a battlefield is not picturesque, romantic or heroic. It wouldn't fash me, now, to have to work in all the muck and gore of the local slaughterhouse or the skin warehouse at the market. I've seen far worse. And I expect I'll see ... but, wait! They're calling me NOW ...!

9   Frivolity and Fate

A move back to west Holland was announced. 'Hope to God it has stopped raining over there,' was the general response.

Tanks had been driven to a wayside railway siding in the Helden area. Long, sturdy, railway 'flats' were waiting for the long line of tanks to be run up ramps and chained securely to the flats.

Crews who had negotiated the narrow ramps, and the vertigo-stimulating view down from a heady summit, now sat on turrets and watched the remainder of the regiment 'come aboard'. Idle hands fiddled with the dials of wireless sets to catch the strains of an American dance band, an English comedian, or even a German oom-pah band. Such wireless listening, off the official net, was illicit, frowned upon, but generally ignored. Even officers wanted to know the latest BBC versions of their exploits.

But there was a news bulletin and a comedian which delighted British troops much more than 'BBC News and this is Bruce Belfrage reading it' or even Tommy Handley and the ITMA show. Everybody switched on to Lord Haw-Haw, the British turncoat who broadcast Nazi propaganda in the English language on German radio stations powerful enough to penetrate any British jamming. Hitler, Goebbels and William Joyce himself, obviously thought that this mind-improving service would promote the Nazi cause. But British troops on active service, as well as civilians at home, laughed and jeered and became optimistic at Haw-Haw's upper-class accent, as he continually prophesied the doom of the British nation. His versions of the news were so distorted as to be obvious lies.

Sitting atop the Shermans, giddily perched upon the flats, crews remembered that it was time for Lord Haw-Haw, and switched to a *Deutschlandsender*. And sat back for the comedy.

'Jar-meny calling,' pealed the snide voice. 'Jar-meny calling. Here is the news ... On the borders of Jar-meny the famous Highland Division' – rows of tank men sitting bolt upright on tank tops, fully alerted – 'have gained a few thousand yards, with the aid of a fanatical armoured division.'

'Fanatical armoured division? Oh, my God. Listen to that!' All along the train of flats tank men clung on to turret flaps and rolled about in agonies of laughter, tears welling in their eyes. 'Oh, my God! Fanatical? Colonel Doug and RSM George? Hank and old Bill Fox? Fanatics? And Spud and Wally and Sergeant Jack and Rex? This Yeomanry shower? And the East Riding Yeomanry as bad? And 144 RAC? Oh, my God. Give him a medal. Good Lord Haw-Haw, OBE; never did anyone prescribe a tastier tonic for weary troops.'

Jar-meny went on calling unheeded, lucky listeners shouted to those still embarking, laughter shrieked where mortar bombs had moaned, and, just then, the Limburg sun broke through.

The train was on its way. Chugging along at an idle pace. Courteously moving aside for more urgent engines to bundle past. Stopping to commune with remote Dutch signal boxes for no apparent reason. Speeding frustratingly through populated stations. At one siding a troop train, similarly loaded but going the opposite way, towards Limburg, halted and joined in steaming, grimy communion.

Shorty Coleman, always ebullient, stood on his turret and yelled to the other train, 'Anybody there from Chippenham?'

'Where's that? Bleeding Australia?' replied a Scottish voice.

'Chippenham, Wiltshire, you ignorant Jock.'

'Yes, I'm from Chippenham,' shouted a West Country voice unexpectedly.

Shorty stared. Gobbled a little. 'Don't believe it! Larry Love! Hey, where's all the other Chippenham lads? Tarrant, Carpenter, Clarke! Here's Larry Love who was at school with us.'

'Well, if it ain't old Shorty Coleman,' came the West Country voice again. 'Ain't you growed up yet, Shorty?'

'He was at school with me,' Shorty informed the world. 'Larry, where are you going? No, don't answer. I know where you're going. Been there. Won't tell you about that! Larry, where have you come from?'

'Italy, boy.'

'Don't be a stupid ass, Larry. How could you have come from Italy on that?'

'On a boat. And a train. And another boat. And another train. And this train. Regiment, brigade, divison, all been transferred from the Italian front to help you useless lot out. Get to Berlin even if you can't!'

A barrage of abuse was lost in the clanking and belching and grinding of the two trains as they jerked away in opposite directions.

Gusts of hilarity seemed to propel the train towards Roosendaal even more effectively than the ancient chugging steam engine.

Hilarity subsided somewhat when the arrival of the grounded tanks at appointed billets coincided with the advent of lorries bringing gallons of paint for refurbishing unmilitary-looking battle tanks. Some troops were located in Leur or Hoeven or Rucphen. Jollity returned as the newly emancipated Dutch civilians gathered to greet the battle-weary troopers. And as local children, learning the meaning of liberty, thronged around the fascinating Shermans, the news came through, 'We're here for Christmas. A month's rest. Leave in Antwerp. Arrange Christmas parties for the kids. The quartermaster is dressing up as Santa Claus. Extra rum ration all round.'

Still unpacking, Spud Taylor looked up and saw a shape speeding past the village church spire. 'Look, chaps! What kind of plane is that? I've never seen one like that before. It nearly hit the church steeple.'

'Plane?' guffawed Sergeant Danny Danson. 'That was a buzz bomb. A V1. Flying bomb. The Jerries are still just up north, loosing off those things. And V2s. Pity the poor buggers in London on the receiving end. Here they're just part of the scenery.'

Yells of delight echoed over the open field where the tanks were parked. Voices shouted, 'Catch it! Get it, lads! It's a stray. Doesn't belong to any Dutchies. Our Sunday dinner!' A squealing, mobile pig, moderately sized but with auras of succulence about it, was evading wild rushes of troopers too long confined to awkward tank seats. The troopers sprinted in straight lines. The pig twisted, turned, leaped, squealed and drew ahead. 'Catch it! Lovely pork shops! It's from the old German mess. It's called Adolph.'

Shorty Coleman heard and ran, shouting, 'Ken! Where's Ken Lyke? He's a scrum-half. Get the rugby players.' As the unruly mob fell over itself and the pig turned to escape, the diminutive figure of Ken the scrum-half darted across the field, launched into a flying tackle, grasped and brought down the porker, the two bodies wrestling together on the grass until superiority of human numbers told.

'What can we do with it, now we've caught it?' grumbled Shorty. Then, 'Ken, you're in the farming business, aren't you? Haven't you ever seen a pig slaughtered? We don't want to share it with too many people, especially pork butchers. Mightn't know what they were extracting.'

'I could try,' mused Ken. 'You have to scrape the hairs off, I seem to remember. Never done it myself, back home in Hereford. But there's plenty of barbed wire about. Chop some up. Twist it together. And we could make a fair old scraper, look.' And, like a foretaste of Yule feasting, with twenty-seven foraging days still to go before Christmas, Adolph the porker supplied a welcome change from tins of standard meat and veg.

A minor sensation was the arrival as a reinforcement of Lieutenant Lord Wellesley. 'Yes,' troopers said. 'He really is the descendant of the Duke of Wellington himself. Will be the Duke himself one day. Perhaps he's come to fight another Battle of Waterloo? Waterloo's not so far from here is it? What about it: the Duke leading the Yeomanry into battle at Waterloo?'

Dick Bates, privileged sergeant and driver, asked Hank Bevan. 'Is it true we have a duke coming to us? Is he related to you, sir? Didn't you say you are a Wellington?'

'No, I'm afraid you're a little wide of the target. I'm not a Wellington. Or any other kind of footwear. But my mother is indeed descended from Marlborough. That's a little further back in military history.'

'Wasn't Marlborough in these parts too?'

'Well, yes. Not too far south from here. But don't listen to all this talk about Waterloo. The Germans have retreated far, far back across Belgium. They are now away in the Ardennes, and Intelligence suggest they may be moving back farther, to reduce their front. By the way, how did the football go? I saw Pedder limping back.'

'That about sums it up,' groaned Dick, whose gunner was Pete Pedder, the squadron right-back. 'We could just about raise a limp between us. Lost a few good players to Jerry guns and sundry accidents. As usual flipping A Squadron won the tournament.'

Hank's operator, Ken Squires, was reclining on the ground with kindred spirits like Harry Graham, planning to resurrect the concert party, now that Harry Brown, the prime writer, had disappeared into the unknown regions of medical care in Brussels or Britain, nobody yet really knew where. Harry was scribbling notes about funny acts which would be comprehensible only to troopers. The regimental Christmas concert for local kids would have to be of a different variety. Ken was writing down a list of possible candidates for a squadron orchestra to play between acts.

'I've always got my accordion on the SQMS truck. If we can get a piano from the local, old SSM Farnham can try out the parade-ground chestnut: 'Right, anybody 'ere play a pye-anner? Right, you lot carry that pye-anner over to the NAAFI'. Can you hear him now! Harry Swift will play the pye-anner, pupil of Charlie Kunz and all that. You, Harry, on the drums. Locke has got his clarinet. Bunny Hare keeps his trumpet in the scout car. Russell on bass. We're nearly there. All we want now is somebody that knows the National Anthem.'

Harry and the other kindred spirits were struggling with a list of irreverent parodies on carols. They had talked about Good King Wenceslaus. Harry Brown had been going to do something on that. What was it? They hummed the tune. Made suggestions. Sergeant Warren must, of course, be the butt of the parody. Words began to fit in. the carol began to flow. They jotted it down. It fitted the tune. This, yes, the troopers *could* appreciate, and bawl out with the full symphony of the Ken Squires' Philarmonic booming behind them.

They would get copies written out by hand:

> *Bad King Adolph last looked out*
> *At Sint-Michielsgestel;*

> *1NY were round about, ready for the battle.*

> *'Mein gott, Goering, what a fright,'*
> *did old Adolph bellow,*

When a peasant came in sight,
and his name was BAL-BO.

Hither, Runstedt, stand my me,
if thou knowest it telling.

Yonder peasant, who is he, why so evil-smelling?

Sire, he was in farmyard born,
and with bulls did wrestle;

So be sure you've lost this war
by Sint-Michielsgestel.

That should bring the house down. Well, actually it would be that barn over there in the corner of the field. That is, if some flaming V1 didn't bring the barn down before Christmas.

Leave! For the first time since landing on the beaches just after D-Day, leave was available to all. For some it would be a week back in Britain. For the majority a brief but wonderful forty-eight hours pass to Brussels or Antwerp. Rotas would be determined not by who was on the squadron leader's most favoured list, but by fair drawing of lots. Staying in Roosendaal area until after Christmas there would be time for everybody.

Spud Taylor's name came up quickly. So did Shorty Coleman's. And Danny Danson. And, among the officers, Sandy Saunders. A Liberty Truck was available for the group going to Antwerp. Liberty Truck was a euphemism for any slow, doddering old lorry from the echelon made available for troopers to travel uncomfortably on its bare boards. But bare boards could not dampen the enthusiasm, delight and frivolity of the selected few.

Sandy Saunders was aware that, with his strong build, light curly hair, and pink cheeks, he had an advantage with the girls. The officer's tunic was no drawback either. But the episode of Vaughan Green's death, and the manner of it, and the promise of more to come for those who survived, all served to render Sandy morose and unexcited by the bright lights of Brussels. He felt more inclined to seek out a quiet *estaminet* and drink away the memories than to indulge in more exacting feats of girl-hunting.

At the reception desk in the hotel, reserved for officers on leave, he encountered a chattery, middle-aged, not unattractive woman who impressed him as rather a delightful old stick. They had chatted easily and she had asked sympathetic quesions about the war. In the evening Sandy found his haven at an officers' club. A table, a glass of decent whisky, a cigarette, and nobody to bother him. Then the woman from the hotel reception came in.

She talked seriously to a younger girl, rather a tart to be in an officers' club, although officers, some of them, did go for the tarty type. The hotel woman, walking past the table, spotted Sandy, stopped, smiled. 'Alone?'

'Yes. And glad to be. Seen too many people lately. Dead friends. Live bloody Boche.'

'I understand. What I had in mind is that you might like to escort me. You're a big man. I have several visits to make and they all involve cash. I always like a guard, if I can get one, in these mad, bad days. Terrible things happen on the streets of Brussels now. Especially to women. Especially if they have money. What do you say? Better than drinking alone, and drinking too much?'

Seems a decent old dutch, thought Sandy. And then aloud, 'Why not? One Northamptonshire Yeoman at your service, Madam!'

They marched off down the street. She paused at another club door. Spoke to an attendant. Collected a small parcel. Dropped it into her large bag. On again. Another club. Another parcel.

It was true, Sandy thought, that Brussels was not the most saintly or safe city on earth just now. Several British infantrymen were brutally punching and stamping on two American soldiers while military police came running up the street, blowing whistles. Several drunken soldiers of different nationalities slept in doorways, or staggered along, bumping into people; or stood in alleyways urinating. A Belgian policeman, strolling past, caught Sandy's eye and shrugged. Sandy strode gallantly along with his companion.

The next stop was at the door of what appeared to be a cheap hotel. The girl on the door was scantily dressed and excessively painted. Sandy thought she had more make-up on her face than clothes on her body. But she had a packet ready for his companion. And the next port of call had a red light over the door.

Some time later Sandy escorted the woman back into the hotel, he always an officer and a gentleman, she always a strict lady. Her bag bulged with packages. She thanked him, smiling, and departed. A man stood at the reception desk. Sandy turned to him. 'Strange lady that. What does she do? Collect insurance?'

'You could call it that.' said the male receptionist. 'Actually, she is the madam of all the local brothels. Goes round every night collecting her percentage. Nice person. Of course, never does it herself.'

'My God,' groaned Sandy aghast. 'I wonder if anybody saw me? I'll never live that one down. And didn't even get invited in for a free sample. Or a cut in the percentage.'

The Liberty Truck was spilling Yeoman off in the centre of Antwerp. The unlucky corporal i-c Liberty Truck announced the rendezvous for the return. A flurry of plans ensued. 'Anybody for the flicks? What's on? Is the local beer any good? Where do we go for girls? Any good services clubs? What about the Sally Anne?'

Danny Danson was going to a cinema. 'Chance to sit down in comfort. If it's anything like the odeon at home, that will be luxury. Oh, lovely. It's the first time for months I've felt safe. Now for the bonus. A film. A soft seat. And a choc-ice. And plenty of fags.'

'What's showing?' asked Shorty, looking at the posters. 'A cowboy film and an Al Capone gangster feature. I don't want that. I've seen enough gangsters in field-grey uniforms these last few weeks. And done enough range riding to last me for life. I'm for finding a nice quiet bar – no bangs or wireless messages or shouting sergeants – and propping myself up. Tired of sitting in a tank. Lead me there and lean me up.'

Shorty's idea seemed popular. Tommy T. alone plumped for a house of girls. Others might find their way in that direction later. Tommy would ask a policeman and head straight for it. And only a young trooper seemed to want to share with Danson the delights of plush seats and choc-ices interspersed with the rattle of guns from cowboys or Chicago hoods. The party split up and good-humouredly went its various ways.

Forty-eight hours soon passes. Shorty was once again propped against the now familiar bar, not having spent *all* his time there by any means. Tommy T. was investigating another interesting house. One or two had gone to see a last film, a Broadway musical, plus another cowboy saga, at the Rex cinema.

Shorty thought somebody had slammed him against the bar. Unused to the extremely strong Belgian beer in such quantity, he turned and demanded, 'Did one of you beggars just punch me?' A trooper drinking beside him responded, 'I thought *you* punched me?'

Tommy T. was sitting naked at the top of the stairs in a strange house. He thought someone had pushed him, and rolled down the stairs, coming to rest at the feet of a resident girl, similarly innocent of clothing, who smiled and said, 'You get used to those here. If you duck it's too late.' That meant nothing to Tommy.

Danson and the young trooper were again in the delightful comfort of the Rex cinema, all the more appealing when one has not entered a house to sleep, relax, eat or perform the natural functions for months on end. Just to sit. Sit well back on the cushions. Breath the air. Smoke a good cigarette. Let the music flow from the screen. This was indeed heaven after so many weeks, and days, and minutes, and seconds of sheer hell.

The broadway musical strummed on. The elegant chorus-girls danced in brilliant unison across the screen. Then something interrupted, like one of those parody films of Hollywood film-making, where the cast and action from one film spills over on to the next set where a different period and scenery are in place. Something foreign. A sound which, high-pitched and fearsome, was not at all Broadway musical. A new radiant whirling on the screen that was not dancing. And the screen rending, like the veil of the Temple, allowing furies to speed and scream out of Broadway and down into the audience, stabbing with red-hot skewers and coughing flame at the audience. These were the brief, sudden, dying impressions of hundreds of people who sat there. Then the darkness.

The V2 missile had plummeted down directly behind the screen, burst its fuse on the stage floor, sent its tremendous force of steel splinters, and blast, and seething heat, down through the auditorium, lacerating, asphyxiating, roasting open-mouthed watchers by the hundred. Until the roof fell in.

To people like Shorty Coleman the imperative thought was that forty-seven hours fifty minutes had transpired, and that ten minutes was necessary to be sure of finding that Liberty Truck just up the road. As the Yeoman hurried to where the truck must be waiting they saw a commotion of people, a pyre of blazing buildings, running policemen, sirens in the distance. A bomb. Or a V2?

At the truck they gave their names one by one. The unlucky corporal i-c truck, unlucky again in the next draw, scratched off names with a bored look. 'Did any of you sods think to bring back a bottle of decent beer for us workers? Or some fags? Or whatever? Now, then, that's only two people missing. What's this? Can't read me own writing. Sergeant Danson. Anybody know him? And a Trooper Blakiston. What squadron would he be? I'll have to report 'em missing. Strict orders not to wait. Any bugger seen 'em?'

'Danson?' said Shorty. 'Danny Danson? Didn't he go to the cinema? And wasn't that the cinema that was on fire? Would that have been a V2? But surely he wouldn't have been still in there after forty-eight hours?'

'Could have gone back,' supposed Tommy T. 'I went back where I was being entertained. Wouldn't miss a second chance. Even when the old francs ran out.'

'Right, then. Two men missing. Mount up. It's a long way to Tipperary. And thanks, mate, for the bottle. Kind of you. Should help us find our way home? Won't have bloody bomb fires to light us all the way.'

For days Danson was missing. And Blakiston. The thought nagged at many minds. Moments of frivolity were jerked to a halt when minds went back to the burning cinema. Could it be? It took days to dig through the ruins. Days to bring out the dead. Days to scrabble in the ashes and find identity disks. Days before the regiment could, with certainty, add to the roll of honour, two Yeoman done to death in the innocent peace of an Antwerp cinema.

Doug Gardner was, however, back from his travels, his ingrowing toe-nail finally rectified. 'You won't believe it,' he told his story again and again. 'Want your leg chopped off and we'll do it here and now. But an ingrowing toe-nail is too complicated for us. So it was back to Brussels. Then given a label for UK. For Blighty. I didn't believe it myself. Loaded into a 1930 vintage bomber. Strap hanging in an aeroplane. Actually, literally hanging on to a strap in the ceiling as you stood.

Doug counted up on his fingers. 'In civvy street, I could

literally have walked down the street, into the hospital, out with the nail, a day or two's rest. Back home. A mile or two. But this lot, apart from the time, I reckon they took me two thousand miles past hundreds of hospitals and wasted gallons of petrol. And I bet our own MO could have done the job here outside the tank if he was really pushed to it.'

Brian Carpenter had also been in hospital. Now back with B Squadron at Rucphen, he was looking forward to an ENSA concert which had been announced. The official ENSA concert parties often had really good stars and were worth waiting for. But the sergeant-major called for him and said, 'Time you did a guard, lad, now you're fit and well.' So Brian and mate disconsolately watched the ENSA group arrive, two males and two lovely girls. As the two guards sauntered on their easy but necessary prowler patrol, varying their route constantly, they managed to pass outside the little local hall where voices cackled in laughter, and a piano tinkled, and a girl's voice soared to the musical heights like a skylark.

'Just our luck!' would be a slogan engraved on the hearts of many front line soldiers when they died.

A flashing of lights and a burst of frenzied activity in the near distance drew the guards away from the ENSA concert. A corporal from HQ Squadron was running towards them.

'Report to the guard commander,' he called. 'We're moving. The regiment's moving.'

'But we're supposed to be here till Christmas. The regiment I mean,' Brian complained to the corporal as he rushed past.

'I've got to stop the ENSA concert. Load 'em up! Get 'em away! Everybody loading up tanks! Moving straight away!'

'What's the matter?' insisted Brian. 'Has Jerry invaded England at last?'

'Worse than that. You'll hear. The American front has collapsed. Von Runstedt's broken through. It's crisis … crisis … crisis ….'

He was still shouting the word to the two retreating guards as he thrust open the door, burst into the hall, and ran to where the comedian was capering around. The concert hall went silent.

At RHQ things were as near to panic as at any time in the war. Hank Bevan and Tom Boardman had gone to Paris with the brigadier himself. Lesser fry were indulging in the delights of Antwerp, or sitting in local Dutch houses,

promising the kids a Christmas such as none of them had
ever seen.

The skeleton of a regiment packed up, loaded, started up
engines, tested gun controls and wireless, lined up in a
straggly formation facing SOUTH. Back where they had
come from. The war gone into reverse gear.

Target hour, and enough tanks lined up but not enough
crews to be fully operational. People arriving back, full of the
joys of life, Belgian beer and Brussels brothels, to be ordered
instantly into fighting positions. But the departure hour
postponed.

More Yeoman arriving back, even more befuddled and
even more urgently ordered to douse themselves in cold
water and mount up. The time of departure again
postponed. All through that turbulent night.

By dawn on 20 December the regiment knew that German
armour had punched through a weak American line in the
Ardennes. As one of the Yeomanry officers put it, 'just about
level with our strategic backsides. And von Runstedt has got
a red-hot poker in his hand ready to shove up our arses, if
we don't move quick.'

You won't meet me often because I'll be up ahead with
the recce troop. We're the boys they push on fast when
a long advance is hoped for. Not a set piece,
wide-fronted attack with phalanxes of tanks and hordes
of infantry sweeping up behind them, and edging
forward at a speed of 500 yards a day. No, we don't
have much to do with that sort of advance.

It's when, as you might say, the commanders can see
a bit of daylight, a mile or two of open road, an absence
of visible German defence lines; then it is 'Go! Go! Go!'
And we are the boys to go. Not in Sherman tanks, but in
the lighter Stuart – as the Americans call it – or the
Honey – as we call it, I don't know why: but it *is* a real
honey for speeding along decent roads. And, for sheer
speed, there is always a two-seater scout car that can
really cut down the travel time between here and Berlin.

Of course, the Honey has very thin armour-plating,
and the scout car's about as resistent to shot as a zinc
bath with wheels on. But speed is supposed to get us
out of harm's way. 'That's it, boys. Just nip up to that
bend in the road a mile away, by that neck of forest, and

see if there's a nasty old SP or Mark IV lurking around the bend.' That's what they say. And if there *is* an SP, or a Mark IV, or even an infantryman with a bazooka, our speed is supposed to get us to hell out of there.

That's alright until you do a bit of simple mathematics. A Sherman can only retreat at about 25 mph. In a Honey we can get to hell at 35 mph. In the scout car we can be damned at up to 50mph flat out. But what does that difference mean when you are facing not another scout car at 50 mph, nor even Sir Malcolm Campbell in Bluebird at 300 mph. You are running away from an 88 or a 75 millimetre shot travelling at maybe 2,000 feet per SECOND. That's, hey! 1,200 miles a flaming hour.

So logic says that although our Honey is a mite faster than the other man's Sherman or Tiger, it's not going to get far in a race against an 88 shot. That's why, at twenty years of age, you may think I'm suffering from Parkinson's Disease. Look! Trembling hands, trembling knees, trembling everything, rude or decent. Because we've now got to go up to that kink in the road, by that death-trap of woods. And think we can hit 1,201 mph coming back, if Jerry pops up and says 'BANG!' A great humourist is Jerry for that sort of thing.

You might think my bit of calculating speeds was a waste of thought and time. But on that one mile open flat racetrack of road before the next corner, there's nothing to look at, after the first study of the lie of the land; nothing to look at; nothing to divert the mind; nothing to drive away the fears; nothing to darken out the vision of Honeys and scout cars blasted to smithereens, with their crews, and scattered all the way from the Normandy beaches to this rotten bit of the front line.

If I didn't invent something to occupy the mind I'd turn into a screaming, ranting lunatic, three-quarters doodlealley, and likely to be shot at dawn for cowardice.

So, 'Driver, advance! As quick as you like. Let's know the worst in double quick time.' And, in the meantime, if an 88 round is buzzing down that one mile of road at 2,000 feet per second, how near do we need to be to good cover, at 35 mph?

10   A Second Waterloo?

There was respect in the British army for Field Marshal Gerd von Runstedt. The average Yeoman knew little of military history and higher strategy but there was a filter down of impressions which left reputations forming, fixed and colourful like stalactites. The reputations may have been erroneous but they influenced even ranker thinking.

So there was admiration for Rommel, now dead; somewhat apprehensive submission to Montgomery; a kind of affection for Eisenhower; a mixture of fascination with, and disdain for Patton; but a profound respect for von Runstedt as the most professional of them all. The news that the elder commander was in charge of the German hosts pouring through the American lines brought a chill to more than one humble trooper's heart. For von Runstedt was aiming *behind* the entire British army, just as the Raamsdonk battle had swung behind a lesser German army, and as the Night March had sought to seal the Falaise trap in Normandy.

Brian Carpenter, deprived of his ENSA concert, and his night's sleep, and several times of the oil change he was needing to complete amid changing orders to move or stay, now checked his speedometer. 'I wonder how many miles we'll do today.'

'Let's make a book on the mileage,' said someone, for tank crews found passing amusement in guessing the day's movements, always so different in reality from announced plans, just as sea cruise passengers enjoyed guessing the ship's daily journey in more leisurely and peaceful circumstances.

'Fifty miles for me. It's panic stations,' said another. In theory a Sherman could do twenty-five miles an hour, which might suggest fifty miles in two hours. But even a Sherman, the best of travelling tanks if not the best planned fighting machine, would break down and shed a track if pressed into top speed for too long. And the most urgent military convoys had to contend with narrow, twisting roads, frequent uncoordinated road junctions, other convoys delayed or ahead of time, the concertina effect of continual halting and starting, as well as changes of orders from on high.

'Aw, no, rubbish,' said a third. 'We was lucky to do 500 *yards* a day in Normandy. Put me down for twenty-five. And we ain't started yet, 'ave we?' It was indeed a weary day, saying goodbye to tearful Dutch citizens, especially the children, trying to explain why Father Christmas would be needing his sleigh somewhere else over the next few days; starting, shunting, speeding, halting, starting, shunting, down congested roads; dust, grit, petrol fumes, sweat, jolting motion, the usual ration of bruises and contusions from hard, metal projections in turret and cab; the increasing cold; the frustration of a cancelled Christmas celebration; the absence of a clear destination; above all, the irrational but persistent fear that Nemesis, in the shape of von Runstedt, was already behind them, and that this was really a race towards another Dunkirk evacuation.

When they eventually halted in the dusk, and parked in formation which presaged an overnight's stay, Brian Carpenter's speedo said eighty-six miles. And the trooper who had bet fifty miles was the nearest guess.

Rex Jackson was climbing stiffly out of his tank when Sergeant-Major Farnham boisterously hurried over to him. 'You speak French, laddo? Come with me.'

'Well, I'm not really good at it,' temporized Rex, massaging his calfs.

'You can say 'Merci' and 'San fairy Ann' and all that twaddle? You can speak it better than anybody else around these parts.'

'*Ça ne fait rien!* What do you want me to do?'

'Trans-a-late, laddo. For your uncle SSM who's going to find us all nice comfy billets to sleep in tonight. RHQ say we are staying until further orders. Don't even know the name of the place. Some say Stockel. Some say La Help or something like that. Near Brussels anyway. Got to defend all those Brussels tarts.'

There were a number of houses nearby. Farnham knocked like a policeman at doors. Rex repeated the simple phrase he had worked out. '*Nous sommes anglais. Nous demandons un lieu*

pour dormir. Peut-être le garage. Un, deux, trois soldats?' Most of
the Belgians were friendly and immediately offered space.
'Well done, lad,' chirped Farnham. 'I'll see you get a nice
house yourself. *Merci* buckets,' beginning to pencil in names
to allocate to shelter available, always excepting the unlucky
guard for the night.

The SSM did allocate Rex, Hickie and Snowy a large
house. The Belgian hosts welcomed them with Latin
exuberance. But when the soldiers hoisted their bedding
rolls and made to go into the garage, the hosts barred the
way. 'No, no! In the house. You are our guests. We are
prepared for you. Only we do not have blankets enough. So
bring your blankets to the bedroom. Then come down for
dinner.' English-speaking hosts made the reception even
rosier.

After a superficial wash, but still feeling unbearably filthy,
the three descended, to find a highly polished dining-table
laid with gleaming silver and sparkling cut glass. And
steaming soup upon the table. As they ate the hosts
explained, 'We are very glad to entertain you. Only
yesterday we dug up from the garden the boxes of china and
cutlery which we had hidden there when the Germans
came. And we are specially glad to be able to provide you a
dinner-table with all good things because, for the past years,
we have had to entertain you poor English with bad food,
poor china, and hurried meals.'

'How do you mean?' asked Snowy, pausing in his
enjoyment of the delicious soup. 'Past years? Entertaining
English? The Germans were here, weren't they? There
weren't any English here?'

'Ah, yes, there were. Many English. Some Americans.
Polish. French. Your air force. Escaping after their
aeroplanes shot down. We had a chain of what we called safe
houses. This was one. A shot-down airman was brought
here. Stayed one day. Two days. Then they fetched him to go
somewhere else. We never knew where. Or when. Finally to
Spain, we think.'

John Pearson, officially C Squadron Corporal Clerk,
normally occupied behind the advancing tanks with his
typed daily orders and squadron records, was guard
commander for the night. Clerks, cooks, fitters, echelon
drivers, everyone pitched in for guard duties on nights like
this. Amid the panic messages, one clear signal had filtered

through from higher command: fanatical German SS troopers were on the loose, dressed as civilians, or even in British or American uniforms, with orders to kill officers, destroy ammunition dumps, report back on troop movements. 'Double all guards! View all unknown personnel with suspicion! Redouble vigilance!'

John, a banker, normally the most placid and pacific of persons, passed on the orders with rather more belligerence than usual. 'I may not be an officer, but I am Guard Commander,' he thought. 'I hope no fanatical SS trooper draws a bead on me.'

'Guard Commander!'

It was the middle of the night. A couple of harassed prowler guards appeared, walking well back from two evil-looking, large civilians who were carefully covered by the Sten guns of the troopers. 'Guard Commander! Suspicious characters. Could be SS. We picked them up in a cafe. They were NOT speaking French. Nor English. Sounded like German. A Highland officer called us in. Not taking chances. Stand still, you buggers! If you *are* SS, here's volunteers for the firing squad at dawn.'

'Hold them carefully,' instucted John. 'I'll rouse the local Belgian liaison chappie. Perhaps he knows German.' In the interim a chill of fear was added to the increasing coldness of the winter's night. To be shut up in a small Belgian outhouse with two members of the infamous SS was not an adventure that any Yeoman would have wished upon himself, even though he had the advantage of a Sten gun and a dozen comrades at his back.

The Belgian liaison man, looking equally worried, came in and surveyed the prisoners with distaste and something almost amounting to horror. Nervously he began to question them in what appeared to be halting German. John caught some familiar words like *Soldaten* and *Spion* and the inevitable *kaput*. The prisoners were wolfishly poised and remained silent. Then the Belgian switched to another rigmarole in some other tongue. 'Polish?' John asked himself. 'Czech? Certainly not quite Dutch or German.' The prisoners responded garrulously. The Belgian eventually had to raise his hand to silence them.

He turned to John, smiling. 'They're Flemish. The other language of Belgium. I don't wonder why you took them prisoner. They seem to have guilty consciences. May be smugglers. But not SS.'

'In that case, let's get them out of here,' said John, unable to feel gracious in the release from tension. 'If you want to take them to your police, do so. But I don't want to see them any more, thank you.'

Hank Bevan roused Bill Fox in their temporary and all too comfortable surburban billet. 'Wake up, Bill. This is a real turn-up for the book. Word just come through. We are to form the final defence line to stop von Runstedt before Brussels, and the coast, and another damn Dunkirk.'

'Where? How far?'

'Just down the road. And where? Where but on the very field of Waterloo. The generals have been look-see, and find that Wellington's ideas can't be bettered. Even by Monty.'

The Shermans quickly moved up past artillery gunners busy digging gunpits in the very suburbs of Brussels. The Field of Waterloo was only a brief trot away. Tanks were very quickly disposed and in position, ready for action. And, within an hour or two, Yeomanry officers were strolling across the ancient battlefield, flicking their riding crops, and tracing Wellington's movements. Troop leaders gazed with fascination at the place names which were coming alive on their maps: Quatre Bras, Wavre, La Belle Alliance, Ligny. Troopers with a notion of military history were ecstatic to have arrived at sites which would have been inaccessible to them on pre-war wages: Spud at La Haye Sainte, Shorty and Wally at Hougoumont, and Rex and Snowy at Papelotte. And B Squadron were surrounded by Gordon Highlanders whose regiment made history there with the Scots Greys in 1815. Officers vied with each other in remembering relevant shreds of military lore.

'Did you know that our regimental badge, the White Horse of Hanover, was worn at the Battle of Waterloo by the 17th Regiment of German Hussars, the so-called Silent Brown Hussars?'

Von Runstedt's Panzers might be just down the road but the fascination of Waterloo prevailed for a while. The cavalry had done wonders at Waterloo. And whist the Yeomanry now rode tanks, they were never far away from horses. Bill Fox, Tom Boardman, Colonel Doug and others were inveterate riders to hounds and to gymkhanas. George Smith and Bill Cole, now tank attendants, were professional huntsmen. Ken Snowdon and Dick Bates, the gentlemen's servants. Eric Good, Charlie Rogers, Balbo Warren and a host of others, hard-riding farmers.

So it did not need a great leap of the imagination, standing there, to see us, the NY, standing there with the Scots Greys, behind this ridge, our horses sleek and well groomed, our chain-mail shining in the sun, our silvery helmets jauntily posed, our swords bitingly sharp. Waiting for Wellington's word of command as he rides by. Watching for Ney to assemble his massive charge. Wondering what Napoleon has in reserve.

Other troopers were less romantic, on that Field where the snow now brought its warning of further icy sufferings to come, when the armoured-steel tanks would be transformed from unventilated summer ovens into unheated winter refrigerators. Other troopers were more concerned with the where and why of Waterloo in 1944, and argued with less military acumen.

'What the hell were the Yanks doing, letting the Jerries through, anyway? Jerry came through that same way in 1940, didn't he?'

'I blame the American generals, not the troops – like our own sometimes. Some of those American generals were only playing trombone in Glenn Miller's band three years ago.'

'Yeah, look at Ike. Nice guy, but only a major, like Hank, a couple of years ago. And now he's got five stars. Not even Monty has five, but five stars on his shoulders.'

'Aye, the Americans have always got to be biggest and mostest. Biggest country, tallest buildings, largest air force. So their generals must have most stars on their uniforms.'

'Seriously though, those Yanks were kind to us. Opening up their food stores on the landing ships. And when we shared the camp with them at Gloucester and they invited us to their cookhouse. And the regiment had to order us to go to our own cook house and eat our own food.'

'Great, that was! Poor old Jark Aris there, with his great cauldrons of rainbow rice, banging a pan and shouting 'Come and get it!' and nobody coming and getting it. And all of us queued up in the Yanky cookhouse, with all the Yanks pushing us up to the front of the queues for a five-course dinner. With free beer chucked in.'

'Next war, I'll be a Yank.'

'Next war you'll be a bloody rheumatic pensioner in a bath chair, get any more of this rotten snow.'

'Happy Chirstmas and "When the snow lay round about" and all that!'

'Bugger me, yes, it's Christmas Eve, 'en' it?'

The mail had come. Piles of letters and Christmas cards, which you couldn't eat. But for Trooper Rushton, A., a huge parcel under which the post corporal staggerd. 'Hey, I want a surcharge on that!' And inside the dear old 'Coon's' parcel were a pie, biscuits, chocolate, and a Christmas cake. The Coon, always popular, especially when he scored goals for the squadron, became THE most popular person on the Field of Waterloo. Yells of excitement, like the war cries of Ney's charging dragoons, greeted the opening of the last parcel within a parcel from Alf's Christmas bounty: one thousand English Players cigarettes, sent by the girlfriend of a fellow trooper wounded in Normandy and now hospitalized in Blighty.

Next day, Christmas Day, at the traditional midday hour of banquet, 1NY were moving on. Von Runstedt, Montgomery, Hodges, Patton and all, did not share visions of a second battle at Waterloo. It might be somewhere nearer Namur. Alf's parcel having been consumed by his immediate retinue, and the crumbs not being sufficient miraculously to feed, if not the Biblical five thousand, the NY's five hundred, rations were basic for the onward march.

Don Foxley, on the replacement Helmdon tank, with a replacement commander for poor Bobby McColl, sat on the outside of his tank while the snow continued to fall, Christmas card fashion, and ate a doorstep slice of bread spread with jam. His drink was a mug of cold, thick, unsweetened cocoa. He finished his Christmas repast and thought, 'Well, at least I can whistle myself a carol. What shall it be? "In the bleak midwinter"?'

Spud Taylor, an habitual charity volunteer, thought of the children back near Roosendaal, who would not get the Christmas party for which he, with others, had been plotting, collecting, and storing up likely items. As the tank rolled along at an average ten miles an hour, when not motionless, he noticed that civilians in the villages were no longer waving, smiling and dancing in the sure spontaneous thrill of liberation. They were looking up the road towards Namur, even more apprehensively than the Yeomanry, and wondering if this bulk of tanks would be adequate to stem the blitz of Tigers, Panthers and SPs, so much more powerful than the older German tanks which had broken through, surging along this very road, in 1940? Downcast, glum faces stared impassively back at Spud.

Jack Pentelow, 'rehorsed' and back within his own mobile, shaking, iron environment, only realized the significance of their advance when his tank halted at the entrance to the local aerodrome at Florennes, their objective for the night. The American air force commander came running to the gate, jumped on to the tank, and shouted 'Jeez! Am I glad to see you guys. If I had a million dollars I'd give it you.' Other American airmen were appearing, mounting Shermans, shaking hands.

'Jeez!' said the colonel again, breathless.

'What's happening here, sir? Where are your own troops?'

'We ain't got no troops, brother. Zero! Zilch! I've sent my Black Widows away. I've mounted their guns around the perimeter. I've put spare air crew in foxholes as infantry. and I've got ammunition for two minutes. Repeat, two minutes. One hundred and twenty seconds pree-cisely. Any wonder I'm pleased to see you guys? Come and have some Jack Daniels with me. I've got a bottle.'

'Jack Daniels, sir? Who's he?'

'Oh, you wouldn't know. That's our Tennessee whisky. Sour Mash. Good stuff. Better than this local 'gin-eever'.'

As often happened, RSM George Jelley, officially located back with rear echelon, made it his business to be up front, ready to take charge of any action which did not involve direct tank shooting. His scout car easily won the race into Florennes. The place was deserted, except for a startled elderly man crossing a street. George halted the car.

'Are you English? Or who?' stuttered the man.

'English, of course. English as they make 'em.'

'Thank God for that. We didn't know who to expect.'

And. in due course, in the allocation of billets, the same gentleman had insisted on the RSM staying at his house. While they sat down to a nightcap later than night George noticed that the man was quietly unpacking a large case full of clothing and other objects.

'Have you been away?' he enquired.

'No, but I was going. Since the Germans retreated people have come to know who were in the Resistance. I was a leader. If the Germans had come back, well ... ' and he drew a finger across his throat. 'So, yes, I was ready to go. Packed up for immediate get out. But now you are here, I shall not need the case.'

'Oh, God, up there,' said George to himself and to a very much Higher Commander, 'pray these people are not disappointed in us.'

Michael Rathbone was also billet-hunting. Lord George, the Regimental 2-in-C, had indicated to squadrons where they might billet, and Michael had studied his map well. The area indicated, when he arrived there, seemed to consist of buildings long abandoned, the site overgown with weeds and brambles. A little way down the road there was a small château. As he walked towards the château, Ratters overtook a stately woman, well dressed, wearing a veil, and carrying a small, black religious book, obviously returning from Christmas mass. Hearing his mission she said, 'You can stay with us, captain.'

'Seven officers, nineteen tanks, and about a hundred tank crews. Plus fitters, medics, and so on?'

'Oh, yes. A large house. Rows of empty loose-boxes. No horses now. A large courtyard. Barns. And as many logs as you like to warm you and bring you Christmas cheer. Come in and we'll talk to my husband, the count.'

Much later the colonel, and Lord George, and the RSM, appeared on their Christmas rounds.

'This isn't precisely the location I allocated to you, is it?' asked the 2-in-C. Ratters explained about the derelict buildings.

'Damn it, George!' laughed Colonel Doug. 'Why didn't you collar this place for RHQ instead of that ghastly brewery we are in?'

Captain Rathbone smiled to himself, for B Squadron were too well installed to offer an exchange. Yule logs blazed in a large bonfire in the courtyard. He went back to the squadron, leaving the colonel chatting amiably to the count about a possible boar hunt, if and when the von Runstedt hunt permitted.

In the various squadrons the cooks had reacted most quickly to the general panic. The Jack Aris's and Harry Claridges had collected together and packed what stores could be saved of their Christmas hoards, arrived quickly in Florennes, lit huge log fires, and, before midnight, were serving Christmas dinner. No crackers, no decorations, no bands, no dancing, no girls. But FOOD. Good, hot, plentiful, wonderful food.

Later, there were girls. Roy Clarke and the crew of Alabama were bedding down on ample clean straw in a wind-proof barn. Brushing the snow off their boots and bedding rolls, they were almost too tired to lay out proper sleeping arrangements. The clean straw and the barn warmed by great log fires outside, invited and induced sleep. Troopers collapsed where they stood, and snuggled into the straw.

A silence, a break in the gossip and merrymaking, drew their attention to the barn door. Local girls, smiling but shy, were standing there, carrying jugs of hot milk, fresh, creamy, warming. Roy saw them through faltering eyelids, but even the thought of a delicious goodnight drink could not drive the sleep away. War, travel, urgency, had reduced lusty troopers to a state of bedraggled weariness where they hardly roused to drink the welcome milk, let alone launch into any other kind of activity which might be suggested by the appearance of the opposite sex.

There was a surprise for Rex Jackson. He was summoned to the squadron leader's tank. Squadron leaders did not normally summon ordinary lance-corporals (which Rex now was). So he wondered what he might have done wrong.

'Ah, Corporal Jackson! Good man! I have some news. You've done some useful things for the squadron. Your action at Loon-op-Zand in bringing back that tank was particularly fine. I want you to be the first to know: you've been awarded the Military Medal. The QM carries a small stock of ribbons for awards in the field. So you can put it up right away. Quite a colourful ribbon. Well, congratulations. Good show! And, by the way, we'll be using you to do some commanding from time to time in the future.'

As the tanks advanced beyond Florennes Rex was not contemplating military glory. He, like everybody else, had been ordered to fire at anything that moved. Nobody seemed quite sure where von Runstedt was. This was not the fault of Regimental Intelligence. Higher commands appeared to be equally perplexed. The Americans might be holding the advancing Panzers better than had been anticipated. But the way ahead was now a potential battlefield. Almost a no-man's-land.

Rex did not fire at the first thing he saw moving, because that was an obviously very aged Belgian man, pushing a pram loaded with personal belongings, and trying to cross the road between tanks. During this German advance there was no panic-stricken flood of civilian refugees thronging the roads. The civilians of Belgium seemed paralysed into inaction by the sudden reversal of fortune, from the heady days of liberation to this threat of renewed Nazi occupation.

Rex watched the old man persistently trying to push between tanks. Even well-designed Shermans are clumsy compared to lighter wheeled vehicles. Slow to respond to controls in comparison. Turning with a swivelling motion and needing plenty of room. One of the Shermans, trying to avoid the aged Belgian, caught the pram and flung it and its load across the road to a ditch, where the pram lay crushed and the parcels strewn in chaos across the ground. The old man stood as though unseeing, unfeeling, not hearing.

The advance ground on. Once again RSM Jelley managed to push ahead. Leading a small convoy of emergency supply vehicles he rounded a bend to see a hunched figure in sheepskin coat and scarf standing in the snow, stopping traffic, turning it back. George decided on the bold approach.

Driving up at fair speed, he bawled at the man, using his best parade-ground voice, 'Get out of the bloody way, there. Who do you think you are? I've got an emergency echelon here. I'm going through. And you're not going to stop me.'

'You cannot go through. The road has been cut ahead. Turn around.'

'Who are you to command? I'll find my own way, roads cut or not,' George shouted at the anonymous figure, toning down his voice a little because the man spoke with authority, and might be an officer rather than a policeman. And at that moment a captain came running along the road, waving to George and pointing meaningfully at the man arrayed like an Eskimo.

'What are you?' the Eskimo figure asked, for in the now freezing weather uniforms tended to be overlaid with all kinds of heat-preserving sartorial additions. '1NY? RSM? Then you must be Jelley. Heard of you! Good man. Dismount, please, and come over here. I want you to stop everything, everything d'you hear? Turn them back. Let'em find other routes. You stay here until I can get some MPs along here to take over. Good man. Hold the fort.' And without further explanation the man turned and headed for a jeep parked nearby.

George caught the sleeve of the captain who was about to follow the other. 'Who on earth is he? Montgomery? I must know in case people question my orders. Couldn't see his badges. Major? Colonel?'

'General! GOC 51st Highland Division himself. General Rennie. Cock of the walk for miles around here, in case anyone argues.'

'Then I can even instruct colonels …?'

'This is the day you've waited for all your life, Sarn't-Major. Yes! Colonels. Even brigadiers if they appear. Not to mention piddling little staff captains,' and with a hearty laugh he ran after the jeep, calling, 'Hold the fort, Sarn't-Major.'

Jim Alcock was a rank lower than George, but of equally short temper when frustrated by human inefficiency or imbecility. Trying to get his large workshop wagons through the snow to their appointed site, he was held up by a traffic block. Three Crocodile tanks had been ditched where deep snow had eliminated all sign of limit between road and verges. A recovery vehicle was trying to tow them out. Standing in the road, and barring the way to any vehicle which might try to edge past, was a group of people, red showing against their khaki uniforms.

'Military police,' said Jim's corporal. 'Afraid we might muck up the other side of the road.'

'There's room to get through. Plenty of room for good drivers. I'll soon sort that lot out.'

'You can't cross swords with MPs,' answered the corporal. 'Sulky, dangerous lot.'

'Nonsense, lad. What's rank for, but to pull a bit of when needed? In this kind of situation, battle requirements supersede everything. Just watch this.'

Jim got down and stalked along the road, shouting, in a voice almost as strident as George Jelley's. 'Move over, you silly buggers. I've got some real soldiers here. Needing to get to the war. There's good room for us to get past. Move your lazy arses.'

The group turned round almost as one man, in total consternation. Jim slowly perceived that the red trimmings were not those of military police, but those of staff officers, one of whom, at least, was a brigadier. There was a moment of stunned silence.

Then, to Jim's intense relief, the brigadier grinned, the

smile of a bird of prey. 'Ah, glad to know we have some REAL soldiers coming up. Go back and rest YOUR arse, and we'll soon have you through.'

It was that sort of day. Everything that could go wrong, went wrong. Without von Runstedt needing to fire one shell at the NY. Wally Tarrant was sitting alongside his mate, Les, a little weary of the constant low-gear advance. But not totally discontented.

'You know, Les,' he commented at one halt, the quietened engines making it unnecessary to use the intercom in the front compartment, 'this is at least an improvement on Raamsdonk. If they fling any hand-grenades, we're under shelter. And if they leave any mines around, we'll see 'em in the snow.'

Lead tanks ahead moved on. Wally's automatically followed. As they did so there was a shuddering and a grinding as of a monstrous mincing machine chewing up iron bars. The tank slewed in the snow. Then sank down rather wearily one one side.

'Blast! We've shed a track!' And to the derisory cheers of other crews churning past, Wally and mates climbed out of the tank, sank deep into the late Christmas snows, and began the heavy, time-consuming task of replacing the track, the nightmare of every tank driver.

Wilf Mylan and little laughing Johnny Taylor almost wished that they HAD shed a track. Their tank was the lighter Stuart whose track was not quite so huge and wearisome to repair. And they crewed the brigadier's tank, so that fitters might be inclined to rush to the brigadier's aid more urgently than to the assistance of lesser fry.

Johnny Taylor had driven the tank up a long slope, with Wilf commanding it in the brigadier's absence. Now they looked down a shorter but much steeper slope the other side. Vehicles were slipping and slewing about on the downward stretch. Snow had been hard-packed under pressure of tracks and wheels and, in places had turned into solid slides of ice.

'Take it carefully, Johnny. Cancel that. I don't need to tell you. Just that it looks a bit dangerous from up here,' said Wilf.

Johnny had the good driver's intuitive knowledge that something was going wrong. Sticks and pedals were having no impact, or the exact opposite effect to what Johnny intended. The Stuart was slithering, not responding, charting its own course, choosing ice tracks through the beaten snow, beginning to speed up.

'Hold on,' yelled Johnny in a voice which could be heard above the striving, revving engine. 'We're going down.'

'Don't tell me,' growled Wilf, grabbing for support.

The Stuart whirled around, almost in its own length, adjusted itself, and accelerated down the slope. The road was straight. The tank was weaving and vacilating, but still staying on the road, Faster. Faster. Too fast. Until the tank became a toboggan, the ice screeching under its locked tracks, the chill air shrilling around Wilf's ears, the tank sliding straight now and ever faster in a child's play of sleighs and slides. Fun! Faster! Fine and jolly!

Until a small lorry, caught in the same ice trap, turned and began to skid straight across the road in front of the Stuart. Wilf opened his mouth to shout. There was no time for words to come. The Stuart, 'light tank' but massive in the eyes of a truck driver, bore down like a dive bomber on the truck, hit it at incalculable speed, smashed through it, the tank tracks folding and crushing the back of the truck, the Stuart plunging on, reaching the bottom of the slope, clashing with one or two trees, slowing to a halt in deep, impeding snow, the tank engine still panting as Wilf and Johnny got out to look.

Back up the slope the cab of the truck stood sad but intact with the astonished driver opening the door, apparently unhurt. Behind the cab was what looked like a large collapsed tent, all that was left of the rear end of the vehicle. Wilf and Johnny did not realize then that they were setting a trend for tanks descending hills in the blizzards of the Ardennes.

That night came with tanks harboured in open country. No courteous countesses and straw-strewn horseboxes. No piles of hewn Yule logs. No milkmaids with steaming hot drinks. No silver service and best china. The only source of heating came from the exhaust of tank engines. There was no strict order prohibiting the practice, so crews ran their engines a little longer in order to sit up on the engine covers and enjoy the warmth. With luck the engine covers might remain at least body temperature for much of the night.

Bill Higham and George Smith were both suffering from

the first bite of truly freezing weather, exacerbated by the reflecting armour plating of the tanks with their own built-in refrigeration effect. Bill and George and others had removed their boots and were toasting their toes, still wearing their socks, over the hot exhaust vent at the back of the tank. Considerable heat could be generated in little space there, and socks helped to tone down the burning feeling.

Swayed by weariness and the welcome warmth Bill was nodding with sleep, his toes almost the only conscious part of his body. Suddenly an agonized squeal woke him from his opium state.

George had roused to find his socks on fire.

No, sir, I'm not brewed-up tank-crew. I'm walking behind the tank because I'm what they call PBI; Poor Bloody Infantry, that means. Footsloggers. I've walked half across the Western Desert with Montgomery. Now I'm walking to Berlin. Except we now get a lift sometimes in these new Kangaroos. Which are really only Shermans with the turrets chopped off.

No, sir, it was the fitters chopped the turrets off, to make room for us PBI on the Night March. August 7th to 8th. Caen. But I've seen some Shermans that the fitters didn't chop off. Jerry did. With those 88 millimetre anti-aircraft guns used as anti-tank. So sometimes we PBI talk about the PBTC, the Poor Bloody Tank Crews. You see, out here, safe on Mother Earth, you can always dive for safety deep into her bosom, so's to speak. And an ample bosom she has. Foxholes – slit trenches to you – ditches, folds in the ground, anywhere is a place of safety we can dive into.

You know, those tank boys don't like walking on Mother Earth. Because Jerry plants unmotherly and unbrotherly crops in the soil. Schu mines. Booby-traps. Nasty surprise bangers. And he covers those traps with bursts of machine-gun fire like fiery cobwebs weaving over the earth. And the tank lads are not trained for that. They'd sooner stay inside their iron forts. Stay and risk the 88s. Have you seen those 88 rounds? Thick as my thigh around, and long as my forearm, and hard steel made to splinter inside the tank.

I remember the first time I saw a Sherman brew. I was crouching down, too close behind it, for shelter, as I thought. Then, BANG-BANG – it's always two BANGS with those 88s – and a real fire-storm, a hundred feet of flame shot up out of that turret. They didn't have a chance. I got scorched. Burned the eyebrows off of me. But I stopped worrying about myself when I smelled the crew roasting inside that oven. 'Tommy Cookers', Jerry calls the Shermans.

So now I keep clear. See, we are fowl and fish, oil and water, Jews and Samaritans, PBI and PBTC, all of us, the idiots at the sharp end of the advance. Fodder. *We* are trained to tread earth and disappear into it. *They* are trained to ride high, and take the risk of cremation as the price of iron armour. But we need each other. They go ahead by day. We dig in and prowl by night. Couldn't do without each other. So we follow close. But not too close.

Yes, sir, I've walked a long way in this man's war. There are times when I'd give anything for a ride. You know, stand at the bus stop and wait for the old number 36 to Camberwell Green. And I don't mind the Kangaroos once in a while. But don't ask me to ride in a Sherman.

Follow at a distance? Yes. Take over at nightfall and guard their front while they replenish? Yes. Crawl through the undergrowth on midnight patrols while the tank lads sleep? Yes, no sweat! Wear out boots and feet and ankles, and develop varicose veins for life, while all they get is bunions on the backside? Yes.

But crew a Sherman? Wait for the 88 to hit? Sit waiting for Jerry to light the cremation oven? And then me get burned alive, down to a black cindery monkey thing?

For all that, sir, I say, 'To Hell with Tanks!'

11 Frozen Purgatory

The regiment was now moving into a land of delirium. A place of frozen suffering compared with which the gentle rains of Limburg seemed positively benign. A region where blankets of hanging snow and sheets of frozen fog hampered vision. A terrain for which tanks had never been designed. A purgatory of bitter cold which, suffered in conditions of exposure and intensified by the effects of living within unheated iron containers, would have been intolerable to human flesh, even had it not been added to by the fear and rage of bloody battles.

At times humans continued to move in the same automatic, unthinking, sliding way as the tanks themselves. Tracks were covered with snow. Extensive forests made outflanking movements hazardous. Identifiable guidelines and rendezvous points were obscured. There was a continual sameness of obscurity and cold and purposelessness that minds were dulled into a frozen state of imbecility.

Phil Wilkinson was one of the sergeants responsible, with RSM George, for ensuring that supplies arrived each night. After the gruesome task of loading up trucks with metal boxes like blocks of ice, and wooden crates which ran splinters into insensitive hands, the echelon began the real task of finding a way forward. Towards a cross on the map, a cross which was thick, straggling, vague, covering maybe thousands of square yards of 'where the squadrons might be'. Even radio messages flashed back were unable to identify the precise locations in a desert of unidentifiable snowdrifts.

The only hope Phil had, in the darkness only made tolerable by the reflections from the snow, was to dismount from his leading truck, plough around in the snow, and find an inhabited hole at which to enquire, for nobody existed above ground during the nights. With luck the people in one of the holes might be infantry, associated with our tanks, who could at least point a blunt, gloved mitt forward to where the tanks might most likely be. And then to see the dark bulks of Shermans among the trees, to shout, be acclaimed as heroes, and then find they were the ERY or 144 RAC and not the 1NY at all.

And, on arrival at last at some God-forsaken spot in the wilds, the only thanks the Phils and Georges, the Jack Aris's and Harry Claridges could expect – comprehended in the circumstances and therefore tolerated without resort to fist fights in the snow – would be, 'Where have you buggers been all night? We're sitting here starving and freezing while you cushy lot are back there, gulping the surplus rations you can't deliver, and smoking all the spare fags. And then expecting us to wake up at this hour to replenish?' And, of course, there was a journey back with empty trucks to a location almost as difficult to find as the tank laagers.

The Shermans were now meeting the foremost feelers of the Germans' dramatic life or death drive for the North Sea. But this was not an advance like any other advance. In Normandy, and to an extent in Holland, the drivers had taken advantage of cover and, by skilful handling of their cumbersome charges, had evaded many an anti-tank shot. Commanders had been able to order complicated movements which sometimes would have perplexed the driver of a wheeled vehicle. But here it was all toboggan work. Vehicles out of control. Or perhaps the vehicles at time IN control of human destinies.

There was not so much difficulty in persuading the Shermans uphill, although even that progress was tortuous and halting, sliding, swerving. On the downhill stretches the machines took over and chose their own route, their own speed, their own destiny. Drivers hung on to driving controls and hoped for survival. Commanders stayed in their turrets and prepared to jump. The rest of the crew ran alongside, often in peril from the sliding, swaying hulk, throwing logs, rocks, any old object in front of the churning tracks to try to give these some kind of grip in the snow or on the ice.

In no way now could commanders order those delicate manoeuvres in the face of the enemy. It was straight up and down country, slide, halt, blast the visible countryside with cannon fire. And then begin the next incredible climb.

Fortunately by this time the enemy were either too strategically extended or too physically chilled to strike back effectively.

'I'll never go to another blinking fairground, however long I live,' moaned George Smith as they slid and slithered somewhere in the wilderness near Waritzy. 'Who would pay to go on any of those fling-you-about funfair contraptions when we've got one here that gives you every thrill of an aeroplane crashing, or a racing car going over the banking, or a racehorse falling at Beechers?'

'I think we've just about seen it all,' said his co-driver. They had not. But the next minute they did! A tremendous thud, hitting the tank under the driver's seat, shuddering through the entire tank, and causing the huge machine to stop dead, threw them all around the tiny space in a way totally beyond the imaginings of any fairground operator. The tower of flame which usually built up instantaneously out of such an explosion, became a vast red-tinted cloud of soft snow, which rose violently as on the wings of a gale, hovered like a gargantuan ghost over the tank, and then began to snow, just like an ordinary snow shower, whiteness replacing the ferocious red.

'Let us out,' yelled George down in front. The engine had stalled and voices could be heard without help from the intercom. 'We're trapped down here. The gun is over the hatch. Bill, traverse, for God's sake.'

Bill Higham found that the power had died out of the traversing system, but the hand traverse still worked. Deperately he turned the handle, expecting every moment that the tank would go up in flames. The gun came level over its usual rest position. The drivers' hatches opened. Bodies leaped out. Bill followed operator and commander in their rapid flight from the turret. They all squatted in the snow, suspicious of a continuing glow at the front of the tank. Gradually edging forward they studied the damage.

'I think it was a mine,' said George, 'I felt it right underneath me. Expected to find myself sliced in half.'

'That fire is probably only something out of one of the storage bins. If she was going to brew she would have brewed by now.'

'Where are we anyway?' asked Bill.

'Somewhere out on a limb. We were moving out away from the rest of the squadron. Nobody is going to find us in this light. We had better sit tight. Maybe until morning. No use trying to walk away in this weather. It's coming on a blizzard that will blot out our tracks.'

'Are we going to sit here in this snow?' said Bill, trembling now more with cold than with shock or fear.

'Well, the wireless has gone. So we can't call for help. But perhaps the engine will start up. We could get in and keep warm, all in the turret together. Might be a sitting duck for any Jerry who's wandering around with an 88.'

'In this weather and light?' queried George. 'Let's get in. Me, I'd rather be a sitting duck than a frozen turkey.'

Out on another limb, at the tip of another tentacle of the advance, one of Sergeant Huitson's tanks had at last taken the wrong route down a hillslide, and had plunged into a snowdrift in what appeared to be a pit or slight depression in the ground. Dusk and snow made it difficult to discern. Intermittent German firing made it inadvisable to spend too much time finding out.

Sergeant Huitson was now commanding a troop, owing to the constant drain of officers killed, wounded or sent on necessary courses. He pressed his microphone switch and ordered the stranded tank to be ready to reverse if his tank could provide a tow. Although they were in what might theoretically be termed the front line, there did not seem to be much possibility of direct enemy interference.

Huitson had his tank driven near to the ditched tank. Then, with his own co-driver, he unhitched their tow-rope, dragged it to the other tank, and linked it on.

'Now go back to the tank,' he ordered. 'Tell the driver when I raise my arm, to take the strain. If I drop my arm, stop. OK?' The co-driver waded back through flurries of snow to their own tank, in that grim murk a figure like Captain Oates going out into Polar oblivion.

Sergeant Huitson raised his arm. Two things happened. His own tank revved up into a thunder of acceleration prior to taking the strain of the other tank's weight. But over that noise there soared first the sudden demonic shrieking of falling mortar bombs. Then the group of thudding explosions. One batch. Two batches. Three batches right among the tanks. His arm still raised Sergeant Huitson performed a classic gymnastic backward roll.

He did not get up. The pure snow around his body was spattered with even purer red blood and then sullied by the fall of smoking splinters, carbonized shards, and charred rags of clothing.

That night, as B Squadron sat on a high ridge in the blizzard, the temperature fell to 37 degrees below freezing. Night guards were instructed to start up every tank at each two hourly change of guard to prevent the engines from freezing. Stan Hilton was one of a number of operators in the regiment who were hardly more fortunate than the prowler guards. The operators had to take it in turns to sit in a chill turret during the night, listening to a silent radio, in case some emergency message might come through. He sat, in the early hours, in what seemed the middle of the Ice Age, his feet warming over wax night-lights which his mother had sent him in a parcel. His mother had been thinking of enabling Stan to read under a bivouac at nights. Stan found the gentle warmth of the lights to be also made to measure for midnight turret foot-warming

Stan himself, to say nothing of the operator who relieved him, viewed the foot-warming as mildly amusing. He was not so amused in the morning to hear that three other troopers were being loaded into ambulances, with severely frostbitten feet.

Next day, as the regiment continued its in every way painful progress, Captain Sandy Saunders, normally a cheerful man, was approached by a solemn Resistance leader at Lignieres. Sandy had met Resistance men who were jubilant or nervous, confident or plainly fearful, all of them resolute. This man had a strange look of horror and seemed to be broken in spirit.

'Thirty-four,' the man was repeating, 'thirty-four.'

'Thirty-four what?' enquired Sandy. But it was simple repetition:

'Thirty-four, thirty-four, thirty-four ....'

The man led him down into the cellar of a house. Partially alerted by the look on the man's face, Sandy came fully alert because of the smell. Sweet, putrefying, all-pervading stench. He took out his handkerchief and covered his nose. He wished he could have decently covered his eyes.

Bodies lay in the cellar. Civilians. In ordinary clothes. All dead. All pitched into a great, untidy obscene heap. All bearing the burning and ripping marks of machine-gunning rather than a rifle firing squad. All only recently dead. A dozen. Difficult to count because they were piled in layers.

Twenty. Even more.

Then Sandy understood. THIRTY-FOUR.

Unable to walk away from a scene which at the same time totally repelled him, the big captain looked closer at the bodies. Each man had been cleanly shot through the head by a small gun, probably a pistol. Once. Then the entire group had been machine-gunned. He was too physically shocked, petrified, even to be sick.

It was 10 January 1945, and at least one Yeoman, favoured by the destinies of war and returned to hospital in England, was celebrating his 21st birthday surrounded by loved ones in a warm reception room. Spud Taylor was still soldiering on. He had left his tank for purposes to which all Yeomen yielded sooner or later. It had seemed a quiet day in terms of actual battle. Then from above came the ominous increasing moan of the aptly termed Moaning Minnies, the multiple mortar bombs. Spud hitched his trousers and prepared to flatten himself on the ground. Before he could do so the familiar clusters of six black smoke bursts sprang from the ground, patched with red centres briefly flashing amid the enduring, drifting smoke.

Sometimes with such explosions a single large piece of shrapnel, which seemed and sounded self-propelled, detached itself from the general mêlée of debris and hurtled away to a distant destination. As it went it gave off a whirring sound, a magnified version of the sound given off by a child's spinning top, but infinitely more deadly. A person could stand and listen to it for what appeared to be long seconds before it fell with an exhausted 'phthwat' of a sigh. But if that person happened to be standing in the direct path of that missile the shred of shrapnel was hard and fast enough to amputate, or even decapitate.

Now Spud heard such a self-propelled, jagged chunk heading directly towards him. He began to run. The noise pursued him. Ahead was a mound in the snow. He threw himself over the mound, even as the missile slowed and speared into the ground where he had been standing. Spud had thrown himself over the parapet of a tiny infantry trench with a couple of men in it. He had speared himself on the bayonet of a soldier of the Black Watch. The bayonet had jabbed right through his leg so that he could not move. Strangely he felt no pain. The Highlander and Spud cautiously effected a separation of bayonet and leg. The knife-sharp point had lodged in the big leg pocket of his thick overalls.

Joe Watkinson had a moustache like two tiny golden bayonets projecting one on either side of his stubby nose. This gave him a look of fierceness only justified when his regiment's fame was impugned in some rowdy pub. He drove Bill Fox's tank, was an excellent tank man, and, under the fierce exterior, was kind-hearted if very forgetful. He had loved and married one of the sweet girls from the Salvation Army canteen in Ogbourne. Not himself very religious, he was still rigid in his moral attitudes. However, Joe believed that soldiers were entitled to filch from the enemy. And what he particularly wanted to filch was a pair of soft leather, high-quality boots as worn by SS officers.

Bill Fox's tank was among those which seemed to be practising for a downhill speed descent on the tracks leading to La Roche. Bill Fox himself had chosen the better part of hiking down the slope and was deep in conversation with troop leaders down there. As Joe brought his tank out of another hectic, heart-stalling bout of mechanized skiing, he suddenly stopped the tank and got out. His co-driver, Kemp, asked him where he was going.

'I've seen them at last. What I've always been looking for. A pair of those officer's boots. Over there, look. By that body.'

'Be careful, Joe, you silly old idiot. That may be a booby-trap. You know the Jerries are always doing things like that. Especially the SS.'

'Well, I'll feel for wires, then, won't I. Be back in a mo'.'

Kemp watched Joe stride through the snow, feel under the boots, pick them up, stroke them. Kemp grinned. 'Good old Joe. He's got his prize at last.' He watched Joe come back to the tank. Lean over Kemp's hatch. Drop the boots in.

Kemp stroked the boots. Admired them. Stared. Stood up, head out of hatch. And was sick. Still holding the boots in his hand.

'What's the matter, boy?'

'Joe, you rotten so-and-so. Didn't you look at these boots? Didn't you check them? They've still got feet in them. Blown-up feet. And frozen solid inside.'

Joe thought for a moment as he put the tank into gear again. 'That's alright. We'll just have to dig 'em out, then, won't we? I'm not letting those bloody boots go, not for nobody, now I've got 'em.'

It was 11 January and the tanks were moving down the touristic scenery of the Ardennes to the pretty, central town of La Roche. Much of the town was in ruins. Few citizens came out from the ruins to greet the tanks. It was not the cold and snow which kept the citizens in their houses. The citizens of La Roche must have been used to cold and snow. But they were not used to being liberated, then occupied again, and then liberated once more. It was all too much to bear.

Wally and his crew were ordered to halt in the shadow of the big hotel, called Hotel de Liege. A war photographer was standing there waiting to take a picture of the row of tanks.

'Hey, cut that out,' shouted someone. 'Last time one of you boys took a photo of us we lost a good troop leader dead within minutes. Go and photograph somebody else.'

'Listen, chaps,' suggested Wally. 'That's a hotel, look. Hotel dee Leej, or something like that. Hotel means beds.'

'Bet your life we won't be stopping long enough to kip,' commented Sergeant Lloyd.

'No, I don't mean that. I mean hotel means beds means sheets. We could whip some of their sheets, couldn't us?'

'Sheets are no good in this weather,' interrupted Les. 'What we need is thick blankets.'

'Will you all shut up and listen,' cried Wally, exasperated. 'I mean hotel means beds means sheets means white, lots of lovely white, means snow camouflage, don' it? See?'

'Well, the paint they gave us wasn't enough for more than a smear or two. Jerry can surely see us stuck out, grey and green, on top of all this snow. Why not?' Lloyd agreed.

They went into the hotel, which was a scene of total devastation. Within a few minutes they had found a chest containing clean sheets amid the piles of bomb-blast filth. Within as many minutes more their tank was swathed with white cloth, leaving only space for the turret to traverse and hatches to open. From a mid-distance view it was quite a successful merger with the clean snow.

'There you are, see,' chirped Wally. 'That's surely worth a mention in despatches. Where's that flipping war photographer now?'

Alf Rushton and crew were fortunate, in the infinite permutations of regimental advances and sideways moves and reserve locations, to find themselves that night in reserve, and placed right at the front door of a luxury hotel in the tourist town. They invited themselves in. The place was uninhabited and partially destroyed. They found bedrooms which could be used. Downy, beautifully quilted, heavily blanketed beds which could be slept in. Almost perfectly working toilets adjacent to the bedrooms, which could be used for squatting and considering higher strategy. There were luxurious carpets on the floor, too, softly sinking under the feet, like the sodden earth in Limburg. So that night they slept in paradise. That is, if paradise has the ceiling and roof wide open to a winter blizzard.

The centre of La Roche was so jumbled with ruins that there was no place through which a 30 ton Sherman could pass. Not by driving the tracks high to crunch down on obstinate ruins. Not by using the nose of the 30 ton monster to nudge aside fallen walls. It would be necessary to wait for specialist bulldozers to clear a way. Meanwhile old friends Charlie Robertson and his battalion of Black Watch climbed over the obstacles and carefully moved through the town, checking for snipers left behind in the second German exodus from La Roche. The Shermans sat behind the obstacles and promised heavy support.

It was that night that Charlie Robertson had a strange adventure. Although closely engaged in battle he had taken it upon himself to organize the porterage of hot meals for his company who, unlike the tank men, had no means of cooking their own food. That night Charlie made his rendezvous with the cooks, collected 80 good, generous hot dinners and loaded them in his jeep. He gave his driver the nod to go. They climbed out of La Roche and were soon on unfamiliar roads. It seemed to Charlie that it was taking a very long time to reach the front-line troops. The bright moonlight among the dark trees only tended to confuse the landscape. They drove hurriedly on, before the meals went cold. For it was really ice-box cold out there. A better night for distributing cold beer!

They rounded a bend and the driver braked, screeching to a stop. At a roadblock. Manned by one or two frozen shivering Germans who were stamping up and down, blowing on their fingers, slapping their arms across their chests. Their rifles leaned against the roadblock.

No orders needed. Driver reversed. Full speed astern. Back round the bend. A tyre-scorching about-turn on two wheels. Then an attempt to beat all speed records out of there.

That night surely must become known as the night when Charlie Robertson almost delivered meals-on-wheels to the Germans.

12 January, and C Squadron moving down towards Hives. 'Ah, I can pronounce this one,' quipped Bill Fox. 'Hives. The Belgians say "Heaves". But I say Hives as in beehives. Only hope there aren't too many damned iron bees buzzing around down there.'

Fingers, feet, brains worked less swiftly, less efficiently at 30 degrees below freezing. Turret crews were numb, drivers still unable to control the wayward tracks on deeper ice and snow. Commanders saw blurred figures through frozen binoculars.

The Germans had had time to dig in. They knew the ranges. They had been able to ensure minimum heating for fingers and feet. A bottle or two of stimulus for tired minds. Amid the revealing snows, Sergeant Warren's Sherman came in sight over that deep, and crisp, and even field of fire. Old Balbo back in the turret once again, hopping to go, and trusting that this was the quickest route to Berlin. When a Panther tank, superb German creation when it wasn't breaking down, fired at nearly a mile's range. Giving Balbo time to see the flash. Time to hear the shot. Time to curse the Hun. But no time to react. Direct hit. Pieces of iron ripping off the inside of the turret as a result of the impact outside, acted as flying bullets, mashing Balbo's legs all down one side. The little man was no great burden to be dragged out of the turret as the crew hastily evacuated the blazing tank. They laid him down and signalled for medics. If the medics came soon enough Balbo might live. But he would never walk again on his own two legs.

That popular joker, McKenzie, was commanding the next tank in line, looking along those blurred woods a mile away for signs of the Panther that struck Warren's tank. Another Panther from another side hurled its armour-piercing shot at McKenzie, smashing the tank, although the crew debussed without major injury.

Other troops paused in reserve for the artillery to put down a heavy retaliatory 'stonk'. In the turrets the waiting crews shivered more violently, cold, horror and appre-hension taking their toll. They had heard of the brewing of Warren and McKenzie over the wireless net.

'Bugger this for a story,' mumbled Harry Graham as

several turret crews were ordered to dismount and stamp around to keep themselves active. 'Why did we bother?'

McGranahan, usually so cheerful, looked grim for once. 'After this lot I shall get up in church and disagree with the parsons. Hell, mates, is not burning hot eternal fires. I know something even worse. Hell is damn, unsheltered, freezing cold, shut up for ever in blocks of ice. What a fate!'

'Send me a message when you get there, Mac.,' said Tommy T., 'and let me know if it really is like that. If it is I'll even give up the whoring and cussing to get to heaven rather than a place like this.'

'Oh, Christ,' groaned Mac. 'Shall I never ever be warm again?'

'Bloody generals had any sense, they'd issue us with hot-water bottles instead of drinking-water bottles for this idiot's game,' concluded Harry as orders came to mount up again.

3 Troop were to find a way through the thick trees and outflank the two (at least) Panthers. Other Shermans were to move cautiously into the woods in support. The artillery barrage descended on the far positions from which the Panthers had fired and troopers watched for a while with satisfaction as a wall of fire seemed to stand fixed along the front of the danger woods.

Shermans moved as the barrage died down. Crashing through trees and crunching over ice. No sound or shot came from the Panthers. Instead the German commander changed to firing artillery and mortar bombs high into the trees above the advancing Shermans' heads. Showered with dead twigs and leaves, and menaced by more lethal fall-out, some commanders closed down.

McGranahan did not. He was seething with anger about Warren. Balbo, the man, he disliked. Balbo, the soldier, he admired greatly. It was not the Panther commander's fault. But, in war, anger must surge, human kindness must shrivel, animal instincts must growl, vengeance must be sought. Mac was seeking it.

His crew caught the enthusiasm and leaned forward more tightly in their tiny seats. Sharing the anger. Until the final shell burst in the trees over Mac's head. Slashing down with red claws of death. Showering into the turret and over the gunner's head, leaves, twigs, grit, shell particles, sharp icicles, pieces of bone, spouts of blood, spools of brain.

It was minutes before the operator could alert the driver, halt the tank, extricate the weeping gunner, move the sagging body of Mac, report over the radio.

'Hello, 4 Baker. Hit by HE high in trees. Vehicle OK. Halted for orders. Regret Sunray killed. Over.'

Away through the trees, Tommy's eyes too were wet. 'My God,' he said, 'and me, silly bugger, just asked him to send me back a message when he gets to hell.'

That was what is often termed 'the parting shot'. Next day, the regiment was bewildered by the news that, as the American front was now safe, 1NY were losing their association with the Highlanders and moving to 79th Armoured Division, the famous division of Major-General Hobart, which specialized in 'funnies', peculiar vehicles designed for peculiar purposes and not normal fighting tanks.

The railway loading siding for the Shermans was back at Ciney. As Michael Rathbone headed a column leading through the little town towards the railway station he noticed that the streets were still empty. None of the jubilation of liberation on that first occasion, only a few weeks ago. For a moment he did not understand this. 1NY had fought a good battle. The Yanks had compensated for the first unfortunate error. In reality the high-risk German adventure had cost them many of their best remaining troops. Already rumours had it that von Runstedt himself never believed that the thing would work. The Battle of that awful Bulge had been a shock and a bloodletting. But it had left the German army weaker. It was time for jubilation again.

But then he saw pale Belgian faces peeping out through windows at the retreating Shermans. Retreating? Ah, thought Ratters. Are they standing there thinking that maybe the Germans will come again?

A Belgian was signalling to him, running by the tank, jumping on. Apologizing. For the sullen looks, the lack of welcome. The SS, there for only a few hours, had dragged out and shot all the local Resistance men. And then left.

A woman at a window shook her fist at Captain Michael Rathbone.

I'm a double act, you might say.

My title is Troop Leader, and so I command a troop of four Sherman tanks. And my troop is one of four troops which make up the squadron, in addition to HQ(F), with tanks, and HQ(A), with trucks.

But I'm also a tank commander. A sergeant and two corporals command the other three tanks of the troop but I command this one. I stand with my head out top, and I give commands to the gunner, operator, driver, in just the same way as the other tank commanders. But, at the same time, I must order the movements of the troop. And I must listen for the squadron leader's commands, developing the battle plan agreed at earlier conferences.

So on my mapboard I must not only trace my own progress and location at a given moment. I must also plot the movements of the other three tanks. And know where the other three troops are moving. And identify squadron headquarters hideout. And have a fair idea of where the hidden enemy may be dug in along my hundred yards or so of front. Or maybe there is no front and no definite flanks and only my troop lined along a lost, empty, worthless country lane, forming the famous arrow-head of advance of which the war cartographers are so fond.

And it doesn't end there, for outside the tank and round about the troop will be a company of infantry with maybe a Highlander captain keeping his eye on me and coming across every so often to liaise. And each of my tanks will be working with a platoon of the captain's men on foot. And the squadron leader back yonder will be wanting strict precise data for artillery barrages and air strikes. And when we were in Normandy it was even battleship salvoes.

And there's the liaison also with the Resistance people who are waiting to guide us; and the enemy prisoners who are often so relieved to be finished with their war that, in a strange mixture of fear, exhilaration and fellow feeling, they may give us valuable information before they clam up further down the line and nearer the cages.

But always there's the need to be as alert as my Able, Baker and Charlie tanks. To spot the unusual shape in the hedgerow, the profile that does not belong on the horizon, flick the microphone switch from squadron talk to intercom, snap orders, guide gunner, alert driver, load, fire, readjust, fire again! – before the enemy commander over there can get off his first shot. And he may have only his own single tank to worry about.

When it's all happening there's not much time for fear. Excitement? Yes! Dread? Yes! Horror? Yes! But the real torment of fear comes before and after. And the concern about missing a trick or botching an order, that haunts one before the action too. In the dead night before action. In the chill dawn. In the torrid or drizzling noontime lull ....

Reward? Little lieutenants don't usually last long enough in this war to ascend many steps of promotion. And there's a queue of more senior officers way back, yearning for a front-line chance. Well, if there are any medals going I shall gain a different coloured one to my Able, Baker and Charlie commanders. If that is of any significance in the greater dispensations of eternity?

Perhaps the worst is sometimes to recollect, suddenly, that a year or so ago I was still at school. Now I give orders, save or damn the destinies of men old enough to be my fathers. Some of them soldiers for ten years or more in the TA, and five years of war service put in. And their own families procreated and reared, and maybe a son fighting in uniform. It is not they who generate the uncertainty. Ninety-nine per cent of them alert, respectful and instantly obedient. It is simply a matter of my own thoughts in the waiting time.

And if you have brains enough to command a troop, you have brains enough to calculate all the chances, even to assessing what an ideal target the human brain is when lofted yards above the battlefield. Brittle brain behind an egg-shell fragile skullbone, when inches of solid steel armour-plating will not deflect that 88mm shot which has one's name on it.

12   Sea Squadron

Dick Bates, prime eavesdropper, was again the first ranker
on the tank crews of C Squadron to hear the news. He also
overheard Hank's little joke about it, made to Bill Fox, as
Dick was checking his tank's track. He immediately found
reason to wander down through the squadron harbour,
acting as unofficial town crier, but a town crier who passed
on his news in an awed whisper. Consistent with the
publicity posters in Britain which said 'Walls have ears', and
picturing Hitler himself standing listening behind the wall.

'We've got to change from being C Squadron,' said Dick,
wetting his finger and tracing a letter 'C' in the dust on the
plating of a Sherman. 'And now we're going to be "Sea"
Squadron,' tracing the word 'Sea'. 'See?'

'You been drinking, Dick, you silly old sausage,' queried
Sergeant Stan Upstone. 'Explain what you ferkin' well
mean.'

'We're going to hand in our Shermans, and we're going to
man ... Buffaloes. BUFFALOES!'

'You mean they're sending us to work at the zoo?' asked
one.

'No, he means we're going off to be cowboys. And old Bill
Fox will be Buffalo Bill.'

'Listen, I'm serious. We're now in 79th Armoured Div.,
which invents all these peculiar vehicles. And the Buffalo is a
tank that floats on water. An amphi-bilious tank.'

'Oh, pull the other one,' guffawed Tommy T. 'In fact pull
all three. A tank that walks on water?'

'Me, I'm always bilious when I'm sailing on water,' said
Johnny Howell, who had rejoined the squadron after
missing D-Day because of appendicitis.

'Oh, it's no use talking sense to you silly lot of BFs!' and
Dick went whispering on.

But, come February 1945, the regiment found itself by the

quiet Willemsvaart Canal (which name Bill Fox quickly and joyfully anglicized), launching the queer-shaped tanks that walked on water. Half boat, half Kangaroo infantry carrier, they looked like iron shoe-boxes with tractor fittings. But they floated serenely on the still canal waters.

The weather was still bitter, although with none of the utterly devastating temperatures of the Ardennes. It was Brian Carpenter who found a new use for the Buffalo. Finding the canal frozen over one morning, and being the first Buffalo to exercise, he blithely cruised around, smashing up the sheets of ice into smaller floes and then into tiny pieces like broken crockery. 'Hey, chaps. I discovered the truth. All this talk of crossing rivers is to deceive Hitler. We're going to invade Iceland. And these contraptions are really ice-breakers.'

Roy Beer was reading letters from home. He had climbed into his driver's cab to read them, partly because it had been raining, and looked likely to rain again, and partly because the road was a sea of mud. A stream of bullets sent a row of splashes up from the mud in front of his workshop truck. Multiple machine-gun fire rattled and a plane screamed low overhead. 'Don't worry. It's a Spitfire,' shouted somebody. 'He's made a mistake.' Fists waved at the climbing plane.

But the flight of Spitfires swooped again and again, criss-crossing the convoy with tracer. The convoy was too far behind the line and too well marked with identification for this to be an error. These must be some of the captured RAF planes which, rumour had it, were being flown, still with RAF markings, by German pilots. Roy Beer did not stop to reason it out. He opened the cab door and slid down under the lorry. More howling engines announced more tracer, and another burst of fire flicked up another long row of mud splashes, passing within inches of Roy's left leg. He hurriedly withdrew his leg under the lorry.

The raid did not last long, but the fury did. Roy was furious because they had been attacked, because the attack came under false colours, because he had dived into filthy mud, because he still had his letters from home in his hand and they were so mud-spattered as to be almost unreadable. His fury mounted several degrees when he noticed that a trail of bullet marks passed right up against his front offside wheel. And that the tyre was flat. 'Oh, my God,' he grumbled, 'a flat in four inches of prime mud. And it's blue-dy well started to rain again.'

Across the road he saw another driver, of a big workshop wagon. The man had been inspecting his own vehicle, was apparently satisfied, and was climbing back up into his cab again.

'Hey, mate,' called Roy. 'Give us a hand to mend this flat, won't you, please?'

'You go get yerself a little monkey,' snapped the other, slamming his cab door, himself comfortably settled inside.

'Mate!' hissed Roy, then set about soiling knees and bruising hands to change the wheel. With a little patience it was done. As he straightened up and moved to get inside his warm, dry cab, he heard a hissing sound as of a monstrous snake. The big wagon on the other side of the road keeled over as one of its great tyres went flat. Slow reaction from the Spitfire attack evidently. The driver climbed down, looked at the flat and kicked it angrily.

He looked across the road. Grinned rather ingratiatingly. Shouted, 'Why don't you give me a hand with this? You seemed to handle your own pretty well. This one's a right bugger. What d'you say, mate?'

'You go get yourself two little monkeys,' snarled Roy, climbing into his cab and beginning to scrape the mud off his letters. 'Mate!'

Mud was a problem for Don Foxley too. Having handed in his beloved Sherman, not as beloved as the original Helmdon, but still a friendly mobile home, he was trying to lavish the same kind of mechanical care on this clumsy iron box. But care needed cleanliness, especially when handling the more delicate parts of the engine. And cleanliness was impossible to achieve in this sea of mud. He seemed to be going through tons of cotton waste, wiping fingers, engine parts, tools, clothes and fingers again. And it was such a chore after the delicately poised controls of the Sherman – in comparison with other tanks. A Buffalo had no dignity on land, it was a crawling, craven, clumsy thing, responding brusquely to any touch from its master. And on water it wallowed and steered like an ancient collier in a storm at sea. Being underpowered, it sailed along happily on the first canal, but, now on the fast-flowing Meuse, you found that you had to point its nose UP river when going in and DOWN river when coming out. And in between you had to turn around without going into a spin like a gush of dirty water swilling down a drain. Horrible beasts!

Brian Carpenter, discoverer of the ice-breaking capability of the Buffalo, had found another ingenious function on the tank-boat. It was a version of the joke where a flower in the button-hole of your coat squirts water into someone's eye. There was an outlet pipe at the front of the Buffalo. You called in some hapless operator or gunner who knew nothing about motor mechanics or seamanship.

'Oh, Bill. Give us a hand, will you? Just stand there a mo', by that pipe and tell me if it's leaking, will you? Hang on while I start up.'

You then accelerated violently, the bilge pump went into excess pressure, and a stream of icy bilge water shot out of the pipe, right in the eye of poor Bill if he happened to be average height. Of course, one day Bill got his revenge. The troop leader, an elegant young lieutenant, was passing by.

'Excuse me, sir,' said Bill. 'The driver, Carpenter here, has been querying whether this pipe should be leaking. Would you mind just looking at it, sir? OK, Carpenter, start her up!'

Which required a very delicate piece of accelerating from Brian Carpenter who had no wish to risk the ire of a troop leader doused in greasy, stinking bilge water.

2 March saw a proving run of the Buffaloes on the river. The river-bank looked as though it was bathed in sunset, so many red-tabbed, scarlet-hatted generals had gathered to watch. There were those whose faces were familiar from the pictorial magazines: Dempsey, the top man; Ritchie of Africa, and Barker, the corps commanders. And a host of major-g's, brigs, CREs, GSOs, ADCs, all watching with a fervour only matched by the Varsity Boat Race spectators.

'What are all them buggers doing, watching us?' mumbled Tommy T. 'I reckon they're weighing up their chances of using us if von Runstedt breaks through again and we DO have another Dunkirk,' murmured a mate.

And the next day, Colonel Doug, with Lieutenant Owen, became the first Yeomen to set foot in Germany, as they took their new scout car up to the banks of the Rhine for a 'look-see'. In the new scout car the colonel smoked his old pipe contentedly.

The regiment was still largely vagrant, not settled into long-term billets, moving forward to rougher waters, fetching reinforcements, carrying out look-see patrols. Jerry was still fulminating in the distance, loosing off long-range artillery shells, or sending up V1 and V2 terror missiles. Civilians were still wary of possible further fighting, even a renewed German occupation as in the Ardennes.

Bristolian John Stenner, another of the significant band of West Countrymen who had found their way into the Northants, had found an empty house for the crew. His commander, Captain Humphries, came in and said, 'Any chance of a brew, Johnny?' John fetched the primus stove from the tank, pumped it up, and set a mess tin of water to boil, squatting quietly on his haunches, glad to be alone for a few minutes until all the gang came in.

Suddenly he was grasped around the shoulders and chest by strong, almost brutal arms. He struggled, but to no avail. Visions of creeping, sneaking SS manhunters crossed his mind. Was this to be his fate after going through so many pitched battles in Normandy and Holland?

Then a woman's voice sounded in his ears: 'Tommy! Tommy! Lovely Tommy!' John trembled. 'Lord,' he thought, 'I didn't know women out here did that to men. What have I got myself into? Ah, well … think of England!'

The arms released him, a hand swung him round. A quite elderly, but still typically sturdy Dutch woman was laughing at him. 'Good Tommy! I am come. This my house. I go away. Long time. From Germans. Now I come. You stay here. All you boys stay here. Lovely Tommies. Germans not come back never no more.'

And all Johnny could think of to say, as he saw Captain Humphries standing in the doorway grinning, was, 'Lady, would you like a cup of English tea?'

It was only a day or two before the squadron moved on, but in that time the lady of the house had become quite maternal. When Captain Humphries announced that they were going, she turned to John Stenner and cried, 'Ah, but you are too young to be in the war. You should be at home with your mama.' Which caused Captain Humphries to blow his nose rather suddenly.

'Some genius at Corps,' said Hank, 'has chosen the code word "Splosh" for our full dress rehearsal over the Meuse.'

'I would have thought that "Beecher's" would have been more relevant,' responded Bill Fox. 'Somebody's sure to fall in. Don't they ride and hunt at Corps these days?'

For 'Splosh' the entire regiment assembled in their battle places, with Buffaloes ready for launching into the vicious-looking river. There was a great deal of the usual good-humoured banter with which troops face an unfamiliar and hazardous enterprise. Suddenly a sharp voice cut through the hubbub. A voice which impressed not by its volume but by its expectation of obedience.

'No parading, Colonel. Just carry on. Battle stations. Everybody where they ought to be. Treat me as a fly on the wall.'

'I'd squash a bloody fly on the wall, wouldn't I?' muttered Cliff Cuthbertson, like most Geordies unimpressed by shows of authority.

'You won't squash this one,' shot Michael Hunt.

This one was a small, abrupt man who came scuttling along like a beetle, talking as he went. Troopers looked at his epaulets and racked their memories trying to identify the rank. Then they looked at the face, and the rank no longer mattered. Monty himself. Field Marshal Sir Bernard Montgomery come to look-see. Only two young officers walked in his wake. No procession of red-tabbed generals this time.

The colonel was standing with squadron leaders David Bevan and Richard Courage, who had recently taken over A Squadron. 'Who do we have? Reliable people?' he questioned. 'Both commander and driver who won't send Monty to the bottom of the river? And who won't flap?'

Before either of the majors could answer, the field marshal, still approaching barked, 'I'll take that one. I'll go over in that one,' pointing an unerring finger at Sergeant Moralee, standing by his Buffalo.

'Steady, son. Don't flap,' said Moralee out of the side of his mouth to his driver, Litster. 'We'll both finish this war either full colonels, or wearing broad arrows and breaking stones on Dartmoor after this.'

'Bugger this one up,' added Bill Fox to Moralee, as the Great Man chatted to the colonel, 'and we'll be a penal battalion serving with the French Foreign Legion.'

If Montgomery was looking for cause to complain, he had chosen the wrong boat. If he was looking simply for a safe passage he had rolled the dice correctly. For Litster happened to be a very good driver who had taken happily to the clumsy Buffaloes. He took the field marshal over and back with hardly a splash of water on the toecaps of his shining shoes.

'Can you swim, sir?' shouted a relieved corporal as Monty was conveyed back towards the starting point.

'I didn't need to. I *am* with the Northants Yeomanry, am I not?' replied the field marshal, a fierce smile slitting his face.

A round of hearty cheering rose from the troops along the bank. The slit smile broadened and curved a little.

'Clever! Bull's-eye for morale!' thought David Bevan to himself.

The field marshal's visit heralded the final move towards the chosen sector of the River Rhine at a point where it was a wide, free-flowing river. The crossing would be almost as adventurous as a minor sea voyage. And the west side of the Rhine, the allied side, was, of course, under direct enemy fire. Squadrons moved up the roads towards German territory in high spirits.

Michael Hunt's Buffalo, one towards the tail of the convoy, ended the day far short of the German town of Calcar where the regiment would be based. Arriving in Nijmegen Mike turned to Rex Jackson who was also on that Buffalo crew.

'Do you see what I see? A bathhouse. A *Canadian* bathhouse. I wonder if they would let the filthy Yeomanry use their marble baths and gold taps?'

'It's worth a try,' agreed Rex.

Of course there were no gold taps. It was an austerity military mobile shower unit, much like similar British units. Mike and Rex enjoyed a bathe, the first for weeks under a real shower. The unit was similar also to British units in that it took in a soldier's soiled, ragged underwear and issued him with the freshly laundered cast offs of a previous veteran who had passed by that way. Mike and Rex went to hand in their 'dirties' and collect some 'cleans'. Mike received a typical pair of British army 'drawers, cellular, for the use of'. As he put them on he chuntered to Rex.

'Look at these flipping things. Full of holes. Falling to bits, Held together by crystals of congealed laundry soap. What silly sod would wear shorts until they fell to bits like this? Wait a minute … there's a name on them. It's … L/Cpl M.P. Hunt, 7952202/22142. Hey, Rex! These are my own shorts. Nobody is going to believe this. I wore them over to Normandy. Traded them in … at a Canadian bath unit – must be this same one – outside Caen last July.'

Up in Calcar David Bevan was complaining to Ken Squires

because the public lighting was not working. It was difficult to press ahead with plans for the Rhine crossing. Some lights would help. So Ken was also in the business of resurrected articles, not clothing but electrics. He was, as he said, 'doing a bit of liberating'. First he liberated some old but usable German signals batteries. Then he liberated a rotary transformer. Liberated cable and light bulb sockets and even light bulbs. Strung along one side of the squadron area this effectively lit the preparations Hank and Bill Fox needed to make.

Brian 'Shorty' Coleman was also into the liberating business. This time it was a large barrel of brandy from a ruined cellar. With one or two helpers he rolled the barrel down the street in the dark. Arriving at their billet, an empty house, they discovered that the barrel was too large to go through the door, any way up. *Nil desperandum.* Shorty was equal to the occasion. He found a narrow zinc bath, cleaned it and dragged it to the door. The troops attacked the harmless barrel with machetes, splitting open a hole large enough to transfer the precious liquid from the barrel to the bath. Which was then formally liberated by the resident crews, indulging in traditional methods of homage to Bacchus, whose name they thought they saw stencilled on the barrel.

Don Foxley, the strict Baptist, became involved in a more serious incident of retribution towards the German nation. Calcar was largely in ruins, but there were some shops in which goods could still be seen. Strict orders were given that nothing was to be looted from local shops, ruined or otherwise. A group of Yeomen had been experimenting with the unknown strengths of German wine, beer and schnapps. Somewhat merry, almost to the point of being abusive to anyone outside their own ranks, they were wandering along in front of a row of shops.

'Look at all that bloody wealth,' said one of them. 'You'd think, if they're losing the war, the Jerries wouldn't have anything left in their ferkin' shops. Look at that china. My folk never had china like that in our house. And we're supposed to be the winners.'

'We ought to take it for ourselves,' said another. 'We couldn' afford that sort of stuff at home. So, why don' we take it. I'm not bloody well leaving that 'ere for some Nazi bugger to enjoy after the war.'

Don, idly listening, heard a third say, 'You can't take it. That'd be looting. That'd be a crime. Shot at dawn. But, you're right. Why leave it for some bloody Nazi, I say. Our artillery didn' shoot straight enough at this china pisser's shop. They ought've destroyed it, house, shop, china, the lot.'

After months of bitter fighting, frustration, loss of friends, wounding, freezing, and now to see exquisite china still displayed in an enemy shop: the mood of the group became fiercer and more belligerent, catching up in their frenzy other troopers who were nearby.

'Finish what the artillery started, then! Bash up the bloody lot. Smash it all to smithereens. Give it hell. Show 'em what kaput really means. Ferkin' Nazis!' The shouts came faster and more furious. Without any special sign or word, the group surged into the ruins of the shop, picking up expensive china cups, jugs, plates, tureens. And crystal glasses. And ornaments. Smashing them one against the other. Throwing them against the broken walls. Treading them into dust on the floor. Two troopers had a fencing match with large ornaments, until the ornaments were worn down to jagged remnants. Suddenly there was nothing left to smash. Troopers began to look around the shop with a kind of despondency, a sense of failure, the beginning of shame. Don stood among them, coming to realize that he too had been swept into the shop and had been smashing china with the same purposeless fury. They started to leave the shop, one by one, muttering their apologies.

'Show 'em! Stupid thing to do! What do we gain by that? Bloody Nazis! As bad as the bloody Nazis. Anybody'd think I was SS. God, what was in that booze? Hope old Hank doesn't find out. What if some widow woman owns the shop – all she's got – we're *worse* than bloody Gestapo. We ought to know better. Shit! That's the last time I ....'

Troopers waking with sore heads after the late-night china shop rampage, were doubly devastated by the news that the colonel had gone. Injured again. Badly this time. Another scout car turned over. Probably the end of the war for him. Our Colonel Doug.

Calcar was too busy a place, and the river operation was too urgent, for Yeomen to grieve too long over the colonel's departure. Rex Jackson was not amused by the preparation which was taking place alongside their Buffalo. A carpenter and a quartermaster of the Highland Division were busy assembling piles of wooden crosses to stick into the ground at the head of temporary graves.

In the turmoil of war, farm animals had been left untended and unguarded. A Squadron saw this as an opportunity to increase their pork ration for there were unclaimed pigs running in and out between human legs. Bill Fox watched several cows lumbering across the main square, lowing wildly and plaintively to the skies.

'Those damn cows need milking,' observed Bill. 'Cruelty to dumb animals, it is, to leave domestic cows unmilked. Anybody here know how to milk a cow?'

'Never volunteer,' laughed Dick Bates. 'But Kemp over there is a farmer.'

'Fetch him. And get me some rope.' A few minutes later Yeomen saw the astonishing sight of Bill Fox's gunner, Bruce Dickson, holding the end of a rope which was tied around a cow's horns. As Bruce held the nervous cow tight, Captain Bill Fox, tough, hard-talking Bill, sitting on the steps of a house, milked the cow into an old petrol tin. 'Cruelty to dumb animals,' he was repeating in rhythm with the hand pulls.

Others rankers were lining up at a cook's wagon in the square. Lance-Corporal Whittles was standing there with his mess tin when a large calibre German shell whistled over the heads of the crowd and crashed into the ruins of the town hall some way to the right. He wondered whether to run, dive or just wait and see. Another shell came down short, the same distance to the left in a bracketing style. The next one would be smack in the middle. Right where the queue was. Some men ran. Others lay down or crouched. A loud whistle. Whittles saw the huge shell hit the church tower across the square. Bounce. Spin through the air. Swoop down. Bounce along the ground with the motion of a rugby ball. Come to rest by the cook's wagon as though waiting to be served. Unexploded. For minutes men in the square remained in a motionless tableau, hardly breathing, watching the shell, waiting for it to explode. The shell also lay there, part of the tableau. Unexploded. Did not explode. Probably was not going to explode.

They left it there, like an outcast leper in ancient times. The cook breathed a brief sigh of relief and then grabbed his ladle again.

Bill Martland was not exactly setting up in opposition to the cooks. But the lads had caught another pig. A trooper who was a butcher had slaughtered it. Now Bill was asked to roast it. This was now a solid Yeomanry tradition, not exactly living off the land but certainly accepting the gifts which an indifferent Providence occasionally bestowed in the form of wounded or stray edible animals. Scobbie butchering a cow outside Caen. Ken Lyke rugby-tackling a porker in Holland. Now Martland to prepare a gourmet pork banquet in Germany. He constructed an oven of old tins filled with earth and saturated in petrol, jointed the carcass and set it to roast, filling the square with the most delicate of smells.

As favoured sergeants, corporals and troopers gathered closer, lips drooling and mess tins at the ready, Squadron Leader Richard Courage was seen to approach slowly, followed by what appeared to be a delegation from the officers' trade union.

'I say,' enquired the major. 'What is that contraption you're working at?'

'It's called an oven, sir,' replied Bill respectfully.

'Ah, yes, of course. They tell me that you are a West End chef. I really must visit your restaurant after the war. I'd love to sample your cooking.'

'Thank you, sir. I'll let you have the address.'

'I say – what is that delightful smell. Can you smell it?'

'Oh, yes,' chuckled Martland, 'they tell me that a shell spilled a lot of valuable perfume at a shop down the road.'

'Ah. Did they? Did it? Tell me, are you happy with conditions in the regiment, for example the food …?'

'No complaints, sir.' He turned to the grinning rankers. 'I don't think officers would want to eat the same food as other ranks, do you? Cooked in the same oven as other ranks' food?'

A young lieutenant stepped forward. 'This war has been a great leveller, you know, Martland. Officers do have to mess with other ranks in the field, as you know.'

The troopers laughed. One of them said to Bill, 'I think we could just about spare a shoulder, don't you. A nice shoulder of pork, sir?' to Major Courage.

'Oh, do you have some pork somewhere? I am astonished. If I'd known you were about to eat, I would never have intruded like this.'

Laughter continued. There was enough pork for all. There

were more porkers running loose. The officers were generally a decent lot. Bill extracted a roast shoulder of pork, done to a turn. The officers' trade union deputation accepted the share, with vain efforts to avoid joining the troopers in their drooling. Honour was satisfied.

Michael Hunt had drawn a leave pass in the latest lottery. A week's leave in Britain. Starting 24 March. But the crossing of the Rhine was to start 23 March. Mike must wait patiently and duck frequently. Stan Upstone, long term commander, had gone down with what looked like food poisoning, intolerable gripes of the stomach. Rex Jackson, MM, was called to command – the tank driven by Mike.

Lord George Scott, a major, returned from his lucky leave in London to find Colonel Doug evacuated, and himself now lieutenant-colonel commanding a regiment about to fling itself into one of the greatest and most complicated military operations in history. He had little time to do more than go round the squadrons, reading out a message from Higher Command stressing the importance of the operation.

In the dusk Major Courage and Captain Boardman cautiously moved along the *bund*, the high bank built up on their side of the river, through which gaps had been blasted to allow the Buffaloes a less steep approach to the river. They checked the last preparations along a bank which was still exposed to direct German fire. They inspected the new, extraordinary, incomprehensible, invisible infra-red light signals which would flash to a screen on each Buffalo the kind of direction signal which hitherto had been given by visible, glow-radiating lights which the enemy sought to douse.

Both officers were reminded of the exposed nature of their tour, for the British artillery bombardment was already roaring overhead like an unceasing multitude of express trains, answered by occasional coughs of German guns.

Remember the old AA man you used to see on the roads in peacetime? With his old yellow motor-bike and sidecar? Always saluted you, like you was a colonel at least? Well, I'm him in wartime.

Tank blows up? Tank breaks down? Send for the ARV! Tank loses its track? Tank thinks it's a duck and goes swimming in one of these bloody deep Dutch ditches or canals? Send for the ARV! That's me. No, not *my* initials. There's one of us in every squadron. Armoured Recovery Vehicle. Really just a tank with the gun turret taken out and a mobile workshop fitted in. Ready for anything. Be prepared. That's us. A cross between the Boy Scouts and the AA.

But I can assure you that we don't paint our ARVs bright yellow so that you can see us coming. Because the person most likely to see us coming would be Jerry. No, true, we don't *start* the flaming battle up front. We start a modest tenth or so in the field. Also-rans. But it is usually the front tank that get crocked, or bogged down, or partly brewed up. Then it's us. No big gun to fight with. No nice comforting Red Cross armband to hope the enemy will let us pass. Not even a white flag we can raise. Only dirty, oily, smoke-blackened bits of cotton waste, to wipe our fingers on.

Some of the tank crews call us 'fitters', with the slightest bit of a sneer on their arrogant lips. Oh yes. Stick an overgrown schoolboy in a tank with a mighty 75 millimetre cannon to his hand – and don't let stories about Jerry's almighty 88s blind you to the fact that the 75 comes a good second in the world-beater stakes. Just a length behind. Close race sometimes. Anyway, give an overgrown schoolboy a gun like that, and immediately he can become a conqueror, a bloody little Julius Caesar, a budding Alexander the Great: when he doesn't know a half about the Sherman that we know, or that the armourer knows. And when things go wrong, he can do bugger-all to put them right. Same with the commanders.

Then it's 'Send up the ARV! Quick! Help! Immediate! Emergency! And bring a bucket and shovel as well,'cos we're sitting here shitting ourselves in case Jerry comes round *that* bend before the ARV comes round *this* one.'

Of course, they're not all like that. Especially the ones that have needed our tow-ropes and monkey wrenches and sky-hooks. You see, those boys up there in the lead position are scared enough when they are ducking down behind the armour plate, and closing the hatches, and loading up the high explosive, and traversing their 75s and Brownings. Who wouldn't be? That's the tight-rope you have to walk, over the fires of flaming hell.

But when they see us, at the flick of a microphone switch, come along in our old overalls, with our toolbags, like as if we were come to mend a puncture. And crouching down there by the tracks, or perched right up on top of that bloody, stupid, Empire State Building of a turret. With no guns, and no armour, and nowhere to hide. Just tinkering with the engine, or hitching on a tow-rope, or shaking our heads in disgust. Then they change their tune, and it's 'Hey, Sarge, have a beer on me next time the QM truck comes up.' Or 'Here's our ration of fags. You need 'em more than us.' Good lads!

And if they see us standing with our hands in our pockets sometimes, it might be because it's a good old way that motor mechanics normally stand, or because we've got no guns to hold anyway, or just because that's the only way we can stop our bleeding hands from trembling.

13   One Last River

On the allied side of the Rhine massed forces gathered like locusts in a ripe cornfield. Infantry waited like one vast football crowd. Buffaloes waited like one vast boat show. Rank upon rank upon rank of trucks continued to arrive with ton upon ton of supplies. Guns, some of them to be fired now, some of them to be ferried, strewed the area like fallen logs in a thick forest. All waiting for the word 'Go'. All waiting for the indicated hour before dawn.

Tom Boardman adjusted his special spectacles which would enable him to see the otherwise invisible infra-red direction signs. His crew checked the screen, with its hatching of cross-wires upon which the infra-red direction could be read. Rex Jackson looked up as the artificial moonlight of searchlights playing on clouds was switched on to guide them over the pathless river, and remembered that at Caen a similar artificial moonlight guided them, behind Tom Boardman, over a pathless plain.

Don Foxley stared through the gap in the *bund*, towards the darkly-perceived river, wondering if its waters would be swifter and more difficult to navigate than the Meuse. Brian Carpenter repeated to his driver, Titch Burnand, just once more the magic formula for Buffalo survival, 'UPstream going in, DOWNstream coming out. 3rd gear *in* the water, 1st gear *leaving* it.'

Half of B Squadron was with A, and the other half with C, as there were to be only two columns or waves. In the dark, at zero hour, in C Squadron Hank Bevan said, 'Advance! Good luck!' Buffaloes in bottom gear groaned slowly up the slopes of the broken *bund*, and lapsed into giddy slides waterwards as they cleared the top. Tom Boardman surveyed and monitored the waves of vehicles, loaded mainly with thronged Highlanders this trip, twelve Buffaloes to each wave, and thought they looked most like lines of crabs, pointing squat prows upstream. Fighting the current. Being driven downriver. But aiming always for the target on the far bank.

Michael Hunt drove his Buffalo to the top of the *bund*, scrabbling up the steep slope which was supposed to be a gap, allowed the vehicle to topple at the top, then pointed down the sheer *bund* into the low, obscure waters. Rex Jackson thought it was the Ardennes all over again, tanks sliding down icy slopes choosing their own route without interference from human agency. But here, instead of deep, soft snowdrifts at the bottom, there was an unseen, unknown, hungry, foaming river. Don Foxley, his craft sliding into the waters, thought this was worse than Raamsdonk.

Brian Carpenter's Buffalo had to load a Wasp, a Canadian flame-thrower mounted on a Bren Gun carrier. There was also a huge load of ammunition, whilst a squad of burly Nova Scotia Highlanders had to squeeze on too. The gap in the *bund* had collapsed so that driver Titch Burnand had to climb up nearly 30 feet from ground level. The overloaded Buffalo poised there, then, at a pedal touch from Titch, it dropped its bows and hurtled like a comet down at the river.

With an explosive splash the vehicle seemed still to be nose-diving to the bottom. Water washed right up over the driver's hatch, which Titch had frantically wrenched shut. Tommy T., the gunner, shouted 'We're sinking.' Even the bronzed veterans from Nova Scotia paled perceptibly. 'Rev, Titch, Rev!' shouted Carpenter. A tremendous burst of engine revolution caused the Buffalo to right itself and come surging to surface level as though it were a submarine surfacing, after which it resumed its normal placid turtle waddle through the waves sent up by dozens of other vessels.

The night was brightened by the artifical moonlight, it was distorted into alternate dazzle and blindness by flashing shells, the scene was reflected and further distorted by the glassy, tossing waves and spume trails, but, as yet, only greyly tinged by the reality of dawn. In this lurid, crashing, battering confusion, Corporal Whittles's ferry came to shore. The ramp was dropped, and Highlanders rushed off the Buffalo on to the mysterious, hidden morasses beyond. Before the tank men could raise the ramp the night was riven by the most brilliant rashes of fire as a Highlander exploded bodily and others staggered, fell, crawled forward, lay still. Another infantryman stood up, and a mine drove fangs of fire into his legs.

'Keep the ramp down!' yelled Whittles, 'and for Christ sake stay on board all of you,' he shouted to the crew. He himself ran down the ramp, trod in what might be the footmarks of the infantry, caught a fallen man by the collar and, heedless of his injuries, dragged him up the ramp. Fetched another. And another. Eight wounded men were back on the Buffalo almost as soon as they had landed. Blood streamed amid the water splashes on the ramp. From a distance a feeble voice cried 'Medics! Medics! Help!' But Whittles's orders were clear. It had to be 'Ramp up! Driver, back off! Full speed back across the river.' With a voice echoing in their ears: 'Medics! Help!'

Yorkshireman Wilf Mylan, sometime squadron pianist, would not be haunted by cries of 'Medic!' But the sight would be burned on his retina like the greens and blues which remained from the brightest explosions. His Buffalo had unloaded on the far bank, and was lifting its ramp, when he saw a wounded British soldier hurrying towards him from about twenty yards away. 'Down ramp,' he called, 'and I'll go get him if necessary.' But a Schu mine burst under the soldier, wrapping him around with flame, a red flare which showed that his foot had been blown off. He staggered forward. A second mine burst crimson and flailing. He was gashed, and burned, and writhed in his death agonies, falling backwards. A third mine blew him bodily off the ground. The body fell in a wild somersault, landing on a fourth mine. Which blew the body to pieces and catapulted the head on to the ramp of the waiting Buffalo.

Rex Jackson and Michael Hunt watched their Black Watch platoon double away across the watery wilderness, where land looked only like a calmer river. 'Up ramp. Back off.' But as Mike responded deftly, another Buffalo, driver confused by the traitorous light and the whirling currents under the bank, crashed into Rex's craft. The engine stalled. The river caught the clumsy iron box and tugged it, spun it, rushed it away downstream. To where the enemy still held the immediate bank.

Mike saw his lucky London leave being spent in a German prisoner of war camp, or even with the fatal Lorelei, entombed on the river-bed. With renewed determination he forced the engine to start up again, exacted dangerous levels of revs in order to drive his awkward charge back into the middle of the river under control. But where were they? After spinning violently several times they were both mentally bewildered and physically sick. Rex could see a bank, but could not calculate if it was the home or away bank, at an allied location or under Jerry control.

But their briefing had been precise, illustrated with a scale model showing a railway line on the home bank, and even a large crane beside the railway line. In their giddy progress around the river in the still uncertain light Rex gave a shout of gladness to see the large crane in black silhouette outlined over the *bund*. Mike might still get his leave. He aimed the Buffalo at the dimly seen bank, struck it at a place where there was no gap, and, in something like an apoplexy of despair, slammed out even more engine revs to drive the vehicle up a mountainous slope which it had never been designed to attempt.

Stan Hilton's Buffalo, like others, was provided with a Polsten cannon on a mounting as their defence. From the cannon led a sensitive trigger cable. Stan was congratulating himself on the first mission calmly and promptly accomplished. River crossed. Load of Argyll and Sutherlands delivered. Craft safely backed off. Turned. Sailing home. Pointing towards safety. The gun also pointing towards the home bank. The gun started firing!

For a moment the crew was in a state of panic. Nobody had ordered 'Fire!' Nobody had pressed the trigger. But their gun was firing, as though handled by some newborn ghost from the far bank, and firing at any Yeomanry who might be stupid enough to watch Stan's Buffalo coming home.

A wild rush to the gun, interspersed with two more bursts of spontaneous firing at their own base, revealed that the hastily-constructed gun mounting had worked loose, allowing the cannon to swing far enough to put sufficient pressure on the trigger cable as to activate the trigger mechanism in a way nobody had thought possible. And fire at their own troops. Stan and crew crept into the home bank hoping that they would not be identified as the dangerous renegades fighting their own regiment. But the sky was still too dark, and the light above the river too inconsistent for them to be recognized and suitably admonished by some highly indignant staff officer.

Les Carr, like Stan, was delighted that his Buffalo seemed to have managed that first crossing without undue difficulty. But there were many more crossings to go. And days to transpire before the engineers could build a bridge across this great river, now that the enemy was excluded from the banks. But Les was cheered and emboldened by the first success. His ankle still ached and came up swollen from his Loon-op-Zand injury but he refused to go back for treatment until this mission was ended. It was worth it. Already he felt he wouldn't have missed it for a fortune.

Waiting for Les was a long 17 pounder anti-tank gun. Basically too large for the Buffalo it was accommodated on two large baulks of timber on top of the vessel. The gun was wedged with kapok-filled floats, and rode above the Buffalo like a parasite bird on a real Buffalo's back. The gun was an enormous weight which made the craft wallow even more than normal. Les drove into the water as slowly as possible. A great cracking sound, like high explosive hitting home, sounded behind Les's ear. One of the timbers had broken. The weight of the gun tilted the Buffalo over, one side shipping water. The craft went into an uncontrollable horizontal spin across the river. It was like going down into the vortex of a whirlpool. Les was considering prayer when another crash shook them to the core. A strange Buffalo, also out of control, had rammed them amidships. The river pulled the two vessels apart as angry cries shrilled from the decks of the other.

'Stupid ruddy imbeciles! Mucking oafs! Morons! Couldn't even find your own mother's paps! Try watching with your eyes instead of your arses! Where d'y' think yer flooding are – the Dodgems?'

Les did not have time to trade courtesies. The collision had snapped the second timber and righted the Buffalo. But the gun, with its incongruously long muzzle and its intolerable weight, had settled down like a gigantic eagle upon the struggling Buffalo in what can aptly be termed the mating position. Beset by visions of imminent drowning, Les carefully nursed more power into the engine. Mercifully the Buffalo grounded on the far bank. Spurred by the momentum, the great gun considerately rolled on and unloaded itself farther into Germany.

It was still early on the 23rd and RSM George Jelley conducted the Highlanders' general down to a returning

Buffalo. The general was no longer the sheepskin-disguised traffic warden of the Ardennes, but paraded in full glory of red trimmings, and surrounded by staff.

'Sail to attention,' smirked a Yeoman from the depths of the landing craft. 'I heard that,' responded the general. 'Never mind the bull! Just you get me over this bloody river safely, and I'll thank you. Good show, Yeomanry, so far. Keep it up!' He sat like an interested tourist, watching the Buffaloes fight back and forth through the currents; refusing to duck when high spouts of water betrayed rather ineffective, but always frightening German shell fire; jaw jutting in the approved but instinctive manner; eyes swivelling again and again to try to penetrate the normal fog of battle which had replaced the darkness of night over the undiscovered land. 'I have had a peculiar feeling, something between pessimism and dismay, about this plan,' he was heard to say to a major, 'wondering if it was to be another Arnhem. But our Yeomanry friends seem to be delivering.'

He and his retinue disembarked, waved in a friendly fashion to the crew, and ploughed through the mud into the wilds of mist, smoke and continuing explosion flashes. The Buffalo waited for wounded men to be loaded. Usually it was one man carrying a comrade, or two stretcher bearers depositing their burdens – some awake and joking, others already stiffening. Fifteen minutes passed. The ramp was delayed, because this time it was an entire procession escorting a single stretcher. The yeomen crew moved forward and stared.

The Highland general lay on the stretcher, his face pallid, his clothes torn, his red trimmings besmirched with brown mire. 'Artillery fire,' whispered a captain to a trooper. 'Killed him outright. Go steady. Take him back.' The returning Buffalo resembled, in the watchers' minds, some medieval funeral barge, taking a dead King Arthur away through the mists and home to Camelot.

The SSM at the home bank was not so poetic. He said to the Buffalo commander, 'Ol' Churchill's coming over tomorrow. For Gawd's sake don't bring that bugger back wrapped in a blanket.'

Stan Hilton's Buffalo was cautiously loading another Wasp, the Canadian flame-thrower. 'Nasty things these. Watch it,' ordered the sergeant. The Wasp on its carrier base was a fast tractor but difficult to control. It failed to brake, crashed into the Buffalo, ruptured the flame fuel container. Liquid, sticky, warming, smelling of petrol splashed over Stan's overalls, across his face and into his eyes. He reacted, raising his fists to rub his yes. 'Don't!' cried a Nova Scotian sergeant, grabbing Stan's arms. 'Get back to the Aid Post fast, laddy. And don't light any flaming cigarettes.' Stan felt himself loaded onto a stretcher, although his lower body was unaffected. He was quickly carried into what sounded like a low cave, echoing with guttural German voices, some in extreme pain.

Firm but kind hands poured a cooling potion over his eyelids, fussed about him, swabbed his face. 'See if you can open up now, trooper.' Reluctantly Stan opened his eyes expecting to see the blackness of the permanently blind. A harassed but smiling medical officer, an unfamiliar Highland Division doctor, pronounced, 'You'll do. You wouldn't have done, if somebody had lit that stuff. Your middle name would have been Guy Fawkes. But you'll need to go down the line for convalescence, sonny.'

'Convalescence?' worried Stan, 'I don't want convalescence. I'm OK. They need me on that silly Buffalo. Not many people can work those awkward things. We're still flat out delivering supplies.'

'What's the problem? Hilton, isn't it?' This was the voice of the NY's own MO, Captain MacIntyre. 'Don't let them send me back, sir,' said Stan. 'You know how important it is for us to keep those ferries running. Just for a day or two. Then I can take a break.'

The two doctors conferred. 'Very well, Hilton. Off you go, if your legs will carry you. But if your eyes play up at all, come back here tout suite. That's an order.' 'Yessir!' snapped Stan. And fled from the gruelling sight of so many wrecked German bodies, exposed and under treatment which, to the layman, was as frightening as the original wounding.

'That's two successful crossings. We seem to have got this job all neatly worked out and wrapped up.' John Stenner, considered by his Dutch hostess to be too young for the war, was standing with Sergeant Eric King watching the second uneventful disembarkation of hurrying Highlanders. There had been just a few flashes and splashes of German response. But 'Pooh!' they thought. Charlie Broadbent stood at the bottom of the ramp, fearful like most tank men of straying too far on strange land which might be liberally sown with anti-personnel mines. Nasty things, those. Even the frail plates of a crudely swimming Buffalo were a safer haven for tank men. Safety is what you know.

With an almost artistic beauty, in the way these things happen, and with the infinite time for appreciation which the watching eye and perceiving mind allow, a sunburst of red glory rose from the ground around Charlie's legs, followed by the rending screech of a speeding shell which had already landed. The sunburst aged into a thunderstorm of billowing black clouds and blinding, spreading light, transforming Charlie into the figure of a glowing messenger from beyond space. He began to rise, disintegrate, topple. The furious blast flung him back up the ramp as though the earth were disowning him. The full ear-shattering rending of explosion, and its grilling blast, tore at John and Eric whilst they were still flinging themselves down on the water-swilled, hard iron plates of the Buffalo.

Eric crawled forward while Stan waited hesitantly. Eric shook his head. 'Never had a chance, poor sod. Equally never knew a thing about it.' Still on hands and knees he said softly, 'Find your way home, Charlie boy.'

John was haunted by the sight. It heightened the natural fear for one's own skin, with which one had been fighting – in a battle as fierce as the outward war – since landing in Normandy. But no way was John going to show it. Nevertheless Sergeant King noticed the look of relief on John's face next day when they were given a different job, ferrying thick steel tow-ropes out to sunken vehicles on the river-bed, prior to special units undertaking recovery work.

Rex and Mike were stranded behind the *bund*. Scraping noises from the tracks had alerted them to damage caused when they had to scramble ashore. There was damage to a number of 'grousers', heavy iron track extensions. They crawled around in the mud, cursing their luck. 'What a way to prepare for homeland leave,' grunted Mike. The grousers were rusty and difficult to unbolt. Damaged ones on one track had to be transferred to the other, at least to enable a short journey to the fitters. They mounted up and slowly moved on to the command post for orders. In a corner of the post the popular C 2nd Captain, Ken Todd, was being treated for wounds. Michael Rathbone was also there, standing whilst an orderly bandaged his elbow.

Rex heard Ratters ask the MO how Todd was. 'Clean

wound on the entry side which encourages him, especially as he hasn't felt any great pain yet. But all tangled up inside the stomach and back. He should survive, but it will be a long struggle. Then God knows for how many years a body can continue like that?'

Outside the post Rex was handed a tin. 'What's this?' he asked. 'Self-sealing hot drinks. New idea. Lovely grub,' was the reply. It was indeed hot, but not too lovely. Between sips he had to dive, clutching his self-sealing drink resolutely, for they were still within reach of German guns and mortars. A shell bored a great hole in Harry Graham's tank which was also parked there. 'Thank God I wasn't inside that death trap,' said Harry, also holding a self-sealing drink. 'Hey, Mike! Not gone on leave yet? You'll need to duck and weave a bit still before you get there.'

Their Buffalo quickly repaired by the fitters, Rex and Mike returned to the *bund*. There was a general order that Buffaloes should cross the river only in groups under command of an officer. However, Bill Fox was waiting at the *bund* and shouted, 'Don't hang about. Damn the standing orders. You're needed. You know the way now. Off you go. Have a pleasant cruise.' At the far bank they found little Trooper Jock MacGregor sitting in a quickly-dug hole. As each Buffalo beached he jumped up, waved his arms and shouted, 'Mines! Dinna gae tae the reet. Mines! Nae tae the reet.' Jock swore that a German patrol had passed only a few minutes before and that one had actually trodden on his helmet as he ducked into his hole. 'Psychiatrist's case,' grinned Mike to Rex.

They almost became psychiatrist's cases themselves. As they drove into the river for Mike's last homeward leg (ending London), a batch of Moaning Minnies fell around them. Mike accelerated into deep waters. More Minnies fell, still at their range. Mike took evasive action, like a naval destroyer at speed. Batches of half a dozen Minnies seemed to follow. 'They must have an observer somewhere,' shouted Rex. 'Damn 'em,' Mike shouted back, 'I WILL go on leave.' Again the long suffering craft was driven beyond regulation revs. This time they found the gap in the *bund*. The Minnies could reach them no longer. Bill Fox said, 'Now shoot off to England, Hunt. What are you damn well loitering about here for?'

The third day of harrowing crossings, with little or no

sleep, found most crews with bloodshot eyes, drooping eyelids and bad breath. Given a brief break – because ferrying went on day and night – Johnny Howell's crew thankfully stripped down, out of their oily, sweaty overalls, lay down on the engine covers and instantly fell asleep.

'Wake up, you silly sods! You'll get court-martialled. The squadron is away,' bawled irate Sergeant-Major Farnham, banging on the Buffalo's resounding hull with an empty shell case. 'You've got two minutes to get this great crate moving and afloat before the major spots you. Squadron is moving downstream.'

The half-awake crew fell off the engine covers, yelling at each other. Johnny Howell took a great leap into the driver's seat, wearing only vest and pants. Started the engine. Began to move as others took their posts, hastily dressing. They splashed into the wake of the squadron. Their engine stalled. That meant the main pump failed to operate. That meant water began to fill the crude vessel. That meant minutes before the ship went under. Johnny fiddled with switches, pedals, gears. Nothing happened. 'Where's the bloody lifebelts?' shouted somebody. 'Back on the *bund*,' replied another voice. At the moment of ultimate catastrophe another even more belated Buffalo hove alongside and cast a tow-rope. In the scramble Johnny saw all his clothes going overboard. Still half naked he jumped to reach them, capsized, and went plunging deep into the Rhine waters. He surfaced, blowing and spitting petrol- and oil-tainted water.

'Come out of there, Johnny,' yelled his mates. 'You're the ugliest looking mermaid in the whole of Germany.'

Charlie Robertson came back from leave: leave, when drawn, was mandatory even for majors, even on the eve of battle, as Lord George had found. Charlie's Black Watch company had been transported over the waters by 1NY and had disappeared into oblivion. Charlie took a 1NY ferry to the edge of that oblivion. Pushing forward Charlie found that his men had rushed a small bridge over another stream. A vital bridge at Empel. Massed German counter-attacks had tried to wrest the bridge back again. Lance-Corporal McBride with only five men had held the bridge for twenty-four hours against odds of more than a hundred to one. But another commander, nerves wracked by months of fatal battles, and powers of judgement dulled by entire days without any sleep, failed to support the valiant corporal.

Charlie launched himself into action, muttering to himself, 'It will be a Distinguished Conduct Medal for one, and home in disgrace for the other.'

Ratters, one elbow stiff with bandages, was sent with a composite force across the river, over the misty ground beyond, to another stretch of flooding which the Highlanders were having difficulty in crossing. The Buffaloes made hard work of it in the shallow waters which hid deep mud. At the far side of the flood Rex Jackson, with an unknown replacement driver from reserve, found himself bogged down with recurring grouser trouble. There was nothing for it but another crawl in the mud, unbolting grousers and swopping them, flattening oneself in the mire as Moaning Minnies responded to the Highlanders' onward advance.

The new driver did not help with the grouser job as Mike would have done. In fact the driver *should* have undertaken the job with the rest of the crew to assist. So the weary, hand-wounding, back-straining task went on late into the night. They slept a while in that wilderness. Then Rex ordered the return. As they approached another stretch of water, water much like any other water in the mist, they passed several grossly-bloated bodies of German soldiers.

The driver went berserk. 'You've come the wrong way. We're in German lines. You'll get us all killed. You're wrong. You're no bloody good. I'm not going any further. Drive your own bloody Buffalo.' Rex, the mildest of men, bespectacled and undemonstrative, slowly pulled his revolver out of his holster. 'Shut up! You'll drive this crate. And you'll drive it where I tell you. If not ... I've never fired this gun at a German yet. But so help me God, I'll fire it at you. Advance!'

'It's my bluff,' thought Rex. 'He'll never fall for it.' But, just as quickly as he had paled and turned berserk, the driver blushed, became sullen, climbed into his seat and started to cross the water ahead.

Time seemed to have stood still. Nothing in the world was distinct. The rushing, greedy waters were eternal. The shades of Hades itself lay beyond this Stygian river. Then the *bund* appeared out of the mists. The *bund* with a gap in it. The first gear scramble up over the rubble. Refuge behind the *bund*.

The mists cleared. The sun shone through. The place was empty. Infra-red signs still blinked unnoticed. The locust army had gone. All of them. Far away into a land haunted by legends from Goethe and Schiller. A land of Lorelei and Erl Kings and Götterdämmerung. And of SS, Gestapo and Hitler.

I never knew it would come to THIS. Driving this crazy iron box that's not seaworthy enough to be called a boat, and not battle-worthy enough to call a tank. It simply wallows in the water, like a great beast in a mud-bath. So, with good reason, they call it a Buffalo.

Yes, I know there isn't the protection you get in a tank driver's seat. But it's still indignity more than fear that I feel just now. I thought it was indignity when I landed on the D-Day beaches, not in a tank but in the back of a cook's lorry, commanded by a cook corporal, as a reserve. But then I was a real tank reserve, a young recruit to the regiment ready to take his place in the real action.

And I know that officially I'm only a 'conscript'. By the time I was old enough for this war everybody of my age had to be registered and conscripted. But most of us who had to go, went willingly, to fight Hitler and all that Hitler stands for. And I know I didn't select the tanks. The army posted me to the tanks after initial infantry training. But when you're trained for a job with a real purpose, and that meant twenty months training for me before D-Day, you begin to take a pride in it. You want to be the best. You want the reward of being up front, doing the most necessary task, you might almost whisper 'the most heroic deed'.

So, what do they do? After months of up front fighting with a jolly good, if a bit unorthodox, assault regiment, they make me the ferryman, without even a decent boat to go with the job.

You need a decent boat to cross this river. Have you seen the Rhine in these parts? It's like a little sea: wide, deep, swept by fast and dangerous currents, not to mention the mortar fire from the German side. You really need a proper boat to do this job.

Yes, I suppose you *could* say I am still up front. There's certainly nobody between me and Jerry on the far bank at this moment in time. I suppose you *could* say that this is a necessary task because the Black Watch, the Gordons and the rest have got to get over this river to be able to rush on to Berlin (with us back in Shermans to support them, I hope). And no Royal Engineers are going to build a bridge over this vast stretch of water overnight. I suppose you *could* say, too, that some day historians will write all this up as a heroic deed, a heroic adventure.

But just look at this ... this clumsy, crawling, wallowing, rusty, misshapen, hurriedly put together, mechanical monstrosity. An insult to decent, drooling-at-the-mouth, fly-blown-eyed, shitty-arsed, mud-rolled buffaloes, to give it their name. A right indignity to put a real Sherman driver in this thing. Couldn't they have used a Marine, or a service corps driver, or a Pioneer?

Indignity. Indignity. Indignity. I keep repeating that word, because it helps hide the fact that really what I am, deep down, is ... bloody scared! Not of Jerry shells. But of this evil-looking, rushing, black-deep river to cross.

See ... I can't swim. And they don't provide lifeboats.

14   Victor Easy

'Victor Easy', in the phonetic alphabet of 1NY, was the way of saying VE, just as 'Able' was A and 'Baker' B. Right from the Normandy beaches to the Rhine *bunds* no Yeoman found himself to be an easy victor. But beyond the Rhine the war tended to diminish, until the day which was also designated 'Victor Easy', or VE Day, or Victory in Europe; *Bevrijding* to a Dutchman.

Two Geordies were discussing the onward route to Berlin with that optimistic pessimism in which Geordies excel. 'This bloody war's going on for ever. When's it going to end?' asked Cliff. 'Why aye, it's still farther from here to Berlin that it is from N'castle to Lands End, man,' observed Jimmie. 'Aye, and I'll tell y' what! We'll be fighting the ruddy Ruskies after we've finished with Jerry.'

The Buffaloes had been returned to compound and the old Shermans restored to the joyful Yeomen. Expecting to bash on to Berlin, or at least Bremen, 1NY found themselves on the long road back to West Holland to guard against rumoured Nazi werewolf raiders over the Maas. On that monotonous road turret crews sat out on top of their dizzy mounts, earphones tuned to BBC radio. Stan Hilton heard the tones of the Palm Court Orchestra playing 'By the side of the Zuider Zee', looked back down the column of tanks, and saw heads bolting everywhere in time with the music.

In the Teteringen area the regiment set up laager. Bill Fox was heard (by Dick Bates, of course) to say to Hank, 'Hope they give us a real rest this time. The lads are shagged.' Corporal Ossie Porter, who patrolled that street in Raamsdonk, had been commissioned in the field and awarded the MM. Sergeant Thompson had won the highly esteemed DCM for the same action. Kenny Jack, the redoubtable Balbo, Falconer and King were among those also obtaining the MM. As well as Colonel Doug's DSO, Military

Crosses had gone to Hank Bevan, Tom Boardman and Lieutenant Owen, among others, whilst Hank and Ratters had both picked up a Croix de Guerre from allies.

Altogether the Yeomen were beginning to dilute their criticism of the regiment as a 'Shower' in the terms of 'Fred Karno's Army, no bloody good are we'. Especially when Corky Calkwell showed Wally Ward and others a cutting from the *Yorkshire Evening Telegraph* describing their 33rd Armoured Brigade as a D-Day 'secret weapon', but now a 'famous name' which had 'made no mistakes' in its battles. 'Does that mean a rise in pay?' asked Wally unhopefully.

The regiment fired another 'All Stations Yoke' barrage across the Maas. Then the abhorrent news flashed through: 'Back to Buffaloes for a crossing of the River Ems'. That day Stan Hilton and Sergeant Falconer walked into the Dutch house which had been their billet, to find the family seated for the meal but bowed in profound prayers, uttered in Dutch. The Yeomen waited silently in the doorway. As the family sat up, looking happy and hungry, the Yeomen knew them well enough to essay a quiet joke. 'Were you praying for Liberation?'

The father laughed and shouted, 'Praying FOR, friends? THANKING for! Thanking God for Liberation of all Netherlands. The Boche has capit ... capul ... *zich overgeven* ... over given! Ask for, you say, armistize? We hear BBC. Thank you God! But thank you also our great brave friends!' And Stan thought, 'That includes me, poor, scared, hardly grown-up schoolboy Stan!'

Meanwhile Captain Rathbone had been summoned for an advance party to Enschede, prior to crossing the River Ems. For the last time in the war, the orders were changed. Destination now: Zwolle by the Zuider Zee.

On 7 May 1945, erstwhile and future film star and stage actor, Ian Carmichael, now Brigade Major, 33rd Armoured Brigade, signed an order to the 1st Northamptonshire Yeomanry. 'Cease fire!'

Zwolle was a fine city for a final destination, with its encircling moat of a river, its attractive architecture, its towering *Grote Kerk*, its neat streets, its friendly people. Tank crews had their official billet in schools but were constantly welcome in Dutch homes. The cheering, honking Liberation traffic was held up again and again by traffic policemen so that a single Yeoman might cross the street. Tank lads found themselves pushed up to the front of cinema queues anxious to view the latest Pathe Gazette war news. Girls, elderly women, even normally staid Dutch men, embraced the Liberators and began to dance with them. The dancing erupted into singing as more and more people persuaded more and more Yeoman – still bewildered from the mists of Limburg, the snows of the Ardennes, the floods of the Rhine – into the wild, joyous, unending ballet, like a pagan rite which, with the coming of darkness, swung into a torchlight revel, frolicking through all the streets of the city and out beyond the moat, consuming in its bonfire of delight Dutch citizens, Northants Yeomen and Canadian infantry.

Michael Rathbone, after months of tinned army food, delighted in smoked eel, was invited into chess tournaments in which the locals prevailed, and also hockey matches, where the NY's ex-international Quartermaster Twigg won the day. Food was still in short supply but Stan Hilton and his crew were invited to a family Sunday dinner consisting of a scanty meat rissole and oatmeal porridge. Their gift of tinned corned beef was received as though it were manna from heaven by the courteous Dutch hosts.

Ken Squires, mobilizing his composite band for a joint jig in the town square, enjoyed the distinctive tones of the 'Dutch Swing Band', and especially the Dutch trumpeter's impassioned rendering of 'Liebestraum' by Liszt. There were no trumpets for Don Foxley. The first reaction of any military unit occupying decent built quarters was to establish a routine of bedmaking, room inspection and, at least, token parades. SSM Farnham, an ex-infantryman, was meticulous in enforcing this after the carefree gypsy, almost bandit life of the past months. A room inspection of regimentally-ranked beds discovered that, amid all the burly-burly of celebration, in his haste to go on duty, Don had left a dirty handkerchief on top of his squared and smoothed bedding. Hank justly but sadly awarded Don three days confined to barracks. But that was much preferable to being confined in that church at Raamsdonk.

And the enemy inflicted the last casualty on 1NY, after the armistice. Hungry, cheery, lustful Tommy T. had, in spite of fiery warnings from puritan Dutch pastors, been infected with VD by a Dutch girl, well known for her association with German troops, from whom she had contracted the then lethal, degrading and militarily prohibited disease.

The final curtain call to this epic pageant of war was to take place, for 1NY, in the presence of civilian authorities and populace, at the vast *Grote Kerk*, a dim Lutheran stronghold which imposed its own aura of disciplined religious awe. Like most soldiers, the NY filed into the great church at something between a proud march and a modest shuffle, RSM George Jelley proudly watching: 'We wouldn't have saved so many in '14-18!'

The oldest, longer-serving men among us were already anticipating early demobilization. The younger ones looked forward to the dubious honour of occupying Germany. Those of us still convalescent in Britain must await posting to a continuing struggle with a worse-feared enemy in Burma, or with vicious, insidious terrorism in Palestine.

The regimental padre, released from his routine of hurried burials, announced the hymn 'Now thank we all our God'. The echoes soared up into the high roof as Dutch, British and Canadian voices caught the magnificent beat of the German tune, accompanied by the Dutch organist.

Lessons were read, good words said, prayers intoned, feet became restless, coughs were suppressed. Until: 'Regiment and congregation will stand whilst the Regimental Roll of Honour is read.' The list of our dead. Our recently dead. 'We will remember them.'

Trooper Shellam, W. The first: round that cursèd corner in Normandy, and into the sights of that waiting Panther.
Lance-Corporal Madelaine, R.H. ... Sergeant Valentine, G.A. ... Corporal Hickson, F.E. Those lovely people. Great comrades. Always reliable, in peace or war. We do remember ....
Trooper R. ... Trooper R. ... Say those names again, Padre, run into each other, overlying, conjoined, as they died and as their bodies were buried, one charred flesh indivisible, unidentifiable.
SSM Turton, S. ... Captain Crofts, R.J. Jimmy Kerr remembering the Night March, the tank hit four times, blazing, a funeral pyre, hatches jammed shut, Jimmy and pals inside. THAT, Padre, *was* a time for prayer.
Sergeant Finney, F.G. ... Sergeant Goosey, J.T. Ray Ager remembering himself driving Tom Boardman's tank on that Night March. Little Ray, the first man in all that allied mechanized host, up front in the front Sherman, yet surviving. Why? When all these names ...?

Corporal Stanley, J.W. ... Trooper Wellbelove, E.W. Fred Gibbs remembering his previous regiment, 148, almost annihilated like 2NY, firing at a Tiger; our shots bouncing off like tennis balls; his shots turning us into an inferno; me, unheroic Fred leaning back into the turret to pull the blazing gunner out by his epaulets. Did he survive?

Sergeant Bamford, C.T. ... Lieutenant McColl, R.S. Cliff Cuthbertson remembering Saint-Aignan, and his commander, Mr Brown, being wounded; and Arthur Dwight taking command, calling Cliff up from co-driver to take over as turret operator; and an 88 shot crashing right through the co-driver's seat, past a shocked Michael Hunt, boring through the very seat Cliff had left seconds earlier.

Lance-Corporal Reboles, G. ... Lieutenant Green, E.V. Johnny Byrne remembering a hesitant German surrendering near Vught; an idiot on our side firing, killing the Jerry, causing a further battle; and thirty human beings – be they Germans – killed unnecessarily, almost criminally.

Sergeant Danson, K.T. ... Trooper Blakiston, J.R. Harry Graham wondering 'Will Arthur Dwight make it?'; Ron West worried about Harry Brown, last seen engulfed in flames; Jack Aris, 'How will Eric Good play golf with only one arm?', all of us hoping they, others, will survive, come home.

Sergeant Huitson, R.A. ... Wilf Mylan remembering a Canadian, leg gashed, body shattered beyond belief, still breathing; wasps swarming on the bloody flesh of his leg, maggots already emerging; the medic saying, 'Best chance is bandage the wasps, maggots, all into the leg; provide some leeching'; the mass of wasps crunching into the raw meat under the khaki field dressing: in battle you learned about Nature's realities.

Corporal McGranahan, H.B. ... All of us wondering: in that eternal moment when time stands still, that moment we had all known as, powerless to move within time, we had watched Death hurtle, flaming and black, towards us, in that moment as the spirit plunged into the darkening tunnel, or hovered a moment at the brink of a bedazzling golden sunrise, did they know of our unceasing love for them? Did they forgive the world's early renouncing of their principles of sacrifice, fellowship and honesty? Did they appreciate their own individual heroism? Did they fully comprehend the diabolical crimes and menace of the regime they helped to destroy? Did they know?

And Trooper Williams, T.H., the youngest of our Departed ....

The church parade ends. Blazon their names on wall
memorials in school halls. Sculpt their sacrifice on stone
monuments in village squares. And may the widows enjoy
their meagre pensions.

The church parade ends. War ends. We rush out into the
sunshine amid the swarming, cheering crowds of Zwolle.
Into a torrent of gaiety and imbecility as powerful as the
rushing waters of the Rhine. But already some of us are
agitated, dispirited, feverish. Gnawed at by virulent maggots
of insanity. Bred by the flies of persisting fear and horror.
Hatched in dank and inaccessible recesses of the mind. The
festering of our invisible wounds.

There will be no first-aid posts for us down the long road
back to normality. No psychiatrists for our unburdening. No
easy return to the confessional of priests. Only our own
ghosts gone on ahead. And waiting for us.

Among our families and friends and workmates maybe we
shall bear the ignominy of shuddering with visible fear,
throwing ourselves to the floor in an epilepsy of memory,
hiding pale-cheeked under some table, as the shells of
lightning flash and the guns of thunder blast the embattled
skies.

There will be no bailing out of the entrapping nightmares,
perhaps causing the assault upon wives at a frenzied
midnight awakening, or the brutality to children after the
stress of daily work. And our vain worship in church, and
our bungled love-making at home, pervaded by the echoes
of the obscene songs the old soldiers used to sing: the
sodomy with Salome and the lechery with Peggy O'Neill.

And in the renewal of the self-seeking, the self-
importance, the self-centredness of peacetime, Rex and Mike
and Harry and Hank Bevan will need to be about their own
business. They will not be there, with their concern, their
forced optimism, their unshirking protection when those
new battles commence.

Nor will Tommy Madeleine (lost in those first shots at La
Taille); nor will little Wellbelove (smiling in that final sleep
beyond Saint-Aignan): nor will Bobby McColl (sliced to
human shambles in Raamsdonk): nor will Hughie McGranahan (cruelly obliterated at the very last under the trees of
the Ardennes): nor will Vaughan Green (his last poem

encrusted with blood in his pocket).

Or will they come softly out of that wiser darkness, to guide us in ways we do not know?

PRE-BATTLE

They talked quietly in groups,
And some made half attempts to joke,
Others sat and smoked apart, in silence;
Each knew the coming hour
Would dictate, in the spate of hate,
Whose existence would terminate.
    The same it was the day before;
    How long since, and how much more?
    Each dawn
    With its dread monotony of War.
        (Ralph Hill, 1NY, invalided, Sint-Oedenrode)

NO COIN FOR THE FERRYMAN

Slowly, like ancient reptiles scenting water,
The lumbering craft move towards the river,
With each its little group of men, each its own small world,
Close wrapped in secret thought, not looking beyond the
      hour.

NOW! the steep bank reached: grinding, gouging tracks,
      they climb
Up, Up, and UP! – noses pointing to the misty stars;
Then, at the balance, tilting downwards, for the smoke-filled
      river,
Black and unseen yet, but a presence felt ominous as the sky.

Down, steeply DOWN, seeming to rush unhindered to the
      bottom,
Till suddenly, feeling buoyant water, the craft rises to its
      task;
Quieter now, purposeful, striking out across the current,
Across the dark unseen waters, seeking out the distant
      bank …

Straining eyes peer … ahead … then … left, right: 'Are we
      keeping station?'
Still the reassuring engine throbs, still the streaming pumps:
'Will the landing be opposed? How much further can it be?'
Time seems fixed, a different plane.

Then: 'What of the men crouching behind me?'
Waiting for the touchdown, waiting for the practised leap,
The leap to bank; on mines? Perhaps to death?
WE only have to touch the bank, wait for them to clear, then
      back.

But they must stay … perhaps only to return
Among those we later carry back with stained bandage,
Or under the grey blanket, silent and unknown,
With no coin for the Ferryman, no coin for their Last
      Crossing!

                (Rex Jackson, 1NY, Military Medal, Loon-op-Zand)

BURN SCARS

No cabbages will grow
   Where 2 Troop burned and died;
no fertile row
   thrives, where '2' defied
      the Panzers. And their olden cremation
      marks still barren each tank's station.

So my inmost soul
   has burned-out places,
the sterile toll
   of war, fear, broken embraces;
      each a Saint-Aignan tank location
      impotent of golden elation.
         (Ken Tout, 1NY, injured, Sint-Michielsgestel)

ROUEN (September 1944)

The flags at the first storey windows,
Dawn-fluttered against the blue,
The waved hands, the unheard voices
As the chariots thunder through;
The fruit and the flowers for the victors,
The smiles and the tears and the fuss:
We read all about it in History,
And now it has happened to us.

For this is the setting for heroes,
The age-old response of the town
To the curved lips, medallion profile
Of the conqueror looking down;
This is Caesar in dusty triumph
For two of the three parts of Gaul:
They told us it all in the Fourth Form
But WE didn't feel that way at all.

For we saw the bridges we'd broken
Where the leaf-green river bends,
And our tracks raised the dust of our bombing
From the shattered houses of friends.
And they cheered us who'd had to shell them,
Thin children with hollow eyes,
And the colourless flesh of starvation;
Oh, it seems it's the victor who cries.

Lord, make us a little bit worthy
Who never had thought to feel thus:
We never were told it of Pompey;
How could we foresee it for us?
(Vaughan Green, 1NY, killed in action, Wessem Canal,
                                        14.11.44)